Together for Good

Other Books by Henry H. Mitchell

Black Preaching

Black Belief

The Recovery of Preaching

Soul Theology (with Nicholas C. Cooper-Lewter)

Celebration and Experience in Preaching

Preaching for Black Self-Esteem (with Emil M. Thomas)

Other Books by Ella P. Mitchell

Those Preachin' Women, vols. 1, 2, 3

Women: To Preach or Not to Preach

TOGETHER
FOR
GOOD

Lessons from Fifty-five
Years of Marriage

Ella P. and Henry H. Mitchell

JUDSON PRESS
PUBLISHERS SINCE 1824

VALLEY FORGE, PA

Together For Good
Lessons from Fifty-Five Years of Marriage

Library of Congress Cataloging-in-Publication Data

Mitchell, Ella Pearson.
   Together for good : lessons from fifty-five years of marriage / Ella P. and Henry H. Mitchell.
      p. cm.
Originally published: Kansas City, Mo. : Andrews McMeel Pub., c1999.
ISBN 0-8170-1489-6 (alk. paper)
1. Mitchell, Henry H. 2. Mitchell, Ella Pearson. 3. African American clergy—Biography. 4. African American Baptists—Biography. 5. Baptists—United States—Biography. 6. Baptists—United States—Clergy—Biography. I. Mitchell, Henry H. II. Title.
BX6455.M58A3 2006
286'.10922—dc22

                                                        2005026130

Dedicated, with thanks to God, to the two previous generations of our ancesters who lived in married togetherness, all the way back to slavery.

And in the fond hope that the tradition may continue with our children and grandchildren, as it has with us and our Pearson and Mitchell siblings.

Contents

CONTENTS

CHAPTER I

Together at First: But Not Love

E *(Ella)* On a hot September afternoon in 1941, I entered an imposing school building whose tower seemed to scrape the sky. Rising high among other huge buildings on upper Broadway in New York City, Union Theological Seminary would be unlike any school I'd ever attended in all my twenty-three years. I had no idea of the awesome reputation of professors like Reinhold Niebuhr and Paul Tillich, or that some people called Union the best graduate school of religion in the world. I was simply impressed that the building had elevators.

Up to now I had been educated in segregated schools by segregated faculties, except for a few White professors at my alma mater, Talladega College in Alabama. I had lived the protected life of a southern preacher's kid. In the swarming streets of New York, I wasn't exactly scared, but I was a bit uneasy. And for the first time in my life I was really on my own.

That afternoon I was headed for an interview with the librarian for a work-study job. Stepping into the tower elevator, I noticed a young man already standing inside it. As we slowly went up, I wondered who he was. What was his ethnic background? He had straight black hair and an olive complexion. Was he a student or a building staff worker? Was he looking me over behind that even stare, or was that just his normal everyday expression?

1

Before I knew it, this stranger had pulled open the accordion gate, to let me get out first. Papa had warned me not to talk to strange men, but I heard myself asking, "Are you enrolled here this year?"

H *(Henry)* I was no veteran of New York either, but I had grown up in Columbus, Ohio, and gone to integrated public schools. As a 115-pound freshman, I'd been one of 13,000 students at predominantly White Ohio State University. I had operated an elevator at a White hotel; both skyscrapers and Caucasians were familiar to me. At all-Black Lincoln University, the majority of my teachers were White, but the Black men of Lincoln were known for their self-confidence. (Some called it arrogance.) For me, Union was a fresh but familiar challenge.

Almost at the instant Ella spoke, I asked her the same question. Her face was pleasant, and her voice even more so. Yet apart from her radiant expression, she seemed to have forsaken all for the Lord. Her shoes were smart, but her homemade clothes were clearly designed to cover the body, period. Her hair was neatly combed but totally lacking in style. I didn't expect high fashion, but I wouldn't have minded a bit more effort, even at no greater cost.

We reached the library. "Where are you from?" I asked. Surely she was a country girl. Ella told me she was from Charleston, South Carolina, but that's all I remember. She stopped at the library desk; I headed down the center aisle of the reading room to the door that led to my rooms, a seventh-floor walk-up in Hastings Hall. Ella seemed like a very nice person, but that was all I thought of her.

E I had no time to ponder this brief meeting. I needed a job, and that day I got one, working at the library's front desk from five to eleven each weekday night. Even though I was living rent-free in Brooklyn with my sister Ermine and her husband, Harold, I needed to earn money.

My folks were pleased that I was entering seminary, but they were already helping my younger sister, Lurline, who was still in college. They had aided me some, but Papa's annual salary as a Presbyterian pastor was only $960. To go to Union, I had sold my 1932 Dodge, which Papa had lent me money to buy. Ermine and Harold gave me a bed. My sister Jessica had not yet returned to teaching after the birth of her baby, but she and her husband, Fred, sent the nickels I needed for subway fares. My sister Beulah, also living in New York, offered me meals from time to time.

My commute alone was exhausting. I had to leave Ermine's house about 5:30 A.M. each weekday for the long tedious trip to uptown Manhattan. In order to get to 116th Street and Broadway from Brooklyn, I had to take two buses and the subway. From the subway station, I walked to the seminary at 120th Street in time for 7 A.M. choir rehearsal. The New York winter was cold and dark; here in the North the snow actually stayed on the ground. Walking home unprotected on the streets late at night wasn't as dangerous as it is now for a woman, but the icy sidewalks were treacherous. When spring finally came and Ermine and her family moved to upper Manhattan, I was doubly glad. It was worth getting up in the dark to sing in a fine choir, but I cherished the extra sleep.

H I sang in the choir with the tenors, right behind Ella. Because she and I were the only two "Coloreds" in the group—there were only six of us in the entire seminary—we soon developed a basic feeling of comradeship. Once, when we performed Handel's "Elijah," I was sitting there half asleep when Ella and her whole front row stood up. I jumped to my feet too. When I looked around and saw I was the only male standing, I felt both tall and small at the same time. Easing back into my seat, I avoided the amused glances of my fellow tenors.

I liked to stop by the library desk and chat with Ella about her encounters with the famous faculty members whose books she checked out. Once in a while I walked her to the subway after she quit work at eleven. She was good company. It was lonely walking back to school without her.

F After choir we'd sit side by side in the 8 A.M. class in New Testament studies. As we took notes, I tried to keep Henry awake, nudging his elbow or knee, but sometimes his handwriting would trail away into a wavy line and I'd look up to see his eyes closing. Our professor, Frederick C. Grant, was a soft-spoken older man and fortunately seldom looked at our faces. Henry said he was like ether, and most of the class agreed, but it was Henry who most often would nod off.

With classes, the choir, and other campus contacts, we were becoming more and more friendly, in a sister/brother way. When we studied in the library, I'd glimpse Henry on the same side of the long table. Once I sought him out to counsel a conscientious objector who was in my youth group at St. James Presbyterian Church. After the Japanese attack on Pearl Harbor that December, Henry was exempted from the military draft because he was preparing for ministry.

H My uncle Vivian Mitchell had returned from France so traumatized by World War I that he spent most of his life in mental institutions. As a boy I had been much moved by his tribulations, and I had seen up close the lingering and pernicious effects of war. At Union Seminary I found a strong group of kindred spirits and became a much more articulate pacifist. My spiritual cell group, the people I met regularly to pray with, were all COs (conscientious objectors).

Suddenly, on "Franksgiving Weekend"—President Roosevelt's attempt to boost the economy by celebrating Thanksgiving a week earlier, to allow for more shopping days before Christmas—I was rushed from the dorm to Columbia Presbyterian Hospital for what turned out to be an emergency appendectomy. I had been sick the previous summer, while working as a domestic servant in Canada. If that second attack of appendicitis had happened while I was in the Canadian wilds, I would not be here today.

A week after the surgery, my white blood cell count went sky high. I was taken back to the operating room with a case of generalized peritonitis, often fatal in the days before wonder drugs like sulfa and penicillin. I developed bronchial pneumonia also, along with other serious complications, and was not expected to live. I stayed in intensive care for two weeks, a place I had never even heard of. A telegram was sent to my parents in Ohio, and they called my cousin, Edward E. Holloway, M.D., who was practicing family medicine and teaching in a medical school in Philadelphia. He immediately called his colleagues in New York to ensure I was being given the best of care. "Orlando, you better get the hell out there and see about Henry right away," Cousin Eddie told my father. "I'll wire you a ticket tonight."

When I opened my eyes to see Pops beside me, I was flabbergasted. He had long declared that he would never fly, but there he was at my bedside, having taken an airplane from Columbus, Ohio, to New York City to be with me when I passed on. To the surprise of my father and the staff, however, I slowly improved. When I finally got strong enough to get on the scales, I weighed under a hundred pounds. Pops's jovial bedside manner betrayed no hint to me of how close to death I was.

As I lay in my hospital bed, I kept worrying about the scout troop I had started at the Church of the Master in Harlem. Earlier attempts to start a troop there had faltered. The problem, as I saw it, was not that the boys were rough; they were like any other boys, with only a small exposure to the gangs who roamed nearer the heart of Harlem. Our turf was on the slightly more comfortable edge, at the foot of the high cliff on which sat Columbia University. I figured our success this time was because I was an experienced scout leader and maybe had a better way with boys. In any case, the troop was eager and active. Then, darn it, I was flat on my back in the hospital, with no assistant to take my place. It was enough to worry any hard-working scoutmaster! I wonder now if I am alive today because I stumbled into worry about my scout troop. If I'd worried about myself, I might have depressed myself to death. God's providence works in mysterious ways.

Pops and President Henry Sloan Coffin of the seminary were my only visitors. They had a great deal to do with keeping my spirits up. Other visitors had been prohibited earlier on; final exams and Christmas vacation kept students away later. Ella never came to visit.

We may not have visited him, but all of us students prayed for Henry every day, in both Lampman (evening) and James (morning) chapels. Reports of Henry's condition were posted on the bulletin board and announced in the refectory at mealtime.

One day in the refectory, I spotted an older man eating alone, with tears running down his face. I went over to his table and introduced myself. He turned out to be Henry's father, Orlando, or Pops, using his son's meal ticket. From then on I tried to sit with him as often as possible and began to look forward to my dinner break from the library.

From Pops I learned about the whole Mitchell family. Pops himself was the son of a well-educated preacher, and his wife, Bertha, was also a PK, as we called preacher's kids. They had three sons, Henry being the oldest, and a daughter nine years Henry's junior. Pops Mitchell was born in Virginia, and Mom Mitchell was born in Ohio of Virginian parents. She was a full-time church missionary/social worker when they were married.

Henry's father was a kind man, gentle and attentive. I relished the chance to tell him about myself, my family, and the South where I grew up. My papa was an educated preacher too, yet in the segregated South he was not allowed to vote. Pops couldn't get over the fact that my papa was the only male in a family of nine. Orlando Mitchell had never been in the deep South; he had left Virginia when he was young. He listened to me carefully when I talked about the dangers of segregation and violence. He was surprised to hear that I had amiable White neighbors as I was growing up in Charleston, and there were small pockets of a strange harmony between races to be found here and there in the South. By the time he left New York, he had heard quite a bit about my life and the bonds and stresses between Blacks and Whites below the Mason-Dixon line. And I was growing closer to Henry by learning about him from his father.

H In my second year of seminary, I had fully recovered from the appendicitis, but I continued to be plagued by falling asleep in class. The school physician sent me to the neurological clinic at my old hospital, where I ran into Ella. She had suffered a concussion in the gym the previous summer and was a patient too. We spent a lot of time talking while we walked to the subway, rode to and from the hospital, and waited to be summoned by the doctors.

One day, after one of our clinic visits, she was running late for her afternoon class and had not yet had lunch. I invited her to my suite, which was on her way to class, and grilled her a cheese sandwich in my makeshift windowsill kitchen. She was fascinated by how I managed to produce the tools and ingredients, and I was proud of my skillet, my electric hot plate, and the golden-brown color of my cheese sandwiches. I entertained her so royally in that small space, and with limited resources, she was able to get to class almost on time, well fed.

E His grilled sandwich was quite tasty. We did more and more together that second year in seminary. As members of the choir, we were given tickets to the Fred Waring male chorus rehearsals for NBC-TV on Tuesday nights. I could trade off work time at the library the nights I would go.

I had long known that Henry planned to marry a woman I had met during my student summer service. I myself was about to become engaged to a medical student I had known at Talladega. As my friendship with Henry ripened, we would discuss our two prospective engagements. One Friday evening in November 1942, Henry came to the library desk and asked me to go with him the next day to help pick out a ring for his fiancée. She was an attractive socialite from a prominent family in Washington, D.C., though I did wonder a tiny bit if, as a chain smoker, she would make a good pastor's wife.

I was sorry I couldn't go with him. I had to stay on the job because I had promised to exchange work hours with a friend. "Please stop by and let me see the ring when you come back," I told him. He made it back before the library closed at five. I gave my approval to the two rings (engagement and wedding), even though he confessed that the dazzling rock was not a real diamond. Henry was my friend, and if he was happy with his fiancée, I was happy for him.

H I gave the ring to my fiancée that Thanksgiving, with the idea that we would get married just before my final year of school started the next September. But before we could print the invitations, we had to face the fact that neither of us had the money we needed for marriage. I was optimistic about getting some kind of job, since the war was on and there was a manpower shortage. Many racial barriers had been lowered during the war, so in theory more varied jobs were open to me. I thought it was only a matter of finding something that would allow me to keep up with my seminary work. My fiancée wanted a professional job, but her Ivy League liberal arts degree gave her no specific credentials or skills that would help her get into the workforce. The social agencies she aimed to work for were operating on skeleton crews. I'm not sure she would have accepted a job where you get your hands dirty.

By summer, her mother was insisting we line up jobs before the wedding could take place. To me this seemed unfair. One moonlit evening when I visited her on her summer service project, we rowed out to an isolated spot in Chesapeake Bay to talk. I felt it was time to put my foot down. "Your mother is a wonderful woman, and I admire her greatly, but you are marrying me, not her," I told her. "You have to decide whose opinion is more important. It's now or never. It's either your mama or me. It can't be both."

"Well, I guess it's never," my intended replied. I was stunned. The voyage back to the dock was long, quiet, empty, and painful.

I returned to school in September of 1943, trying to mask my broken heart and bruised pride with classwork. I hated it when people asked me about the marriage I had so anticipated in May. One of the hardest things I had to do was cancel the reservation I had made for an apartment in married student housing. When it first happened, there wasn't anybody around I felt close enough to share my feelings with. I couldn't discuss it with Ella, because she was away at Lookout Mountain in Colorado, working with the Lisle Fellowship summer service program. When she returned we were both inundated with work. She was adjusting to her many tasks as full-time staffer at the Church of the Master, and I had my old jobs again at the seminary and at Concord Baptist Church in Brooklyn.

When I went home to Columbus for Christmas, I was still hurt—and also anxious. How could I ever be called to a church after I graduated from seminary the coming summer? In those days, Baptist churches did not usually call bachelors as pastors.

E While Henry was nursing his bruises, I was working in Colorado, having already traveled to California by car with two women friends. I was the sole driver of a Yale professor's new 1942 Pontiac, clear across the country—which took awhile; to save gas, the wartime federal speed limit was 35 miles an hour. The fact that Hazel, one of my companions, was White didn't help with the problem of finding places to sleep during the seven-day trip. Because our threesome included two Black women, we couldn't stop at hotels or motels. Our first night out, to no one's surprise we had to bed down in sleeping bags in a farmer's field in the Shenandoah Valley.

In Little Rock, Hazel was excluded from the parsonage of a "Colored" Presbyterian preacher where Gerri and I were made welcome. The pastor, afraid of trouble, arranged a room for Hazel at the YWCA. In Oklahoma, we were not allowed in Hazel's uncle's house; he arranged for Gerri and me to stay in the home of his Black maid. Even in South Carolina, I'd not witnessed such outrageous denials of dignity.

Toward the end of the trip, we slept in the car in an Arizona Highway Patrol parking lot, where they watched over us until dawn. It was years later before I fully realized how risky it had been for Negro women to be on the road unprotected, especially in the South. In those days almost every Negro was equipped with a kind of blinders that kept us from living in perpetual terror. Without such blinders we could not have moved about at all. However, I must have had some notion of the danger, because I carefully waited to tell my parents about the trip until I had arrived safely in California. I had more drive and spunk than even I was aware of. In a way, I didn't dare face the fact that there was in me an adventurous and rebellious woman trying to be free.

I wanted to spare my parents worry for another reason: In March 1943, Papa was stricken with a cerebral thrombosis. We four sisters were all summoned home to Charleston; Papa was in a coma and not expected to live. Mama needed help around the clock, because he could not be moved to the hospital. I fed Papa with a medicine dropper while the others bathed and changed him. He stayed in the coma for fifteen days. I was with him when he came out of it, talking as if nothing unusual had happened. I was amazed and extremely happy to have been the one on duty during his resurrection. Like the women at Jesus' tomb, I got the honor of bearing the good news.

Henry called me in Charleston in early May, to ask why I hadn't been at commencement to receive my diploma. I was pleased that he was concerned, and I did return to New York in time to march in the Columbia University commencement. (My degree was jointly conferred by both schools.)

While I was in Colorado that summer I had learned of Henry's broken engagement. I was not really sorry it had happened. Several people with me in the Colorado Lisle summer service program knew and liked both Henry and his fiancée, but we felt divine providence had intervened at a critical juncture. Henry's fiancée was a lovely person, but she was not really dedicated to the church and its mission. A role as wife to a pastor or missionary would have required of her an overwhelming amount of adjustment and sacrifice.

Before Christmas 1943, when I was back in New York, working full-time at the Church of the Master, my boyfriend from college days came to visit from Meharry Medical College in Nashville. I knew he had a ring in his pocket and intended to ask me to marry him. Since I had received my master's degree in religious education the previous May, my beau knew I would be ready to think about marriage.

Unfortunately, he arrived four days early, while I was still working on church activities. I had planned to complete my various Christmas parties and Advent programs by December 17 and had gotten tickets and passes for a string of Broadway shows and other affairs. When he had to kill four days by himself, he fussed the whole time, bored to tears. "You spend all your time at church. You might as well be married to the church," he complained.

"I guess you're right. In fact, I know you're right!" I told him.

There was a cold and eerie feeling between us for the remaining

11

days of his visit. He kept his ring in his pocket. We left New York on the same train, but we hardly spoke to each other.

Back home in South Carolina, Mama wanted to know, "Are you heartbroken?" To my own surprise, I had to say, "Not really." My intended and I had been good buddies at Talladega, when he was president of the college YMCA and I was president of the YWCA. But I had never been madly in love with him, and somehow I couldn't see myself as the wife of a wealthy doctor.

H One night after dinner, during Christmas of 1943, I was complaining to my parents that I didn't know any young Negro woman who had both the intelligence and the spiritual values I felt I needed to seek. I told my folks that in my fat file of photos and letters from girlfriends up and down the eastern seaboard, I knew no woman I thought could share the risky ministries I felt called to. I didn't want to be married to a wife who longed for fur coats and fine homes and cars but thought she could sacrifice them for love of a young preacher. I had seen this bond crumble under the weight of a spiritual vocation the wife didn't share.

I also told my family that I knew a White student whose aspirations might match mine. We had been spending a lot of time together. I had helped her defend herself after she waded into one of the fierce theological debates that occurred in the student lounge. We were just good schoolmates so far, as Ella and I were, but we had come to look forward to each other's company. We took walks along Riverside Drive some evenings after dinner. Then, just before Christmas, I had had a dream, more like a nightmare, in which she was with me on a city bus when I was harassed for being Black and she didn't come to my defense. I felt abandoned. I took the dream for an omen regarding my doubts about her, and my interest cooled considerably.

During dinner, Pops laid into me about how there were spiritually sensitive and intelligent women everywhere. I just had to do a better job of looking for one of my own race. Then he said, as a kind of afterthought, "What about that Pearson girl?"

"Pops, she would make some preacher a wonderful wife," I told him.

"Why not you?" Pops wanted to know.

"Pops, she's fifty pounds bigger than me, and she's almost two years older." It was true. Ella was, it turned out, 189 pounds to my 135.

My mom jumped in. "What's size got to do with anything?"

There could be no question why she asked; she had been much larger than Pops when they married, and she was still taller. They both went to work on me so fiercely that I hightailed it out of the room. I did not bring up marriage again. There was something about Pops's suggestion I couldn't avoid, and I knew Mom's challenge was sound. But I didn't want to dwell on either one. I put it all in a mental file called "inactive."

I marvel now, as I look back, that I was so resistant to Pops's suggestion. All during my late teens and early twenties, I had anticipated marriage and spoken to God about it. "Lord, I don't have any idea who she is or where she is," I prayed, "but make me worthy of her and help me to make her happy. And Lord, please, let me know who she is as soon as possible. I am eaten up with curiosity."

All through those years I had a recurring daydream: looking from my pulpit at a wife with a radiantly happy countenance, sitting in church, left of the center aisle in the third or fourth pew from the front. Under a napkin spread over her breast, she was nursing a baby. Now, I realized that my problem went deeper than my superficial objections about Ella's weight and age that I had offered to my parents. I also held the traditional view that marriage should begin with a wildly romantic attachment. Friendship was not, I thought, what made for a happy romance and a lasting marriage. Friendship was a nice beginning, but very soon flaming passion should take over. Of course, at twenty-four I didn't know what I was talking about.

More than a dozen years later, I had a conversation with our son, Hank, when he was maybe ten or eleven years old. We were just returning to our home in Berkeley from a trip to show some visitors the redwood trees in Marin County, north of San Francisco. I had been telling our guests how so few married couples really seemed to enjoy each other's company. Hank sensed that I considered Ella and me to be very happily married and really good buddies. He butted into the conversation. "You guys aren't the only couple in the world that are really happy and enjoy each other."

I agreed, but I suggested that the number of truly contented couples was still very small. Then I challenged him. "Think your way up our side of our block and back down the other, and stop when you come to a radiantly happy couple."

He accepted. "What about our neigbors two doors up?" he asked. At this house, a garbage-truck driver from Ireland pulled up for lunch every day at noon, to be met by his chubby Georgia-born wife. We all heard their joyous laughter echoing down the block. "See there!" Hank gloated. "You *know* those guys enjoy each other."

Hank was right—so far. "Tell me when you get to another friendly couple."

I watched as he considered the people on our street—including his own grandparents, Mom and Pops. He had to skip them, just as he skipped the others. There simply were no more really joyous couples. He was frank enough to admit it, adding that his grandparents were very loyal and supportive of each other, but they weren't boon buddies. It was a sad conclusion for me too. We both wished there were more couples in our neighborhood like the garbageman and his wife and Ella and me.

Together at First: But Not Love

When Henry and I look back over a marriage that can stand the keen scrutiny of our own son, we thank God that we didn't start with a stereotypically passionate romance. Instead, we had three years in which to season and ripen a friendship based on our common values. During our two years on campus together, our main focus was on our call from God, our studies, and our field work. There was none of the pressure that comes when two people are heatedly preoccupied with each other. It was not love at first sight that yielded the jovial, happy bond that continues to blossom between us after fifty-five years. It was only after a slow, healthy growth toward a deep relationship that we heard from heaven the orders to move on up to love and marriage.

Friendship is far more important than we ever knew when we got married. Lasting love is not something people fall into. It is a combination of growing and climbing, and that happens through a profound amity that grows in the fertile soil of common values and interests. Together we have grown far beyond anything either of us had in mind fifty-five years ago, because God nourished our friendship and set it to blossom.

15

CHAPTER 2

Equally Yoked:
Friendship to Courtship

E *(Ella)* What a difference our Christmases at home made in both of our lives! That winter of 1943–1944 left huge snowdrifts at the curbs in New York, in shocking contrast with my balmy South Carolina holiday. Even in Henry's Columbus, the snow didn't make mountains at your door and cover your car. Both of us were up to our ears in snowdrifts of work and riding out the aftermath of our failed engagements, but we didn't get together and jointly assess my relief and Henry's hurt. We were still just friends; I had no inkling of anything else.

My friendship with Henry was initially based on the fact that, without self-conscious to-do, we both felt called by God to some form of Christian ministry. My intended hit the nail on the head when he said I was married to the church. Shucks, that was true a long time before I ever met him *or* Henry. It became true for me when I was a little girl, the daughter of a preacher.

In my childhood, I was happy making the rounds of parish visits with Papa. As the first colored pastor of the Olivet Presbyterian Church—his predecessors had been White ministers heading a largely Black congregation as a kind of mission work—my father faithfully cared for more than a hundred souls, most of them lower-middle-class

16

to poor. Charleston as a whole was an old tradition-laden town, and the small community Papa served was near its heart. Most of the members lived close enough to walk to services, and the parsonage was in the churchyard. When I knew Papa was going to visit the older congregants, I would hurry to finish my homework so I could go with him. We Pearson girls had no playmates in our immediate neighborhood, so I was happy whenever Papa went to make calls on Short Street, only three blocks away from our house, because the Coaxum, Giles, and Bryant families had children my age.

Mama made me a big thick pillow out of mattress cotton so I could sit sidesaddle on the frame of Papa's bike as we rode from one street to another. Mrs. Bailey and the other ladies would give me tea cakes and other sweets to take home and share with my sisters. With these warm encounters so central to my childhood, the idea of full-time Christian ministry began to gain a hold on me as early as nine or ten. I knew I couldn't be a preacher; girls were not allowed. I never struggled with the details of how I would serve God. The attraction was not to any particular aspect of ministry; I liked all of it, especially the people. The service of the Lord appealed to me because service was about "two or three coming together," the way Jesus said.

On Saturday nights, Papa and I walked some eight blocks down to King Street to get our weekly peanut supply. We had to pass the shops on Beaufain Street and the wolf whistles of the loitering brothers on the block. At twelve, I looked older than I was. "Ol' Big," Papa advised, using his affectionate but problematic nickname for me, "you are well developed for your age, and these men don't know you're jailbait. Pay no attention to their flirting. Just to smile back could get you in deep trouble." It was a few years before I understood all of what he meant, but I could tell even then that he was dead serious, and I said obediently, "Yes, Papa, I'll be careful."

Grandma Wright became my roommate when I was five, after

Grandma Pearson moved to Washington, D.C. As soon as I learned how to read, Grandma Wright had me locate and read many of the Bible passages she had learned by rote earlier in her life. This led me likewise to spontaneous memorization of many treasured verses, which I still recall with ease. Now, seventy years later, Henry and I preach and teach all over America, and people tell me they are deeply moved by my readings. Whenever I read the Bible in public worship, I think of those formative years when I shared it with Grandma Wright. I believe this God-given gift of dramatic Bible-reading appeared way back then, in the mid-1920s.

With words came music. From the time I turned eight, Mama and Papa encouraged me to play the piano. Many times I was excused from my house chores in order to get in that half hour of practice. Papa would wait for me to finish before we went on our parish visits. My piano teacher, a minister's wife, challenged and motivated me, and I became good at sight reading. At age thirteen, I was drafted to serve as pianist for the Olivet Sunday school, which drew me deeper into ministry. Eventually I played for as many as four different Sunday schools. Though I was not conscious of my inner drive at the time, I now realize that I was a determined little sister about serving in the church. Music became my means.

About the age of fifteen, I became organist for morning worship at Olivet, so I started taking organ lessons from the wife of another minister. She died before I had many lessons. I played for her funeral and was asked to replace her as paid organist at the nearby Fourth Baptist Church. This was a major challenge, since my feet hardly reached the pedals of that majestic organ. But I loved that great instrument's worshipful sound. I wasn't just performing; I was pouring out a youthful and growing love for God and God's work. I practiced all the time, opening up the organ stops and letting the sound ascend. People would come in off the street to sit and listen.

At this time I was soprano soloist with our glee club at Avery Institute, a highly rated mission high school for "Colored" children, sponsored by a Congregational group, the American Missionary Association. My mother had graduated from both the high school and the "normal school" program there, but I was the first of her daughters to attend. My sister Lurline followed later. All five Pearson girls finished high school and went to college, in spite of my father's three-figure salary per year, plus parsonage.

Before I went away to Talladega, Papa invited me to preach Olivet's Youth Sunday sermon. I was seized with fear. I had won a local contest in public speaking, but preaching was hugely different. I had never even heard a woman preach, and I couldn't imagine what it would be like for me to stand there and proclaim the Word of God for the people of God.

Moreover, I sensed in Mama an undercurrent of quiet opposition. Girls were not supposed to put themselves forward, her manner implied. But after I spoke, most of the older women of the church were very encouraging. After that, when I was home, Papa had me lead worship or give the message at most evening services. Every time I came home from college, I knew I should be prepared to preach.

During the Presbyterian summer conferences for youth at Haines Institute in Augusta and Bethune-Cookman College in Daytona Beach, I was asked to give vesper messages around the campfire. I had no notion at the time that there would be so many lives touched as the result of the seeds sown in those early years of my ministry. More than sixty years later, as Henry and I were visiting retired United Methodist Bishop James Thomas, his wife, Ruth, announced to all of us, "Miss Pearson used to preach at vespers in the summer conferences in South Carolina during my teen years. I always looked forward to those evenings. She was such a delightful speaker, and we learned so much."

Despite my preaching, I never once said anything in public about being called. But there can be no denying that in my heart I felt I was being summoned to ministry. I knew I enjoyed doing it, but in the late 1930s there were huge barriers against women in the pulpit. I knew of no religious body where women were preaching. Even my parents were divided on the subject. Papa in his own way affirmed my embryonic ambitions. He was careful not to press me, but I felt his strong support of the longings that I myself had not fully defined. We both knew Mama was not to be approached on the subject, then or later. Her silent but staunch resistance weighed heavily on me. It was not until after she died in 1976 that my spirit felt free to accept the call to full ordination to the ministry, which came in October 1978.

During the thirty-five years from my seminary graduation in 1943 to my ordination, I never had anything but encouragement from Henry. He was already a rebel against sexist barriers, and he insisted that I override my timidity and accept every preaching invitation that came my way. He told me often how effective he thought I was as a preacher, using embarrassing adjectives like "great" to this day. At no point is he competitive with me, and he seems to enjoy my successes far more than his own.

When I first went to Talladega College, I had hoped to major in music. I wanted to be an opera singer, inspired by the pioneering Black diva Marian Anderson. At the time, it didn't even cross my mind that I could major in religion and become a preacher. Then something happened my freshman year that started me rethinking my education. One afternoon, as I was washing my face to go to dinner, I looked in the mirror and I couldn't see anything. I was devastated. Fortunately, this blindness lasted only three days; just as abruptly as it began, it departed, and my vision returned. Two weeks later, Papa took me to a special eye, ear, nose, and throat hospital in Washington, D.C. I will never forget hearing Papa and the surgeon chatting in Latin during the operation, while the polyps that had caused the blindness were being removed. I think they were just showing off.

Losing my vision, even temporarily, made me take my spiritual calling even more seriously, though I still wasn't sure how. By this time I had been informed that I didn't have quite the voice to be an opera singer, so a music major was out, even though Professor Harrison was kind enough to let me do most of the soprano solo work in the college choir. At the end of the school year I received the class's fourth highest grade in physics. That made me feel good, especially since I was the only woman in the top five. Even so, I didn't feel led to declare science as a major. As I faced blindness I had come to want to concentrate in religion, but a religion major was not available when I entered my junior year. I chose what I saw to be closest to it, a major in humanities with a minor in sociology.

However, my calling became more and more clear. As a junior I was elected president of the Young Women's Christian Assocation. I traveled with the College Quartette, but my real interest in singing was in the chapel choir. My other passion was a Sunday school I organized in Furnace Quarters, a nearby community of twenty families living in shacks beside an old steel mill furnace. This place was dark and dirty, and the students I invited to help me begged off. I taught the ladies' Bible class myself. Because not a single male student would come near the Quarters, there was no men's Bible class. Some of my female schoolmates did help me with the layettes we made for expectant mothers, but I always went down to the Quarters alone. It was said to be a dangerous place, but I was not impressed by the supposed risks. The only people who ever bothered me were the town police, who stopped me one Sunday and insisted that no college student should be down there. The next week I was right back at my class.

When I told Henry about this experience five years later, my story deeply affected him. I learned later that Mom Mitchell had taken the same risks in her mission work. That quality of willingness to engage in risky spiritual adventure was what Henry had been searching for in a woman.

When I went back to Talladega for my senior year, Buell Gordon Gallagher, the college president, called me to his office. "I am happy to inform you that the major in religion you requested is now available," he said. "We will do all we can to assist you in completing the necessary courses in time for graduation." The college had recruited Joseph W. Nicholson to be head of the Humanities Division. His doctorate was in religion, and he had coauthored a famous book, *The Negro's Church,* with Benjamin E. Mays in 1933. I was speechless with joy.

That year most of my classes were homelike one-on-one tutorials in the new religion courses. I was made assistant to Dr. Nicholson in the chapel and also enjoyed close ties with his wife, Mae, and their daughter Joan. I stood frequently before the students and faculty as leader of worship, and I learned all about the liturgical year as I sewed pulpit covers and Bible markers for the chapel. I was like Abraham's servant who got his final directions late in his journey: "I being in the way, the Lord led me" (Genesis 24:27). I had found my niche after three years on the way. In 1939, I graduated with a major in religion. My commitment was firm. I would serve in some capacity in the church, in spite of the barriers to women.

Again I was launching into the unknown. I knew of no woman who was engaged full-time in ministry. I had no models to follow. The illustrious president of Union Theological Seminary was known to suspect that every woman enrolled in the theological division was really working for her "M.R.S." degree. But how could they give their lives to work in the church if they were not married to a preacher? Even the more visionary overseas mission groups insisted that women appointees be married and accompanied by their husbands. Still, I was not consciously looking for a husband in seminary. Henry would say that if I were I would have dressed better!

In my two years between college and seminary I taught high school English when my sister Jess got pregnant and had to leave her job. (Her marriage had been a secret, because women known to be married were not allowed to teach.) I then served as a missionary for the Presbytery in rural Sumter County, South Carolina. I helped establish Sunday schools and did parish work. It was like being Minister of Christian Education for six small rural congregations. That meant teaching on porches and under trees. Unlike a modern VISTA volunteer, I was allegedly on full salary and expenses, but given what I was paid it was hard to tell.

In Mayesville, South Carolina, one of my mission stations, I finally encountered a woman farther down the path I wanted to travel. Mary McCleod Bethune was the first Black churchwoman I had known in a top position of church leadership, yet she had come from a poor and tiny place. Our chats on her front porch greatly enlarged my vision of what a woman's role might be, even if she was Black and from humble beginnings. Mary McCleod Bethune founded a college, championed the rights of children, and wielded influence in places as high as the nation's capital. For the first time I saw there could be more to a woman's call than Sunday schools, church music, and meetings of the women's society.

I needed to learn much more about how I might serve God. I applied to Yale Divinity School, which replied that they could find no placement in field work for Black males in New England, to say nothing of females. They felt Union Theological Seminary could place Black students because it was in a larger metropolitan area. Union accepted me on probation, because they had no previous students from Talladega to compare me with academically, but I was happy to be enrolled on any basis. Little did I suspect that this place would not only change my life and focus my calling but give me a lifelong companion.

Just to be allowed to study there made me rethink who I was. I had always seen myself as a low-profile plain Jane. Despite my high grades and vocal solos, I suffered in comparison with my prettier sisters. They teased me about never using any makeup and wearing whatever our mama put on me. Even Papa called me "Ol' Big." Somehow I had accepted their view of me. But now I was away from my roots and free to soar. I could create a new self in the world.

Two days after I met Henry in the tower elevator at Union, we applied for the same field work placement at St. James Presbyterian Church in Harlem. Although Henry had the usual male advantage, he was a Baptist, and I was, after all, a Presbyterian preacher's daughter. I was first cousin to Robert Pierre Johnson, who later became Stated Clerk of the Presbytery of New York. He had done his field work there during his seminary years. And Aunt Etta, my mother's sister, was a very active member of St. James. I was given the field work placement and a scholarship of $75 per semester, a small amount even then, but equal to a semester's tuition for as many credits as I could carry.

Henry laughed off losing the placement at St. James, and I sensed that we grew closer just by having gone through the rather clumsy selection process together. It made me admire him for his unselfishness and his keen sense of humor. He teased me that I'd been chosen out of nepotism, but he acted as if he was actually glad this woman had bested him. It boosted my sense of self to get the job. It was a reassuring initiation into the big city and the seminary.

H *(Henry)* Knowing how hard it was for women to get placement, I was glad Ella was chosen. I went on to get placed at the Church of the Master, also Presbyterian. It was hardly five long blocks down the hill from the seminary campus. The pastor, James H. Robinson, had also graduated from Lincoln, six years before me. When I first met him, he was emerging from a furnace he had been repairing in the church's ancient building, which made him seem easy to relate to. We hit it off right away, or so I thought.

But my rejection at St. James did stir a thought in me: "How odd of God / to choose and use / a dude like Henry Mitchell." My calling had never come easy. I had been a frightened, lonely kid, with one part of me very ornery. My foul mouth and sneaky side compensated for my small stature and the taunts of my schoolmates as I walked to school. I can still hear them singing about my squinting eyes and the oriental-style bangs that resulted from my father's bowl haircuts: "Ching chung Chinyman, eat dead rats. / Chew them up like gingersnaps."

I may have been short and innocent-looking, but I was also a juvenile delinquent in training. Part of me enjoyed the excitement of slipping past the streetcar conductor without paying the five-cent fare. I would chat up a store clerk, distract him, and steal chewing gum. I actually stood down by the public market on the east side of Columbus one Saturday night and picked the pocket of a boy who was bigger than I was. He never had any idea what happened to his dime. When I was ten years old, I took two envelopes out of an offering plate at the church. The whipping Dad gave me did not completely erase the excitement of buying pocket knives for my brothers with the cash I stole.

I had made a sincere and moving public confession of faith and been baptized when I was only five and a half years old, so I would ask myself why I did such awful things. But my concern always arose *after* the deed. I never stopped to think before I stole. It is called compulsive behavior, and all ages do it. The apostle Paul phrased it this way: "but the evil which I would not, that I do" (Romans 7:19b).

I've been making amends ever since for the rascal I was then. The only people who knew both sides of me in those days were my two brothers and, at times, my parents. My brothers sarcastically called me "Deacon Do-Right." Most other people warmly patted the back of the nice little boy they saw me to be. Dad had the three of us sing when we visited the elderly. Mom would have me recite portions of the Bible at her meetings. Everybody was sure I was going to be a preacher. But the older I grew, the more insistently I denied any such possibility, in part, I suspect, because I knew I sinned.

I don't have a specific recollection of when I started stealing and lying, or when I promised God to go straight. All I know is that I was in a constantly nourishing spiritual environment, at home and in the church, and I was sincerely taking part in it. Just as I had slipped into thieving without a conscious decision, so I slipped out. By the time I was about fourteen, I started praying, "Lord, what wilt thou have me to do?" I was pretty sure even then that the answer was "Preach the Word." I just felt it in my bones that I was called.

I backed off suddenly, however, when our pastor, who was my mentor and hero, was accused of having an affair with a young woman. I had confidential knowledge that he had undergone surgery that precluded such a liaison and could not be guilty. Still, he was forced to resign as pastor, which left me disillusioned about the church in general. This was the man who had given me my first ball and bat. In his seventies, he demonstrated an athletic vitality that recalled his college football successes and much impressed me. His encouragement had been the greatest influence in leading me to consider choosing the ministry. My namesake grandfathers were also preachers, yet I loved them more for their jovial and permissive ways and their skills with carpentry tools than for their ministry, which was merely a general part of their presence for me.

My deepest religious experience occurred in my twelfth-grade physics lab. Our teacher, old Mr. Bailey, held up a drop of water on a stick. He asked us what would happen if he heated the drop. "It will expand," we told him. Then he asked what would happen if the water was cooled. We shouted, "It will contract!" When he challenged the truth of our answer, we backed it up with the Law of Expansion and Contraction. He teased us and made us realize the drop would contract as it got colder, but only down to 32 degrees Fahrenheit. After that it would freeze into ice and expand.

"What difference does this make?" he asked us. "What if this exception were not true?" He helped us to see that without this one exception to the rule, ice would sink. Water passages underground would freeze shut, which would stop the heat exchange between underground masses of water and the water on the earth's surface. The temperature of the earth would be unbearably warm in summer and impossibly cold in winter. The planet would be uninhabitable if it weren't for this one exception to an otherwise global law.

By now, there was a drop of water in the corner of his eye. He said, "This is a public school, and I cannot take our inquiry any further. But I'll never believe this exception just happened." The lump in his throat and the tear in his eye made it unmistakably clear that he saw the hand of God in Creation. He would have liked to go further and testify to his faith, but he had gone far enough for me. I could now take full ownership of his scientific belief on my own. Suddenly I saw that natural science, which I loved so much, was not the enemy of my cherished faith, as so many of my elders seemed to think. This manifest scientific evidence of divine intelligence and power answered all my intellectual questions and brought me great spiritual healing and joy. I felt like shouting right there in the lab. And I had a drop or two of water in my own eyes. (Little did I dream that I would one day marry a woman who was similarly fascinated by the sciences, especially physics.)

However, my definitive calling to ministry did not come in my church, school, or home. The call came in a warehouse. Soon after I finished high school, a friend of my father's, Jack Fields, a foreman for a regional distributor of tractors and farm implements, created a job for me when he really didn't need another employee. He was expressing his gratitude for Pops's help around the house when Jack had been recovering from a near-fatal auto accident. He hired me at 25 cents an hour, and I wound up cleaning the showroom, offices, and shop; warehousing carloads of farm implements; packing and shipping parts; and occasionally serving as mechanic's helper on tractor motors and other farm equipment. When there were no obvious chores, I was sent out of sight, up into the warehouse, to bolt steel-forged cleats onto unmounted tractor wheels for reserve stock. (High-tread rubber tires for tractors would be developed later.) It required no thought to push that ratchet wrench, and I had unlimited time to daydream.

I had already told everyone my ambition: to become an electrical engineer in South America. I had long talked of going there, because I took for granted the fact that Blacks were not allowed to practice engineering in this country. It did not matter how well trained they were. We Blacks could not even become apprentice electricians.

In a fifth-grade geography text, I had seen a picture of a boy who could have been my Peruvian twin, and I knew I would be accepted in South America in spite of my skin color. Yet when I envisioned myself abroad, I was always at an African mission station. When I pictured myself at work in America, I always saw myself in a church. At first I ignored these scenarios, but they persisted in my daydreams. When, sitting in Jack's warehouse in the summer heat, I finally accepted the fact that I was being called of God, a huge load fell from my shoulders.

I had been denying my call so loudly that I insisted on keeping it a secret. It embarrassed me to admit my change of heart. Of course, I had to share it with Mom. She herself had once felt called to the mission field in Africa, but failing health forced her to abandon her ambitions. I waited until nobody else was at home and asked to talk with her. "Mom, I have something I must tell you, but remember it's a secret," I said.

"Son, you know you can tell me anything."

"Well—uh, I really didn't want to do it, but God has called me to preach, and as soon as I gave up fighting it and said yes, I felt so much better."

Mom responded with a serenity that took me aback. "Henry, you know already that I am delighted. But of course I'm not terribly surprised. Before you were born, I offered you to the Lord and prayed that you would be used in Kingdom service somewhere. Of course, I was careful not to try to press you in that direction."

I was a little bit disappointed. I wanted her to shout in boundless joy. "When I asked for some private time to talk, did you have any idea what was on my mind? What did you think I was going to say?" I had never asked for a private conversation with her before.

Mom smiled. "To tell you the truth, I was afraid you had fallen in love. I had no idea you were up in the warehouse praying, or I would have known what the end would be."

She had *expected* me to be a preacher, but she just hadn't told me or tried to make it happen, as so many others had. She felt there surely ought to be one preacher somewhere among her three sons, and when the first two showed no signs, she tried to influence the third by having him take Latin. We two older boys were allowed to take industrial arts—and we are the ones who ended up preaching.

My secret didn't last four days. I told our pastor, the Reverend C. F. Jenkins, who pledged his silence. But the next Sunday morning worship service, he managed to mention that "one of the Mitchell boys has been called." The same afternoon, Grandpa Henry Estis came to town and sat in on our Baptist Young People's Union meeting. I had been president for a year and felt in charge, so I steered the session to a close with no intention of calling on him for remarks. I knew too well how he bragged about grandchildren. However, several adults *insisted* that I give Reverend Estis the same respect I would show any other visiting minister. So I asked Gramps to have a word.

"Ever since he was a little fella, I knew this boy was called to preach the gospel," my grandfather announced. My heart sank. I couldn't deny him. I had to confess. "I hadn't planned to tell it just yet, but it's true," I said reluctantly, avoiding eye contact with my audience. "I tried to get away from the call, but I just couldn't. Please pray for me."

Less than a year later, while I was a freshman at Ohio State University, a friend of mine, George "Gatemouth" Moore, who was also a Black Catholic layman, told me that Union Theological Seminary in New York City was the greatest Protestant seminary in the world. "If that's the case, that's where I'm going," I declared. I have to believe that the Spirit guided me to break out of what was then my reflexive distrust of Catholicism, so I could be open to Gatemouth's advice. Four years later, in New York City, I'd be sitting at the feet of Paul Tillich and Reinhold Niebuhr, perhaps the two greatest American theologians of the twentieth century. At the time, of course, I had no notion of just how blessed I was, or how much influence these two giants would have on my future development. Or that I would meet Ella Pearson at Union.

I transferred to Lincoln University because I wanted to study away from home, and I preferred the compulsory Bible courses at Lincoln to the compulsory field artillery courses in the ROTC at Ohio State University, a land-grant college. Lincoln was also the alma mater of Grandpa H. H. Mitchell, class of 1876. He was the third oldest living graduate at the time, and I expected to get some scholarship aid just for being H. H. the Third. (It didn't happen, unfortunately, but I made do.)

When Reinhold Niebuhr came to preach in our chapel at Lincoln, I was proud to tell him that I had already been admitted to Union. I looked forward to being his student, and I was, just two years later. I also studied under Tillich, John Knox, Sophia Lyon Fahs, Harry Emerson Fosdick, and George A. Buttrick. Fosdick was featured on national radio and was probably the best-known preacher in America at the time. Buttrick was later the editor of the highly recognized twelve-volume commentary, *The Interpreter's Bible.*

My first year at Union ended darkly: My scholarship was removed, and I was actually advised not only to drop out but to consider another vocation. The letter came from the seminary's pastor/president, who had faithfully visited me in the hospital after my near-fatal appendicitis. I read the letter as I stood by a cooler, during my summer job at Indian Point Park, up the Hudson River. I was stunned. It seemed I had acquired a terrible reputation somehow, and I rushed back to New York to clear it up.

It turned out I had two fierce enemies close to the president. One was the school physician, who resented how I had pressured him to return me to seminary after my release from six weeks in the hospital. No doubt this Black student should have been patiently thankful that a White doctor would drive him back to the seminary, no matter how long he made me wait. He also reacted sharply when I told him I knew an error had occurred in my surgery. It never dawned on him that I couldn't possibly have made up the medical terms I used to describe what had happened. The surgeon professor on his rounds would never have used such technical terms at my bedside if he hadn't thought I was in a coma. I had to suspect, again, that the doctor was indignant that a Black man would dare to complain about anything a White man did.

My other enemy was Annie, the Irish-born maid on my floor at Hastings Hall. She also served in white apron during socials at the presidential parsonage. As she reported to my roommate's mother, she had fixed an opinion of me after a prank by my floor mates. They decorated the whole floor for St. Patrick's Day with *orange* shamrocks— a Protestant insult to any good Irish Catholic. It was a cruel trick, but I didn't know their plan when I drew the shamrock pattern for them and then left for my boy scout meeting. Annie saw the shape cut from some green paper on my desk and blamed me.

I thought she had forgiven me when she brought me some home-made marmalade. But her misjudgment of me didn't stop there. Coming back from a scout meeting one night, I found New York City firemen extinguishing a blaze in the dorm's dust chute. Some wag said, "I bet Annie caused it by shaking her dust mop in the chute from the top floor for the first time in twenty years." I caught the spirit and raced up the seven flights to my room. There I typed up "Proceedings of the Union Theological Seminary Night Court," with floor mates as the jury and Annie as the defendant. The charge was that she had broken her rule and actually put dust in the chute from the top for the first time, "thereby disturbing the adjustment of the dust particles in the chute, setting into motion the spontaneous combustion which resulted in the fire on the said date." A floor mate urged that I add this judgment: "She shall not again molest the dust."

Annie's boss saw it on the bulletin board, confronted her, and wound up calling Annie "dirty shanty Irish." When Annie finally pried out of Woody, the biggest square on the floor, that I was the culprit, she was furious. That's when she probably reported to the powers that be that I was too cruel to be studying for the priesthood.

After completing my detective work, I replied to the president's letter.

Dear Dr. Coffin:

I am regretfully in receipt of your letter of June 24, 1942. I also regret the apparent misinformation on which the letter's decision was based. Suffice it to say that to the extent that I did engage in presumably harmless pranks, with utterly unexpected results, I do humbly apologize.

As to my considering changing vocations, let me assure you that I am not studying for something lightly chosen. I am called to preach beyond any question whatever. And as to the withdrawal of my full-expense scholarship, I'm certain that the One who called me will also provide for me.

I fully understand your invitation for me not to return this September, but unless you literally refuse me registration, I shall return.

Yours in Christ,
Henry H. Mitchell

After a conference with Dean David Roberts, I was admitted for the fall term and given a work-study job on the Hastings Hall switchboard/reception desk. That, with my new field work assignment at the Concord Baptist Church in Brooklyn, assisted in tuition, subway tokens, room, and board. Despite the burden of the two jobs, I made the best grades of my life.

Union Seminary remained for me a mountaintop experience, but it had to end. I was to graduate at the end of summer, 1944. Could I be called to a Black Baptist church as a bachelor? I doubted it. I needed to find my divinely chosen wife, and I needed to find her fast.

One night at the end of January, I set about praying the matter through. I had never prayed so seriously or so long in my life. I asked, and then I struggled to hear a response. It was hard work; I broke out in a sweat. In all sincerity, I was trying to seek God's will, not mine. I prayed prostrate before the Lord from ten-thirty in the evening to three the next morning. *Lord, lead me to a companion whom I can lovingly help to be very happy and yet serve with all my heart wherever You call me to serve,* I prayed. *And please, Lord, make me worthy of her.*

What about that Pearson girl? It was Pops's question, repeated in the very voice of God. For a split second I thought, *Lord, that's not what I had in mind.* But I knew better.

The message became clearer and clearer. I promised God that I would call Ella the next day. Then I rolled over and slept like a baby. God had confirmed the fatherly advice I tried to ignore.

E When I returned to New York after Christmas 1943, Henry gave me no inkling of what his folks had put on his mind. He was busy finishing up the semester's work. I was busy with my four jobs in one at the Church of the Master. By title, I was Minister of Church Education, but I also coordinated the daycare program, served as girls' worker in the center, and acted as church social worker. I did just about everything at the church but preach regularly; I did preach on special occasions. (Women, of course, weren't expected to preach regularly.) I really had no time to think about my failed engagement.

Before my Christmas encounter with my intended, I put money down on a set of Lunt sterling silverware for my hope chest. I planned to finish paying before sales tax went into effect in April and then set it aside until my marriage. Now I decided to pay it off sooner and give the silver to my younger sister, who was getting married in February.

One day, riding on a city bus, I described the flatware to Henry and told him I was giving it to Lurline and Wendell for their wedding. Henry looked at me, astonished. "Why don't you just keep it? That's not the only man God has. You don't know *what's* liable to happen to you in the plan of God."

I was taken aback. "I don't expect to have any need for silverware," I told him. "Eventually I'm going to leave the Church of the Master and go home and help Papa manage his property." It wasn't that Papa had that much property; I was just resigned to spinsterhood.

Henry pressed me. "Now, Ella, you know that's a sick excuse. Why would anybody come way up here and get all this training to go back and manage a little bit of property?"

I could feel the anger in his voice, and I felt so crushed I couldn't say anything. I just let him rage on, oblivious to the other people on the bus and how he was hurting me. "How can you be so sure you will never need that silver?" he demanded. "I can't believe you think so little of yourself!"

I couldn't respond, and he finally quieted down. We rode the rest of the way home without mentioning hope chest and marriage again.

H I felt a bit frustrated, but I also felt embarrassed at how I had insisted to Ella that she was wrong. After all, Ella had a right to do whatever she wished with her sterling silver. I was fully aware that the service in my home in Columbus was Rogers silverplate, not solid sterling. All the more reason why I should stay out of Ella's business.

Just a few days later, I heard from the Lord about the woman I should marry. At the time, I was reacting to what could be thought of as a slight suspicion; it was an effort to keep this valuable property within reach. Had I known the answer to my prayer that day on the bus, I would have been as quick to reveal my intentions as I was later.

E When he asked to see me on a cold Saturday night in late January, I hadn't a clue as to what Henry wanted. I went downtown that day to audition for a singing slot with Phil Spitalny's all-girls chorus and orchestra. I didn't expect to be hired. I was doing it for the cause; it seemed that Phil should have to consider some Black singers like me. By the time Henry and I finally got together, it was much too late to go anywhere. We just stood in the lobby of the apartment house where I had moved to live with my godmother, Emma Wallace, on St. Nicholas Avenue at 157th Street, uptown Harlem, and what began as a casual chat turned into our most profound heart-to-heart conversation ever.

We talked until about 3 A.M., leaning against the wall by the steam radiator, greeting the tenants as they came home for the night. (God-mother was sleeping in her own living room. During the war every bedroom in the apartment was rented out. She also boarded children whose parents were in show business and traveled.) Our conversation was a more intense, late-night version of what we had discussed for years: our hopes, our ambitions, our families, and our faith. Then I mentioned that I had wanted to serve overseas as a missionary.

H It struck me like a bolt of lightning. Ella was casually talking of my own heart's desire. "When I first entered seminary, I applied for a year of study in Japan," she said. "I still think it would have worked out if the Japanese hadn't bombed Pearl Harbor."

I couldn't hide my excitement. "Girl, you never told me you were interested in missions. You mean you actually filled out the papers?"

"Sure, and I was accepted," she said. "I would have spent my second year over there and been back by now."

I was amazed. "I wonder why we never talked about this before, in all the talking we've done. I'm interested in missions too."

E "Oh, that wasn't my first attempt," I told him. "I took a shot at it when I was at Talladega. I applied for service in Africa with the Student Volunteer Movement, but they said I had to be married before I could go overseas."

H My mind was raced when she said Africa. This was the sort of woman I had been looking for all these years. But I managed to keep my cool. We had a whole lot more to talk about, but we were both very tired. I escorted Ella to the third floor via the elevator. Then I surprised myself and did what I had never done before. I put my arms around her, and kissed her good night, on the lips!

When I left her, I was ecstatic. "I've found her!" I told myself. "Here is one who will go *anywhere* the Lord sends." And for size-conscious little me a voice said, "Wow! I can actually put my arms all the way around her! With ease! Mom was right. What difference does size make? Besides, she has the face of an angel."

[E] My heart was beating so fast I could feel the pounding in my ears. That unusual encounter at the door set my mind spinning. What on earth could Henry mean by suddenly kissing me? And a lip-to-lip kiss at that? I was beside myself with excitement. I could hardly keep my mind on my work. I spent hours daydreaming of Henry, trying to figure him out.

Over the next weeks, we were both busy and could talk seriously only in snatches and only in public. Yet every time I saw Henry my heart tensed with hope. On February 29, I called Henry on the telephone. "Henry, let's get married. Tradition says it's respectable for ladies to propose today. It's the last chance I'll have to pop the question for another four years."

"When shall we have the wedding?" Henry asked quickly. "You set the date."

I was dumbfounded. Then I managed to blurt out, "Down, boy! I was just joking."

I couldn't believe he was serious. Imagine Papa's "Ol' Big" being singled out and sought after by a man most of my girlfriends thought was a prize catch. There were other girls who were much more attractive. Here I was, more than fifty pounds heavier than he was at the time. And besides, I was older. To me, he was a little brother in both size and age. Unaccustomed to male attention, I felt quite uncomfortable, and on that February twenty-ninth I beat a hasty retreat to cover my embarrassment. I didn't consciously distrust Henry's motives, but I was uncertain enough to decide that my leap-year proposal was a fearful mistake.

Sudden and unlikely love encounters generated deep suspicion in me. A few years earlier, a dear and homely friend of mine had been swept off her feet by a handsome old boyfriend. They were married before she found out that he wanted her for her family's money and already had a wife in California. Fortunately, my friend was able to get an immediate annulment. I always wondered why she didn't see through him from the start. She had known him since elementary school. Could I fall into the same kind of trap, even without the allure of money?

Now, half a century later, I know how little self-esteem I possessed back then. Lack of inner confidence causes many good women to make great mistakes in marriage. They don't think they can compete with men, even when they have a great deal to offer, so they surrender to some slick operator whose hot pursuit overwhelms their feelings of inferiority long enough to get them to the altar. Then these women find themselves exploited and they are left, as Terry McMillan so famously put it, "waiting to exhale." Our self-esteem ought to be based on our own standards of character, not on our culture's popular notions of what is desirable. We should apply those same standards to our choice of a mate and not react out of fear or desperation.

H If Ella wouldn't take my leap-year response seriously, I decided I'd have to woo her in print. I began sending her typed letters of as much as three pages single-spaced. One of these oddly theological epistles ended with the declaration that "every conversation with you could well be held between cross and candlesticks." This wasn't just poetry; I was trying to tell her that for me she represented a happy synthesis of divine call and human commitment in love. I suggested that she was overlooking what could be a providential downpour of blessings. I dared to think, with profuse apologies for my presumption, that I just might be the agent of that providence.

E What holy chatter! Was he a smooth operator? Or a bloomin' "agent of providence"? I was nonplussed. I didn't know what to do, so I asked for some help. Godmother Wallace said, "Take your time. You don't have to be in a hurry about this." I shared the letter with one of my girlfriends. "That guy is out to win all the girls sooner or later," she warned me. "And you're the only one who hasn't fallen for him already." It didn't occur to me that she might be jealous. And so I waited—but not too long.

H Without even an inkling that we were dating, James H. Robinson, Ella's boss and my former boss at Church of the Master, blasted me. As she rode in the back seat of his car, Ella heard him tell his friend, "I had to get rid of that Henry Mitchell. He was too arrogant and considered himself an authority." Ella said she didn't challenge Jim Robinson, but she couldn't imagine he was talking about the same Henry Mitchell she knew.

Ella shared one of my letters with a close friend. Ella's friend told a mutual friend of ours about the letter and her theory about my ambitions. My friend confronted me about it in his room one afternoon. "Man, I don't believe you actually wrote that girl a serious love letter, actually put it on paper where she could show it to people! What on earth were you thinking about?"

I didn't have the nerve to tell him flat out, "The Lord made me do it." I just closed his door and wandered back to my room.

E Henry got a better rating from some Barnard College students I talked to. On the Saturday before Palm Sunday, I took a group of them up to the Church of the Master's Camp Rabbit Hollow in New Hampshire. We were there to ready the camp facility for the summer season. Henry had helped us with the luggage as we were leaving New York. All during that work week, the girls badgered me with questions.

When I told them he said he was serious, they wanted to know why on earth I was so hesitant to marry him. These girls worked hard to get me to confront my fears. I simply could not believe it was real, that I was the one he wanted. Why would a person with his unlimited options choose someone like me? It didn't occur to me that in the male mind there could be a set of values other than the ones that prevailed on Hollywood movie screens.

During the train ride home, I got to thinking seriously about my conversation with the girls. Suddenly I wanted to find Henry as soon as possible, to see if I could get some answers to my many questions. I got off the train at 125th Street, hoping to reach him at the seminary. The girls went on down to Grand Central, where, it turned out, Henry met them and helped them with their baggage, as he had done the week before. When I called the seminary, I was told he had gone to Grand Central to meet us. I never did reach him that entire evening.

The next day, Saturday, I heard the rhythm of his footfall as he bounded down the steps to my office in the Church of the Master. "It's twelve-thirty in the afternoon. Workday is over," he declared.

"All right," I said, "but I have to deliver some Radio City Music Hall tickets for the Easter Sunrise Service. One of us can stay in the subway station, to save the fare, while the other delivers the tickets to the senior citizens." We had dropoff points at the 72nd Street Y and several other places.

After that we went to 155th Street, to the Palace Mission. Father Divine, a famous cult leader of that era who claimed to be God, had opened many public ministries. He helped people get off welfare and learn trades. I had left a suit jacket at the Mission's tailor shop, to have some machine-made buttonholes put in. After we picked up the jacket, we went over to the Mission's restaurant for a chicken dinner with all the trimmings, which only cost a quarter. The secret for getting bigger servings was to order by this formula: "I'll thank Father for a chicken dinner." Father's minions were pleased by that and ladled on more.

We took a table and sat in one of the secluded balcony booths. We weren't allowed to leave when we were finished, because Father had the building sealed during his visits, which were limited to weekends. (He was having some trouble with New York tax authorities and had taken up residence in Philadelphia.) We watched as Father made an appearance that sent the dancers who welcomed him swooning to the floor. He said very little, but every word he uttered set off a great response. The beat of the music was powerful. There was some reason to suspect that it was designed to sublimate the urges of his faithful followers, whom Father Divine had decreed must be separated from their spouses. It had the opposite effect on the two of us, sitting close together in this strange setting and watching the rites that went with this cult leader's good works.

It was late evening when we trudged through the Saturday-night street crowd, up the hill two blocks to my godmother's apartment on St. Nicholas Avenue. Once again we stood by the steam radiator downstairs in the barren but clean lobby. The night before I had thought I had many questions, but once we got together they all seemed to evaporate. As I reflect, the questions had been about me, not Henry. His warm attention seemed to answer them all, despite the unromantic setting.

It all came to a conclusion when Henry took my hand, looked me directly in the eye, turned on his best soft resonant baritone, and declared, in a most un-Hollywood manner, "Ella, darling, I have thought and prayed a great deal about us being together. I am convinced that God is guiding us to make it a permanent relationship. I'm not wildly, madly in love, but everything I know about you makes me certain that we were meant to be together."

I stood there stunned. Henry seemed so convinced and so sincere. Finally, I got myself together and calmly replied in the words of Paul to the church at Rome (8:31): "If God be for us, who can be against us? Not even I."

CHAPTER 3

Love and Marriage:
The Wedding and the Honeymoon

H *(Henry)* Ella started the summer directing Camp Rabbit Hollow in New Hampshire, but she came back to New York City to make the final plans for our August 12 wedding. We had aimed to marry around Christmas, but I had proposed a new date just two days after my commencement. This meant my family could attend my graduation and our wedding on the same train ticket from Ohio. Ella agreed, and her parents had the invitations printed. Three weeks before the wedding, when I happened to ask how long it had been since Ella's family mailed the invitations, Mama Jessie Pearson said she still had them. I nearly flipped! Etiquette prescribed a whole month's notice, but Mama thought it was too soon to send them—people might forget to come. She was planning to hand-deliver the ones in nearby New York the week before the wedding, and mail the others a bit sooner. I was very much put out, even as I was trying to make a good first impression on Ella's family.

E *(Ella)* I had never seen Henry so upset, and I was terrified at what he might do. But he fumed only briefly before he blurted out an ultimatum. "Those invitations will be in the mail tomorrow, or I will bring a crew of friends and do them myself!" What a relief! He didn't storm out. Mama stammered out a promise to comply. I was glad not to be caught in the middle.

43

I was the last of the five Pearson sisters to get married, except for my adopted senior sister Beulah, who was considerably older than the rest of us. She seemed beyond the prospects for marriage already, given the conventions of that era. My family told me they had decided that since none of the others had had a large wedding, mine must be as big as we all could manage. I didn't offer any protests, and the wedding just grew. Sister Jessica would be the matron of honor, Beulah the maid of honor, and Ermine and Lurline bridesmaids. Henry's sister, Marjorie, age sixteen, would also be a bridesmaid. Together with our school friends Charlotte Hanley and Jane Pakenham, and an assortment of cousins, I would have nine women as attendants. One of the flower girls was Jessica's three-year-old daughter, Andrea.

In the wartime manpower shortage, Henry had to rustle up nine men to pair up with our women. For groomsmen he recruited six schoolmates, plus two six-foot teenagers from his Concord Baptist Boys Club basketball team. Since Elbert was in the South Pacific and Louis in California, Henry chose Pops as best man. Ermine's two young sons, Harold and Edward, were the ringbearers. With Papa and Dr. J. B. Adams officiating, and Jess's husband, Fred, to walk me down the aisle, and, of course, the bride and groom, the number of wedding participants rose to twenty-seven. To this must be added our musicians, the celebrated contralto Carol Brice and the now-famous Sylvia Olden Lee, accompanist, both from my Talladega days.

Though half of the wedding party have departed this life, an article in the October 27, 1997, issue of *Jet Magazine* declared that the four married Pearson sisters were still with their first husbands, with a total of 227 years of marriage among them. The article stated that Mama Pearson had told each of her daughters she was marrying "the right man," but Henry's approval came later. In any case, all four couples found themselves to be good friends first, before marriage. The total of years together reached 231 before Ermine's husband, Harold, died in November and Jessica died in December of 1998.

H With my two brothers out of reach, I asked Pops to be my best man. Although I preferred informal dress, I was outvoted by a wide circle of family and church friends and wound up paying for twelve tuxedos, each retailored to fit at cuffs and shoulders, which cost me a total of only $84. Of course, all that wool cost us all a lot of sweat that hot August evening.

Ella's gorgeous wedding gown, train, veil, and twenty-five yards of ribbon cost $75. Her sisters made the nine bridesmaids' dresses and hats. The large iced fruit cake that served as wedding cake and sliced into wrapped souvenirs cost $25. Ella's father paid for the reception, hosted by relatives of the Pearsons who were in the catering business. The whole affair was amazingly deluxe for so tiny a total budget. This turned out to be a foretaste of all of our abundant life together. If you're aiming for a genuine experience and not just trying to show off, simple creativity, with taste and talent, will leave you joyful and satisfied. People will remember the spirit and the faces, not the frills.

H Henry and I spent hours choosing vows, prayers, and the Order of Service. We selected passages from several pastor's manuals and wrote a bit ourselves. For instance, we declined to use the word "obey," from the widely used Episcopal service. That decision was pretty radical for that era. I was no militant feminist back then, but we wanted our marriage to reflect our equal yoking and the authority we would share. Our most memorable phrases came from a prayer by Walter Rauschenbusch. We still recite it to each other:

> We pray thee to make their love strong, holy, and deathless,
> that no misunderstandings may fray the bond, and no gray

45

disenchantment of the years may have the power to quench the heavenly light that now glows in them. May they ever discern the true values of life, and may no glamour of cheaper joys rob them of the wholesome peace and inward satisfaction which only loyal love can give. . . . Thus may they reverence themselves and drink the cup of joy with awe.

H I worried that if we repeated the vows, phrase by phrase, as the ministers intoned them, we would sound wooden. If we really believe what we vow, we ought to be able to say it without having someone put the words in our mouths. Ella and I decided to memorize the vows. Even today, whenever we do a wedding, we ask the bride and groom either to memorize the vows or read from a card they hold. Definitely none of this repeating "I, John, do promise . . ." / " I, John, do promise . . ." and "I, Jane, do promise . . ." / "I, Jane, do promise . . ."

Having natural-sounding vows was a part of our larger concern that the wedding be a service of true worship, not a mere spectacle. Carol Brice would sing the simple hymn "O Perfect Love" and the Lord's Prayer during the ceremony. The male and female participants had prayer before entering the sanctuary. We did, however, request the traditional secular processional and recessional, from Wagner's *Lohengrin* and Mendelsohn's *Midsummer Night's Dream*.

E The wedding day arrived. My god-sister, the actress Ruby Dee, was at the church, helping the ladies get ready. She had lent us her home, just two doors away from the church, where Mama and Cousin Emily Gibbes were getting me dressed for the occasion. Mama still smarted from Henry's anger, displayed over her delayed invitations, and she couldn't resist one last word of counsel: "It's not too late to change your mind, you know." My husband-to-be "spoke with an open mouth," she said; he was brusque and outspoken. And he was, after all, only a Baptist, not a proper Presbyterian. Standing there in my wedding dress, experiencing the mixture of joy and terror that all brides feel, I couldn't help but feel wounded at what she said and when she said it. I took a deep breath and looked down at her graying head as she knelt before me, arranging the folds of my dress. She loved me, I knew, and she was losing a daughter to marriage, after all. I wouldn't let what she said get in my way, and so I didn't respond. I finished dressing, and Mama and Emily walked me the few steps to the church, where Fred, Jess's husband, met me in the vestibule.

At the back of the church, I watched as the bridesmaids and grooms-men processed down the two sides of the sanctuary, and suddenly the truth of this whole affair came crashing down on me. The white Bible in my hand was quivering, and I narrowly escaped stepping out of one of my slippers. I clutched Fred's arm and set out down the aisle. It seemed a mile long, but ahead of me were Papa and Henry, smiling. I had somehow settled down when Henry and I joined hands and faced the presiding ministers.

H Ella's countenance had never seemed so angelic; there was no visible trace whatever of her nervousness. Just seeing her moved me deeply. A lump rose in my throat, and I struggled to be sure my vows could be easily heard. When my main vow came up, I looked her straight in the eye and said with all my heart, "I, Henry, take thee, Ella, to be my wedded wife, and I do promise and covenant, before God and these witnesses, to be thy loving and faithful husband, in plenty and in want, in joy and in sorrow, in sickness and in health, as long as we both shall live."

As Ella repeated the same vow, I soared. Though I am not one to cry or show much emotion, I was awash in tears. But nobody could tell, not even Ella. I was already bathed in the perspiration of a hot August evening, thanks to my woolen tux.

By the time we came to the exchange of rings, I was joyously calm. Dr. Adams intoned, " Bless, O Lord, these rings, that they who give and wear them may abide in thy peace and continue in thy favor unto their life's end, through Jesus Christ our Lord. Amen." Without any trembling of hands or any of the usual fumbling that marrying couples make, we each slipped a wedding band on the other, saying, "This ring I give thee, in token and pledge of our constant faith and abiding love." Both these words and our recited vows were right out of the Presbyterian Book of Common Worship. This would have pleased Mama greatly, if I had thought to mention it. But we chose these words only because they said what we wanted to say.

Our wedding bands had special meaning for us as well. While I was working at St. James Presbyterian Church, I was introduced to a Mr. Lanz, a wholesale jeweler on Maiden Lane, in the financial district of downtown Manhattan. The church often sent me there to purchase gifts for the church's weddings at the same 50 percent wholesale discount given to dealers. When we needed gold wedding bands, I took Henry to see Mr. Lanz. He seemed to be delighted to be included in our wedding plans. The two wedding bands cost us a total of only twenty dollars! Mr. Lanz also laid aside a diamond that could be placed in a ring that Henry would send for later, after we had had a chance to earn some money.

For the pledge of our engagement, Henry had given me a large opal pendant. Several months after our marriage I lost it, much to my dismay, but I still have that nearly half-carat diamond Mr. Lanz laid aside. It is now worth many times the $75 that Henry paid for it the Christmas after our marriage. Mr. Lanz claimed he was letting him have it for the prewar price, but we knew he was just being generous. Years later he sent a ring at the birth of our son, Hank, and later sterling silver spoons to each of our children. We still rejoice as we look at that diamond. It was the providence of God, working in World War II, through a German jeweler.

H Over fifty-five years, Ella has worn out two mountings of her stone, and I have worn thin my wedding band and replaced it. But we will never outgrow the joy of sensing God's care that we felt on our wedding day. The passion of being madly in love, which I thought I had missed, was more than replaced by the bond I sensed with my bride as we recessed back up the aisle. I was gripped with an awesome feeling of togetherness.

Of course, the festivities were not yet over. We were driven to the reception at the Church of the Master in what, during the war, was the rare luxury of a private sedan. It was owned by Navy Chief Frank Collier and his wife, Fannie, dear friends from the Concord Baptist Church in Brooklyn. The reception was a beautiful occasion, laced with the love of Ella's cousins, who catered it, and complete with a wonderful collection of wedding gifts on display. Fifty-five years later, after moving repeatedly to new homes across the continent, we still have a piece here and there from those presents.

E The Colliers continued their role as our gracious chauffeurs. As we were driven down Riverside Drive, headed back to Brooklyn for our first night of wedded bliss, we loosened our wedding finery and sat back to enjoy the breeze coming in from the Hudson River, a marvelous relief in those days before air conditioners. Henry was so grateful he sighed and allowed as how he "could ride like this for the rest of the night." Saintly sister in the front seat shot back with "Some people *do* ride all night when they get married." We all laughed. Soon we were delivered to the residence of the Reverend Thomas J. and Mrs. Jean Boyd, dear friends and associates at Concord. It was too late to catch a train upstate to our honeymoon cabin. As we prepared for the night and packed for the morning, Henry asked for a pair of pliers, to pull a nail that had somehow gotten stuck in the heel of one of his moccasins. But, of course, our gracious host didn't hear the reason for the pliers, if indeed Henry bothered to explain. Tom's comic imagination made much of a man's need for pliers on his honeymoon.

Our host also favored us with a special selection of hymns, which he sang through the hall and up and down the stairs from time to time: "Nothing Between My Soul and the Savior," "Love Lifted Me," and "I Surrender All." In the midst of our laughter, Tom let loose with a hymn I had not heard before I came to Concord Baptist Church, "Is Your All on the Altar?" After four meaningful stanzas, the chorus included this refrain: "Is your all on the altar of sacrifice laid? . . . / You can only be blest and have peace and sweet rest / As you yield Him your body and soul." We still enjoy Tom Boyd's humor whenever we are guests in his home.

H Starting with our laughter at the end of a profoundly spiritual day, our lives have always been full of joy. Twenty years or so after our children left home, they confessed to occasional eavesdropping on their parents in the middle of the night. They could never figure out what we found to talk and laugh about so heartily at 2:00 A.M. I tend to be the primary jester in our family. As the son of Orlando Mitchell, who knew when in life to laugh, I believe I inherited a saving grace of humor that matches me well with Ella, daughter of the mischievous Joseph Pearson. This could have kept me from becoming a hopeless, humorless workaholic.

"A merry heart doeth good like a medicine" (Proverbs 17:22), and good humor is healing. A marriage without merriment is a burden and a bore. People who enjoy life abundant can afford delight—in love and in sexuality. It greatly enriched our union.

E The next morning, we took a train from Penn Station to Cuddebackville, New York, to begin our honeymoon. In my bag was a small book I had bought by a man named Butterfield, *Sexual Harmony in*

Marriage. Henry and I had studied a lot about marriage and family in classes at school, but neither of us had any "road experience." Somehow Mama Pearson came across this little text among my wedding planning materials. She must have been shocked and thought I should not be reading about such things, because she hid it. Before long I was asking if anyone had seen the book, because I had read it and wanted to pass it on to Henry. When Mama owned up to having taken it, my married sisters couldn't believe she was so prim. "Were you going to give it back to Ella *after* the ceremony?" Ermine asked. "Are you expecting them to read it on their wedding night?" Then they portrayed the newlyweds, each holding the book in one hand and embracing with the other. We were all shaking with laughter, and Mama reluctantly surrendered the book.

H That name Cuddebackville sounds like a joke, but it isn't; it's an actual town on the Delaware River, across from Middletown, New York. We had a one-room lakeside cabin reserved for a week. Here we were, just Ella and me, one-on-one for days; our only occupation to be with each other.

Being together was awkward at first, even embarrassing. What do you say and do for sixteen waking hours? All we had to read were some magazines, including a supply of back issues of *Esquire* magazine, back then a para-pornographic journal with some genuine sophistication. And, of course, we had a couple of Bibles. We slept, ate, read, and swam. The small lake on the premises had ample shallow water for Ella to splash about in, yet grew deep enough for me to swim. I cavorted in the lake as much as possible, but it wasn't exactly warm.

In our many daylight and evening hours of close contact, we continued to discover and explore each other. My curiosity was great, but so was my timidity. The fact that all I had in mind was fully legal and even righteous did not free me from twenty-five years of fear and inhibition. My one comfort was that Ella felt the same way.

E That's the truth, believe me. I was nervous and uncertain day and night. Was I doing *anything* right? First of all, it seemed I was married to a fish, whereas I had been content just to fulfill the college swimming requirement. How was I to know I would be married at all, let alone to a professional lifeguard? I dreaded our time in the water, and it seemed he wanted to spend half the honeymoon in the lake.

Henry was sensitive to my discomfort and tried to teach me how to swim. After all, he had taught dozens of people in his summer jobs. But, as we learned, it is definitely not a good idea for a man to teach his wife to swim or drive a car. Husbands just can't be objective, and an unspoken response to the failure of a loved one will tend to make the wife freeze and block out all the lessons. We both knew this, but we dared to try to be the exceptions. At least when it came to sex, Henry was as dumb as I was. Since we had read the same books and seen the same movies for a couple of years, we were equally yoked in our ignorance.

Sex made me anxious because I was so afraid I would fail. I had always felt overweight and underattractive—how could my husband ever feel a magnetic pull toward me? I dreaded getting undressed. I was almost as bad as my mother, who bragged that after fifty years of marriage and four babies her husband had never seen her in the altogether. Our honeymoon was nearly half over before I bravely revealed my entire body to my husband.

Painfully aware of my self-consciousness, Henry strove to reassure me I was desirable. "You were predestined for the worthy purposes of snuggling," he told me, "and I am a genuine, pure-bred snuggle bunny." Even after fifty-five years together, and all the physical and other changes, he still says he is a snuggle bunny, and he still seems to mean it. Back then I greatly appreciated his attempts at comforting me, but no one can erase twenty-seven years of feeling inferior with a few kind comments. It took years of Henry's affirmation before I felt confidence in my body.

H I myself had grown up knock-kneed, squinty-eyed, and something of an ugly duckling. With their pretty curls and lighter complexions, my brothers were always considered the cute ones. Ella's praise of my looks didn't cure my "ugly" complex any faster than my insistence on her comeliness cured hers. It did make us equally yoked, of course. And both of us are still working on each other's self-esteem even now, after fifty-five years. We still have some failures, but it's lots more fun to raise a partner's self-image than to deflate a mate who is arrogant, presumptuous, and self-centered.

In the dance of lovemaking, we started by stumbling. No matter how much we had read or how much we tried to reassure each other, we still felt oppressed by deep-seated fears that we were not performing as we should. Fears piled on top of fears, especially for me, each time I responded all too soon. Even so, we both enjoyed a naive fulfillment, covering up what for me was a seemingly endless downward spiral of anxiety. Anxiety is the opposite of faith, but they are alike in that they both arise out of experience. I found it difficult at the outset to have faith-producing experiences, but little by little our life together grew toward our dreams.

E Women don't measure themselves by the same sexual performance standards as men do, but my sense of failure was still strong, no matter how much I showed my desire for my husband. I felt a lot of responsibility for Henry's problems. Either I was not as desirable as I should be or I was not doing something right. The first two nights were most disappointing for both of us.

Then my anxiety began to melt down, and so did Henry's. As we fumbled through our encounters, we learned a lot in a hurry. We found out that Henry's snuggling had excellent effects. We learned that anxiety is best talked out rather than kept hidden. We learned that it is never good to be in a hurry, and that the Spirit cannot be held to stopwatch precision. We began to have more patience with ourselves, and to our surprise things improved mightily. By Friday, we were wondering if we could stand it if our loving got much better. Now, more than half a century later, we know that this worry was ridiculous. But at the time, we had no previous experience with which to compare our lovemaking. We wouldn't trade our history with anybody, even though we dare not be judgmental toward today's majority of young people whose sexual experiences come earlier than ours did.

We left Cuddebackville on Saturday and returned to our apartment at 1447 Dean Street in Brooklyn, which Ma Warren, pastor's widow and *dear* friend, had temporarily vacated so we would have somewhere to live. Henry's folks had stayed there while we were on our honeymoon. When they greeted us at the gate, we guessed they were curious to see if Henry could actually carry a person my size across the threshold. They must have forgotten that he was once a freight handler. He scooped me up and laid me across his chest and marched all the way through the house to the back door. I wasn't too heavy after all.

H We were two wide-eyed children, hand in hand, exploring a wonderland of surprises. No matter what we were doing, between us there was a constant undercurrent of physical magnetism that culminated at the day's end in ever greater unity in both body and spirit.

Without even a hint of self-conscious piety, our sex life took on some of the qualities of a sacrament. One night while we were living in Durham, North Carolina, after we concluded our lovemaking I found myself soaring on a kind of ecstatic inspiration. I couldn't go to sleep; a brand new sermon insisted on assembling itself, with some parts arriving verbatim. Only after I put it on paper could I sleep in peace. Again and again, after we made love, the Spirit would visit me. I began to keep a writing pad beside the bed. I never knew when such a blessing would invade my consciousness. Ella began to share in the joy of the pouring out. She made sure I had Bibles and a concordance within easy reach. After I had roughly sketched out the night's revelation, we would kiss good night and fall asleep grateful.

M Maybe this too was a gift of the Spirit: I outgrew my shame with dazzling speed. I looked up one day, and our closeness had blown away all self-consciousness about my body. I saw nothing dirty or unworthy in my husband seeing me in the altogether. With him, I could also reveal my thoughts. I had never expressed my ideas to anybody, anywhere, the way I did to Henry. The man Mama said spoke with an open mouth was forthright and revealing with me in ways he had never allowed himself before. I even went so far as to take the initiative in sexual encounters, which put me light-years beyond the beliefs I'd been raised with. In every way, our romance made us feel *healthy*.

H As for false modesty, I had lost mine years before, as I sat on a public pool's lifeguard chair and worked, the same summer, in a hotel in Columbus. It was all too common for female swimmers to float in front of my post and act as if they didn't know that the white knit underskirt of a princess bathing suit became transparent when wet. It was all too common in the hotel for hookers to operate across the courtyard with no regard whatever for window shades. I had been exposed to every possible combination of humanity, becoming something of an inquisitive expert as I lost a part of my innocence. But these exposures were at a distance; my personal inhibitions had remained until Ella came along.

Beyond our private wonderland beckoned the world of work. My sudden and serious problem after our honeymoon was a job. When we landed back in Brooklyn, I discovered I was unemployed. The assistant pastorate I had assumed Dr. Adams intended to create for me was lost from his recollection. Yet, before we even had much chance to worry, Dr. James E. Shepard, the president of what was then officially known as the North Carolina College for Negroes, now the great North Carolina Central University, invited me to be acting dean of the chapel. I went to Durham immediately, leaving Ella to await Ma Warren's unexpectedly necessary early return. She did not wish her apartment left empty.

In Durham I found a cozy two-bedroom brick bungalow on the campus, available because the dean of the chapel was on sabbatical. I loved it, but it was terribly empty before Ella came down to join me. My only remedy was the fact that I was soon up to my ears planning worship services and student assemblies, preparing lectures, and grading papers.

E Still in Brooklyn, I was busy acknowledging wedding gifts, and I missed Henry terribly. I actually ached for him, and was overjoyed as soon as Ma Warren returned and I could rush down to Durham. When we did get together, it was as if we had been apart for a year. We wasted no time in enjoying our new love nest to the fullest.

In the midst of newlywed joy, I was cooking and supposedly keeping house for a breadwinner for the first time in my life. Three weeks in Brooklyn had not been long enough for Henry to teach me how to cook. The older women in my childhood home had insisted on doing all the cooking, so my childhood duties had kept me away from the stove. On Saturdays, Henry helped me to cook much of the food for the week. Our honeymoon continued amid much more practical responsibility. Weekly washing, ironing, and ordinary housecleaning chores were all quite new to this newly married lady, and it took me awhile to develop a household rhythm. Even so, after just six months, the senior girls would ask me to teach them how to be wives. I was surely no expert at that stage of our marriage, but we must have been doing something right.

Now, after fifty-five years, we are still on a kind of honeymoon with, from time to time, spontaneous special events, like our unforgettable experience in 1959, at the Baptist bathhouse at Hot Springs, Arkansas. We were returning to California by car from my twentieth class reunion at Talladega. Henry was curious about this spa, owned by the National Baptist Convention, USA, so we stopped for two nights. As part of the usual treatment, we were packed in warm mud and then bathed in the hot springs and given massages. We felt cleaner and more relaxed than either of us had ever been before. Our togetherness in the nights that followed was unforgettable. In 1966, just after we were called to serve the Santa Monica Calvary Baptist Church, we experienced more awesome oneness. Our hosts were away on vacation, and we had the run of their comfortable home. Our children were out of the nest by then, and we were free to focus on each other, the way we had on our original honeymoon. We knew a lot better what to do with the hours we spent together than we did in Cuddebackville in 1944.

In the early 1980s, when we were both doing lectures for the Tabernacle Baptist Church in Detroit, the pastor, Dr. Fred Sampson, put us up in a deluxe hotel. We were free most of every day because our presentations were already prepared. We gave some time over to swimming, and one day we took the hotel's free limousine to the 'hood, to buy a pair of barber shears. For years we had trimmed each other's hair, but that particular day the act had a special quality that electrified our togetherness.

Still, while special occasions are indeed special, our day-to-day, night-to-night oneness remains a constant joy. The joy is even greater when it is constant. We still cut each other's hair, fix meals together, and bathe in our large tub with Jacuzzi. When we thank God every morning for our blessings, we dare not fail to include our still rich and extended honeymoon. Age is just a number, and God is good all the time. With God's help, we have kept the divine spark alive with which we were united fifty-five years ago.

CHAPTER 4

Together Starting Out: Creating Couplehood

H *(Henry)* My introduction to Durham was not auspicious. In early September, I took the train to Raleigh and then did the final twenty miles on a bus. At the station that Sunday evening I was met by a company of upper classmen I knew had to be bent on hazing incoming freshmen. As soon as I asked how to get to the college, they moved in for the kill. "Dog, where you from?"

"Sorry, I'm not a freshman, and I come from Brooklyn," I said, as casually as I could.

"Then you must be a sophomore."

Still amused, I countered, "No, not a sophomore either."

"Well, you couldn't be a junior transfer, could you?"

"Right. And I'm not a senior."

My reception committee now decided that I didn't have proper respect for big burly upperclassmen. They felt I was playing games with them and advanced on me. It didn't help when I said, "I'm a member of the faculty." This seemed to be sure-enough disrespect, and I felt definitely in danger. Before they got too close, I picked up my bags and hailed a cab. "Take me to the president's house, please," I said loudly. My attackers did a double-take when it dawned on them that I might be telling the truth. From that night until the day I left Durham, they carefully avoided me. Fortunately, all my English classes were for freshmen, so none of them had to face me for a grade.

Safely settled in the cab, I sat back in relief. The president greeted me warmly and referred me to the proper people, who opened an office and found the keys to the home of Reverend and Mrs. J. Neal Hughley, where I was soon safely settled. It was my first night away from Ella, and I missed her terribly.

I reported for duty the next day. My last-minute appointment had left me no time to make the major transition from student to faculty member. I was only three weeks away from being single, and now I was the old married minister on campus. It was important to convey that I was romantically unavailable. I could tell from their direct inquiries that the girls in the senior dorm needed to know I had a wife in Brooklyn who would be arriving soon.

When Ella arrived I was ecstatic. Now I could leave the dining hall and eat in my own kitchen. I could cuddle in my own bed with my new wife. This was the actual beginning of our nitty-gritty life as a married couple. We'd been marking time those first three weeks, with no job to go to and no responsibilities.

E (*Ella*) I said farewell to Ma Warren and boarded the train for Durham with a mountain of luggage and wedding gifts. When Henry picked me up at the station and drove me home in a borrowed car, I had to pinch myself to be sure it was for real. We unpacked everything in record time.

The house had attractive furniture, drapes, and rugs. But it didn't include basic things like pots, pans, and table service, and our wartime wedding gifts hadn't provided them either. There were six coffee makers, but we didn't drink coffee. We did have bedding and linens, but kitchen supplies were very limited. We consulted Mom Mitchell by phone, and she was quick to respond with some extra equipment, some of which we still use today—a small cast-iron skillet and an ice-cream scoop, for example.

H Early in our marriage, we realized we had very different ideas about how the family's money should be handled. Pops hadn't been very successful when he tried to manage the family finances, so Mom had taken over. Her know-how came from working with her father in his hay, feed, and grocery business. Pops brought his check home, and Mom paid the bills and did the shopping. When Mom was ill in 1934, I got the job of paying the bills in cash after she decided how much to pay where.

She had a tough time stretching the money, but we Mitchells never felt deprived. There were no missed meals; she made grape jelly from our grape "harbor," as we called it, and we ate dandelion greens we pulled from the yard. Pops always had a small garden. We had what we needed, if not what we wanted. We were clothed, even though we felt others had nicer clothing. And I'm an ice-cream fanatic today because as a child I could never get enough. We boys loved to visit Grandma Estis because she didn't try to control how much food we ate. She could afford to let us eat what we wanted, because she and Grandpa Estis had a bigger garden and we were there for just a short time. Otherwise, our appetites would have bankrupted anybody.

When I started helping my mother manage our money, I knew the inside facts about the family finances. That helped me to worry less about how we'd make out. Mom's attitude of faith in God buoyed me when I struggled through college in the great Depression. Once I'd done all I could, from cleaning toilets to serving as teacher's assistant, it never occurred to me that God would fail to do the rest. Meanwhile, I learned to laugh off months without pocket change for a nickel Pepsi, as long as I wasn't thrown out of school. Most of my school-mates were about as poor as I was. We made it so fashionable to be poor that the few fellows from comfortable families tried to hide their good fortune. Poverty is relative, and God has come to Ella's and my rescue amazingly throughout our life together. I may get anxious about some other things, but I tend to be cool when Ella and I are having a financial crisis.

Papa Pearson handled *all* the money in our family. Most of the time I remember, Mama didn't even shop for groceries. Papa bought flour, sugar, and rice in huge quantities and had it hauled in. Sometimes we got so much day-old bread from the bakery we shared it with families from the church. But we kept all the raisin bread Papa brought because it was extra good and made wonderful cheese sandwiches.

I realize now that we ate very well, even though none of us children ever had money in our pockets. Our family economy was based on bartered blessings. It wasn't unusual for us to find a large bucket of fresh shrimp on the back porch when we got up in the morning. These same fishermen, some of them Papa's church members and some just friends, kept us supplied with fresh fish and crabs in season. We had peaches and figs from our own trees. Papa brought beans, peas, squash, and fruit from John's Island, eleven miles away, where he taught school. In many ways, we ate better than many people do now, decades later.

My allowance was ten cents a week, which meant it took ages to save up enough to buy even a pair of knee socks. We made our own dresses, slips, and bloomers; the shoes Papa bought were the kind he could repair. He was trained as a cobbler, which his college required along with his academic degree, following the famous injunction of Booker T. Washington that no educated person was truly free unless he had a manual skilll to fall back on. I'd wake up in the early morning to hear Papa mending our shoes and the shoes of many children from the church. Even with Papa's ingenuity, we were limited to two pairs, one for school and one for Sunday-go-to-meeting.

During my teen years, I worried about not having the gewgaws to keep up with the other girls. I also worried about having to walk, instead of taking the trolley, as my slightly more affluent classmates did. Then and later at seminary, walking to save a nickel subway fare was a major inconvenience, but I had no choice. Thinking back on these long hikes, it's easy to see why I sometimes get overly concerned about making ends meet even now. It's not habitual, but from time to time I get a little anxious when there's a problem with the Mitchell family cash flow.

H That all depends on what you mean by a "little." If anxiety means getting tense and having your stomach start to rumble, then this is definitely a worrier sister, whether she's aware of it or not. Of course I enjoy urging Ella to talk through the "demon" of money worry. As soon as she sees what's going on in her gut, she names the demon and casts it out, as Jesus did in the Gospels.

I'm happy to report that in fifty-five years Ella's anxiety about money has yet to generate an argument between us. I think it's because her concern is never about frills and nonessential material things. There can really be no debate about paying things like the light bill or the mortgage. Financial fusses in marriages usually revolve around issues like "I want this," rather than "We really need this." We are blessed in having similar values, so it isn't hard to avoid conflicts.

Starting back in Durham, we decided not to follow either parents' way of handling finances. We began by putting all the bills on the kitchen table, together with all our resources; two small paychecks and an occasional honorarium. Ella compiled the list of obligations, and I totaled them up—without a calculator. If the total we owed was more than the cash we had available, we numbered the obligations according to their priority. We had no cause for argument, because the facts and figures usually spoke for themselves. Since neither of us had any ambitions to be the sole manager of the family's fortunes, we were spared the problem of jousting over who would take charge. So we've always had just one checking account, and we take the tithe off the top. The rest is disbursed by checks that Ella writes, because she's the one who can write so people can read it. As far as I know, she's never dreamed of writing a check we didn't agree on, and she's never been tempted to buy unaffordable material things to bolster her security. Even when there's a crisis with one of our grown children or a needy student, we try to work it out together before deciding to help financially. We generally arrive at the same figure for how much help we should provide before we even say it out loud to each other. We work like one mind.

All too often, marriages go sour over money. The breakup usually results from a combination of power hunger and worry over finances. I've always felt that this worry itself isn't truly innocent; it's simply a gut-level fear that God will not take care of us. You might say, it is the idolatry of trusting in money in place of trusting in God.

E The very last place I would put my trust is in money and material things. From the time I was a teenager I've admired Lincoln Continentals, but I had no gnawing ambition to own one. We have one now, but it arrived after my seventieth birthday. Meanwhile I have thoroughly enjoyed driving whatever God provided to take us from place to place.

Henry probably took more control of our financial situation when we were first married. I expected to go through life saying yes, yes. Like my mother, I assumed the man of the house was supposed to make all the decisions. But Henry would have none of it, not even at the beginning. I remember how he'd go through the motions of being in charge at the outset. He had no choice; *somebody* had to take the lead. Henry did it reluctantly, and he always insisted that I say what was on my mind and cast my vote. I got the hang of it pretty quick, and now I sometimes think he'll appear to be henpecked, which of course he'd never allow.

I have to remind myself that we now have a line of credit that lets us write checks without a balance. And I tell myself that in all our years together, with all our narrow escapes, we've never felt that providence failed us. We've always had whatever we really needed. The financial embarrassment my gut seems to fear has never once been a reality. I fall asleep before I ever have to count either blessings or bills. When it's time to sleep, even my gut knows that God will provide.

H Once we bought a new 1954 Ford station wagon that we enjoyed a great deal. We drove it across country and back, with as many as ten of us aboard at one time. This trip, the fulfillment of a dream, included both sets of grandparents among the passengers. Nevertheless, when we compared the bills and paychecks on the kitchen table, the bills were much too high. Our parents couldn't help us at this point, and we knew we'd have to give up our treasured wagon.

My mom felt terrible. "Henry," she told me, " I hate to see you part with that station wagon. It's been so useful hauling things to the convention camps, and we really enjoyed the trip across country. Isn't there some way you can work out to refinance it?"

"Mom," I said, "I feel the same, but I've tried everything I know, and I just don't see any other way out. I have the lowest payments possible already. Refinancing would only make things worse, and we're already over our heads." I added a little emphasis by waving my hands helplessly over my head.

Suddenly her voice took on a sadness. "I hate for people to see you going down financially like this. You work so hard. You don't deserve this kind of embarrassment."

"Look, Mom, we aren't terribly concerned about appearances," I said. "The only thing we'll miss is the handiness. But it still has been a spiritual lesson for us. We shouldn't have bought it prematurely. In a way, losing the car is a blessing in disguise."

We got rid of the wagon and fell back on our old second car, a 1951 Studebaker. But now we could afford to repair it and make it dependable enough for all the traveling I had to do back then on my job. It was a kind of deeper spiritual discipline, and we both felt blessed to have had the restraint to part with our shiny new car. We never again overstretched our budget in an effort to get material things, no matter how much we thought we needed them. The next new car came in less than a year, when we were blessed with the means to make the payments. We may have been behind the Joneses in cars and clothes and housing, but we had everything we *needed*. And we were way ahead of many folks in the things that really count.

O One of our favorite Bible verses fits in here. We believe quite literally that when we seek first the will of God for our lives, all other *needed* things will be added (Matthew 6:33; Luke 12:31). Both of us believed this long before we ever met, and our trust in God's provision only grows deeper as the years go by. One experience after another reinforces our faith.

I In Durham, I had an interesting opportunity to witness this faith to President Shepard. One morning as he and I waited to start a campus assembly, I mentioned that we planned to have four children. He was shocked. "How on earth can you raise and educate four children on the income you make or can expect to make?" he asked. He knew he was paying me only $1,500 for the school year. I had some knowledge of my prexy's own background, so I asked him, "How many children did your father have?"

"Eight."

"How many of them finished college?"

"All eight."

"What did your father do for a living?"

"He was a Baptist preacher."

"That's just what I thought. He wasn't rich, either, was he?"

"No, not at all."

"Well, Dr. Shepard, I serve the same God your daddy served, and I expect he'll provide for my kids the same way he provided for your daddy's kids."

Dr. Shepard's jaw dropped all the way to his chest. "You are a sound young man! I didn't know young people talked like that anymore." He was even more surprised because he had me stereotyped as a flaming radical. I made headlines speaking against Durham's racial prejudice and injustice. At a conference on counseling military personnel returning from World War II, I simply suggested that Blacks in uniform were treated far better in Europe than they were back home in the country for which they had fought. It was radical to suggest these veterans would have problems readjusting to riding at the back of the bus. I don't suppose President Shepard ever considered how very radical Jesus was, how little he was concerned about things like a place to lay his head.

E Beyond the material needs we've been discussing, we've felt God was with us in every phase of life. Most people don't talk about it the way we do, but we've been on a kind of divinely arranged honeymoon ever since we were married. This is especially true of the conception and birth of our firstborn child, Hank.

We were anxious to start a family soon since we felt like we had a late start. I was almost twenty-seven when we got married, and in those days we thought that meant my biological clock was already running down. I can't forget Henry's attempt to hide his tears when I had my first menstrual period in Durham. He didn't dare say it out loud, but he feared providence had forgotten us temporarily.

One Sunday afternoon a month or so later, Henry got so sick that we called our new family doctor, LeRoy Swift, who gave Henry a thorough going-over. After a few more questions, he asked me, "Why don't you come by the office tomorrow morning?" It seemed like an odd request, but I did as he asked. The next day, after he did the test, he told me I was definitely pregnant.

We were overjoyed at the news, but that didn't stop Henry's illness, which turned out to be a kind of morning sickness. We learned later that it is common in some cultures for the father-to-be involuntarily to take on some of the expectant mother's pregnancy pains. But neither of us had ever heard of such a thing. As Henry's sympathetic malady progressed, I ended up having to teach his classes a few mornings. It looked as if we really became one when we married, and now we could enjoy our pregnancy together.

Of course, one thing Henry could *not* do was carry the baby, but he was very diligent about observing the process. Some of my happiest memories came from watching him watching me at choir rehearsals. We sang with three different groups: the college choir, a community chorus, and the choir of the White Rock Baptist Church. Sometimes when I was singing, the baby responded by stretching out against my diaphragm, and I'd get winded. I knew that in the bass section Henry was watching for what he called "that radiant look on my face" in the soprano section. It came when "Wait'll" (wait'll you see if it's a girl or boy) stirred things up. Those moments combined two of the greatest shared passions of our togetherness, our beloved child en route and our music. In every way our honeymoon continued throughout the pregnancy, and even my Victorian mama was delighted to see how much we enjoyed each other.

H Seeing Ella pregnant and radiant and singing was even more than my early vision had offered me. I had envisioned Ella seated in the third pew back, on the left side of the center aisle, nursing our baby while I led worship. She had her breast covered by a linen napkin, and her face glowed with a happy, angelic smile. But here I was in White Rock Baptist Church in Durham, seeing the same expression even sooner in the context of the magnificent choral music we were both singing. It was almost more joy than I could take. I sometimes got choked up and couldn't sing my bass part. I'd mouth the words and try to hide my embarrassment.

For no really good reason, I was convinced that Wait'll was a boy, and I was almost as bonded with Henry the fourth (as he was sure to be named) as Ella. I got to where I talked to him, touched Ella's tummy to feel him moving, and prayed for him. I asked that he might be fully formed and healthy and, if the Lord so willed, that he might be a bright and gifted child. Then I asked, if it wasn't too much, that he reach back to my mother's father for some "tall" genes. Grandpa Estis had been something like six-three or six-four. I hoped our son wouldn't be as short as my five feet seven inches, at the same time thanking God that I was a bit taller than my Pops, who was five-five. I didn't take these petitions too seriously, and even before he was born I became awesomely attached to my dream-fulfilling son.

E Henry was no more attached to Wait'll than I was. In fact, I had a considerable advantage over dear Daddy Henry because I had Wait'll with me twenty-four hours a day, and the glow the child's father could see on my countenance was only a pale reflection of what I felt in my soul. I wanted to shout the Magnificat of Mary, mother of Jesus: "My soul doth magnify the Lord, and my spirit doth rejoice in God, my Savior" (Luke 1:46).

My term was moving toward its end, and so was Henry's year as interim dean of the chapel at the college in Durham. He asked me one morning where I'd like to go for our next tour of service. I remembered my Lisle Fellowship experience during my seminary days and quickly replied, "Let's go to California."

Quite matter-of-factly he said, "Okay. We'll go to California." I figured it was nice of him to be so agreeable, but I hadn't the faintest notion that he'd pull it off. And neither did he. He was just talking, letting me know he was trying to please me.

When he came home from class that afternoon he jauntily called through the screen door, "Okay, Ella, it's all set. We're going to California." I just knew he was joking, but he slapped a letter down on the kitchen table with a mischievous look in his eyes. "You think I'm kidding, don't you? Read that!" I read it and my jaw fell apart. Henry was being asked to consider a post as field missionary for Northern (now American) Baptist Blacks in Northern California.

The awesome chain of events that led to this offer had started in the 1880s when Grandpa H. H. Mitchell helped to found a college and seminary in Lynchburg, Virginia. Three graduates from around 1908 were involved: Dr. J. P. Hubbard of Oakland, California, who wrote Dr. C. T. Murray of Washington, D.C., for a recommendation. He turned out to be a member of Dr. C. F. Jenkins's congregation in Columbus, Ohio. The nomination was confirmed when Dr. Hubbard happened to ask his guest youth preacher, named Louis Mitchell, if he knew anything about a Henry Mitchell.

Based on his brother Louis's good word, Henry was offered the job sight unseen. The letter had what we needed to move across country. We had to decide what to do about me, since I was nearing delivery and dared not risk a trip that long. Besides, we had no support system in California and no certainty about health care or hospitals there. For all we knew, California was no better for people of dark skin and modest means than South Carolina was. We decided I should be in Columbus, in the care of Henry's parents and family, until after our baby arrived.

H We packed our few belongings and sent Ella to Columbus two weeks before commencement. En route to Oakland, I said farewell to Philadephia, New York City, and Columbus, where I visited Ella and my parents. When I landed in Oakland in early July and saw the difference between the churches of the East and West, I would gladly have gone back east. The African-American congregations of northern California were small at best and few besides. The largest in my new field had maybe five hundred members, compared to the fifty-five hundred at Concord in Brooklyn. I was summoned because they needed help in ministering to the thousands of immigrants from the South who came to work in the war industries. I had said I wanted to be a missionary; I had serious premonitions that I was called to serve overseas. I even saw God as giving me the kind of wife whose partnership would stand the test of missionary life and work. Yet here at home I was discouraged by small, poorly maintained church buildings.

I think I would probably have been better prepared for the culture shock of Africa. At least I would have expected it. I would have been bolstered by the call and a lifetime of models from the mission fields overseas. Here I felt called, but the call was so different from the language and images of "foreign" missionary service that for a moment I wavered.

I thought, if I turn back, I could be with Ella in my hometown for the birth of our child. There would surely be better church opportunities; maybe I shouldn't have declined the invitation to stay another year in Durham. But then there was the brutal fact that I just didn't have the money to go back. I prayed, and was once again convinced that the California call was God's providential will. As it turned out, although we had many opportunities to move east, our service in

California came to a total of thirty-four years! We obviously found ful-fillment in service from one end of California to the other. Everything we ever needed was provided, and much more in due season.

E I wasn't sorry I stayed in Ohio for the birth, since it gave me more advanced medical care than I might have gotten in the Carolinas. It also gave me time to get to know the Mitchells better. Pops Mitchell took me for daily walks to his garden plot, and Mom cared for me as her son did; she tried to do my labor for me. Wait'll finally made his debut in the wee hours of the morning on July 26, 1945, after a long and painful night of labor. Our dream son weighed nine pounds, two ounces, and—in answer to Henry's prayer for added height—meas-ured twenty-one inches! Mom Mitchell was ecstatic when she saw her first grandchild, much relieved that our shared labor was at an end. Even so, I stayed in the hospital for fourteen long days because of stitches, even though it was not a cesarean section. After that, Mom Mitchell and her sister, Aunt Arlene Harris, took excellent care of baby and me. There were no further complications, and Wait'll, now officially Henry IV, settled down to regular plenteous breast-feeding. Henry's sister Marty (Marjorie) later gave the baby the nickname "Hank," and it stuck the rest of his life. I stayed in Columbus until our son and I got our six-week checkup. Meanwhile, we soaked up the tender loving care of the Mitchells and their extended family, plus the entire Second Baptist Church family.

There were no direct flights from Columbus to California, so we took a train to Chicago, where my sister Lurline and her husband, Wendell, cared for us that night. The next evening, in the expectation that Hank would sleep his way west, they bundled us onto a TWA pro-peller-driven overnight flight, along with a bassinette and diapers. I carried my own milk supply. This was the first time I had ever flown, and it was with Hank, not Henry. Hank slept in his bassinette almost all the way, undisturbed by the noise and vibrations, awakening only for feeding. The ride was more comfortable than I had expected, and I too slept most of the night.

H I had a meeting across the bay in San Francisco the morning after I received the exciting news that I had a son. This announcement was joyous to a lot of local people because the memory of my grandpa, H. H. the first, was still fresh in the minds of many earlier settlers in the Bay Area. He had left the area seventeen years ago, but quite often when I was about to speak they would actually talk more about "old Dr. H. H. Mitchell." They hardly even mentioned me, although I was the one who was there to preach. But I didn't mind; I rather enjoyed being a part of the Mitchell tradition.

I couldn't wait for Hank and Ella to get to California. On my twenty-sixth birthday, September 10, in Pacific Grove, word reached me that Ella and Hank were flying in from Chicago, to arrive on the twelfth. That morning I drove my brother Louis's 1931 Pontiac to the San Francisco airport. It was about 9 A.M. when I hugged Ella and held Hank for the first time; it was like heaven all over again. What a reunion! Ella and I hadn't seen each other for nearly three months, and it seemed like a millennium. But we were back together, praise the Lord! Of course, now there was a third party named Hank on the honeymoon, but that only made it more deeply fulfilling.

CHAPTER 5

Together in Ups and Downs: Family and Mission

H *(Henry)* In spite of the severe wartime housing shortage in California, we found ourselves blessed with places to lay our heads. Our first home was a tiny cottage occupied by our friends the Fords: Marcella was returning east to teach at Shaw University in Raleigh, and Jesse was working around the clock as a Pullman porter, so we were welcome until providence located us a more adequate space.

On Saturday, the very next day after we moved in, my sister Marty and my brother Louis arrived from Ohio. Louis would live in the dorm at Pacific School of Religion, but Marty camped with us. I went to work on Sunday, preaching in San Francisco morning and evening. So began fourteen years of high times with our family in the Bay Area. Then my work would take me away for days in the "field," a six-hundred-mile stretch of northern California, where I was doing everything I could think of to help provide for the spiritual needs of a huge number of African-Americans who had arrived in the region to work in the war industries.

We worshiped one Sunday at the church where the co-pastors were Ella's old college prexy, Buell Gordon Gallagher, and my college classmate, the Reverend Roy C. Nichols. One of the members was a staffer in war-emergency temporary public housing at Codornices Village, in

Berkeley, near Oakland. When she learned of Ella's training in Christian Education and music, she proposed that Ella help on the staff of emergency ministries serving the village. This would qualify us for an apartment there without having to go to the end of the waiting list. In one providential stroke we solved our housing problem and got Ella a part-time job that was within walking distance of our apartment and had largely flexible hours, except for Sunday worship. She played the piano and planned the worship, along with doing visitation, with the other ministers, among the villagers. She was happy beyond our fondest expectations.

E *(Ella)* After a year in Codornices Village, we were advanced from one to two bedrooms to make room for Marty, who had slept in the living room. It wasn't a bit too soon. A few weeks earlier, in our first apartment there, she answered a knock on the door at 2 A.M. Thinking that the only person who would knock at such an hour would be our brother Louis, she got up from her sofa bed in her shorty pajamas and opened the door, only to be confronted by a drunken White sailor, six feet three inches tall. When he saw her, scantily clad and easily mistaken for White, he was sure he was at the right address. It took all of her considerable muscle to close the door, after which she stood guard with a butcher knife.

Henry joined her, as the sailor yelled and tried to beat down the door, and I called the police, who came and hauled him away. By then Marty, who had acted so bravely and calmly, was a bundle of nerves. It took us awhile to help her relax and get ourselves back into bed.

Marty was busy studying at San Francisco City College and working on Longfellow School playground in Berkeley. We put Hank's crib in the bedroom with her, and they became good buddies. Soon, however, she found another buddy, a schoolmate named Harold Wilson, and they were married. I missed her helpfulness with Hank and her company while Henry spent so much time on the road.

Dr. Gallagher's network brought still more miracles. His family's outstanding pediatrician, Dr. Percy Hall Jennings, was swamped with new patients and not accepting any more. But he did accept our children, first one, then two, then three. Dr. Jennings, in turn, referred me to his church, after he learned I had studied under Sophia Lyon Fahs at Union Seminary. I ran an eight-week training course at the Berkeley Unitarian Church, introducing the "Martin and Judy Series," a widely recognized new children's curriculum written by Dr. Fahs. This was the second in a happy series of diverse places I used my talents during our fourteen years in Berkeley.

In his prayers about our dream family, Henry went so far as to ask that our second child be a girl, and sure enough, God gave her to us on April 23, 1947. The labor pains started when Henry was eighty miles away in Sacramento at Louis's ordination. I left Hank in Marty's care, and a neighbor drove me to the hospital. The baby came in a hurry, in the labor room, before I could get to the delivery room or the doctor could change into her surgical clothes. We named this baby Muriel, my middle name, and once again I saw the hand of a provident God, giving us the daughter Henry and I prayed for.

This delivery was much easier than the first, and I found little or no problem with combining my professional activities with my brood of two.

H My parents came to live with us in 1948, after Pops fell ill in Columbus, so we moved to a three-bedroom apartment. Elizabeth was born in September 1949. Our public housing was deluxe, with hardwood floors and attractive yards. We enjoyed living with my parents as built-in babysitters. We put the two older children in the third bedroom. After Pops had recuperated somewhat, they bought a home nearby on Jones Street and moved out. And after seven years in public housing we moved into our own cozy ranch-style home in Berkeley, across the street from Mom and Pops.

E In 1948, doctors east and west diagnosed Pops with incurable cancer and gave him six weeks to six months. He lived nineteen years.

Muriel was a happy, healthy, active child. Imagine my shock one day when I looked out the window into the yard and saw that my six-month-old baby had climbed out of her playpen. She walked at nine months. She and Hank soon formed a pair of Katzenjammer Kids. He was quite active too, hanging from doorknobs and the like. These two characters were inseparable.

When the temporary housing at Codornices Village seemed to be becoming permanent, the temporary church ministry closed. I was then hired by the Oakland-Berkeley Council of Churches as an instructor in their program of Released Time Religious Education. Not only was I teaching fourth, fifth, and sixth graders, I also drove a huge bus, outfitted as a mobile classroom, from one elementary school to another, whenever no large classroom was available in a nearby church. The bus did not have power steering, and I suffered several strains just from steering it, but I loved the work. I was free to design much of my curriculum, and I helped other teachers plan theirs.

H Ella could do wonders with children. One day I happened to drive her to a class she was teaching in a long, narrow, storefront church, deep in the 'hood in West Oakland. The White teacher had arrived earlier but failed to bring order to the seventy-five children present. It seemed to be an impossible situation, with the children in the last row hardly able to see or hear. Then Ella arrived, and bedlam soon gave way to near-absolute silence. I was astounded. What on earth was she doing? She was up front, radiantly smiling—and almost whispering.

The children had hushed and were straining eagerly to hear their beloved storyteller's words.

In addition to her teaching, Ella enjoyed serving as a member of the Commission on Children's Work for Northern California Baptists. She became more and more involved not only in meetings but in workshops and training courses. After she and I joined the McGee Avenue Baptist Church of Berkeley, she was invited to organize and direct a youth and young adult choir on a volunteer basis. She also served occasionally as fill-in organist at Beth Eden Baptist Church in West Oakland, where Dr. Hubbard (who sent for me to come to California) was pastor. Later she was the regular organist at Parks Chapel A.M.E. Church, also in West Oakland.

E While I played the organ, I had "on-site" babysitters in West Oakland, like Marty and Harold, who lived hardly two blocks from the church and who soon had a child of their own, Stephanie. I could leave Hank and Muriel with them when Marty wasn't at school or working. There were also other church families of willing babysitters in the neighborhood, such as the Haddens, Turners, and Johnsons.

When I played for and directed the youth and young adult choir at McGee Avenue, our children often went with me to rehearsal. It wasn't long before we had thirty singers, well balanced between male and female, many of them capable of reading music. One of them was Henry himself, age twenty-seven, who sang in the bass section whenever he was in town. I had always just played organ or piano, and now here I was directing classical anthems, spirituals, and gospels, with a wonderful reponse from both choir and congregation. It was one of the most enjoyable and challenging things I ever did. Friday nights couldn't come around fast enough.

Henry, who was on the road much of the time, was pleased that I was so fully and happily occupied and so well supplied with child-care volunteers. Even before his parents arrived in Berkeley, the Browns, George and Lela Mae and their three teenagers (Herb, LaVerne, and Barbara) cared for our kids as their own, and were insulted when we offered to pay. What they did was beyond anything money could buy. We still marvel that our children were returned with all their clothing freshly washed and ironed and their hair carefully combed and styled. It was almost as if our children were the Brown kids' pampered dolls, except that sisters were too old for dolls. When they learned to drive, they took the children to music lessons and other appointments. Every family should be this fortunate—to have the loving support given us by Henry's parents and the Browns during our child-rearing years. It made it easy for Henry, when he was in town, to be fully present with the whole family, and especially with me. We never had to feel that our treasured time together was stolen from our children.

H In my work I covered six hundred miles of northern California for $1,800 per year, $300 more than my college salary but for twelve months of work instead of nine. However, I quickly lost sight of this underpayment, as well as of my negative first impressions. I plunged into work, with nineteen already established African-American churches and sixty new ones I eventually helped to start, over the fourteen years I served. My work continued full tilt after the war, since almost none of the thousands of the African-American wartime workers in northern California returned south. Most of them had been underemployed and underpaid in the South and had little to keep them there. Those with skills had come to California to find better ways to use them for more pay. They were also escaping violent oppression in many cases; lynching was still a reality in those years. In a sense, my constituency were like the Pilgrims and other immigrants: They sought freedom and a better way of life. Like other immigrants, they were an asset in their new home. It was my job to help provide ministries with and for them.

I had no car, at first, but made do by borrowing; then I got bargain used cars, and even cars with motors I rebuilt. I also traveled on one of the few free annual passes issued by the Southern Pacific Railroad. One of the greatest pleasures of my entire life was the joy of stepping off the train at the Berkeley station, not far from our public housing, to be greeted by Ella and the children. My heart would leap as they ran full speed down the platform and jumped into my arms.

There were other pleasures, but they were sometimes mixed. For instance, I had the great privilege of being asked to preach a revival each September at the churches in the lumber-mill towns of Weed and McCloud, on the north slopes of Mt. Shasta. This was the beginning of deer season, and I could hunt in the early morning, before I took a nap and preached in the evening. Even though my rifle was said to be out of line and I thought I was just going through the motions, I shot a buck one morning at a distance of a hundred yards. My partner, with a much better gun, had missed. Suddenly I was a hunting hero. The whole Black neighborhood turned out to cheer me as I checked my deer in at the ranger station.

I planned our Thanksgiving dinner, both guests and menu, as I waited for a truck to pick up my deer. I could hardly contain myself. Imagine my grief when the ranger counted only two points on one of my deer's horns. I was at a station where both horns had to have three points. My deer was confiscated and I narrowly escaped arrest, while at a station five miles away, my kill would have been legal. Between the terrible disappointment and the look in the deer's eyes as he died, I haven't picked up a rifle since.

We lived frugally and worked happily for two years. Then, in early October 1947, came my first big storm. My work was primarily with the self-defined Black caucus of American Baptists called the General

Baptist Association, but they paid only a third of my operating budget. The rest came from the American Baptist Home Mission Society and the Northern California Baptist Convention. The storm arose from the General Baptist Association.

On the first morning of the annual meeting, their executive board held a closed session and voted to ask for my resignation. I was charged with not properly reporting work, even though I had already caught up on my reports. A White executive had joked to the chairman about my lateness, and the board had taken his offhand comment seriously. I had gotten behind in the first place only because this board had donated my services to the National Baptist Sunday School and Baptist Training Union Congress, meeting in June 1947 in Oakland with an estimated attendance of 10,000. I worked hard, without paid help, doing this over and above my regular duties to the Association. My office was still at home, and Ella graciously took my calls and helped out as much as she could. From April through June I had been as busy as a cat on a hot tin roof.

I was summoned to the afternoon session of the board and asked for my resignation. They would let me stay on for a few months until I could find something else to do to support my "fine little family." I managed to rebut the charges. "Has anybody present bothered to read my late but voluminous reports?" I asked. The only yes came from the wife of the board chairman. "Is there any dissatisfaction with my efforts to do the work of four or five men?" There was none. "I am quite willing to resign my position, but I refuse to do so under a cloud. If you insist that I leave at this point, you'll have to fire me."

At that moment a phone call came from Dr. J. P. Hubbard of Beth Eden Church, the man who brought me to California in the first place. He threatened to withdraw from the association in protest at their treatment of me. The board agreed to scan my reports for the first time, whereupon they rescinded their request for my resignation.

They appointed a "review committee" to see that "the late reports never happened again," but this committee met only once, without a quorum, and never scheduled another session.

It was a victory for me, and the final turn of events was clearly providential, but I didn't perceive it that way. I was heartsick at the thought that a whole board of people I considered good friends could be so hoodwinked by the twisted report of what one White man had said. I was also hurt by the board's failure to read the reports and their timidity about taking a stand against the conniving chair and in my defense.

For two weeks following the meeting I was sick at home, with many of the symptoms of a peptic ulcer. I know now that my malady was actually massive depression, with gastric side effects. If only I could have opened my mouth and vented my pain to the board in the vocabulary of my street days, I would probably have survived the encounter without such emotional scars. As it was, I suppressed and internalized my rage, and it made me sick.

Fortunately, Ella was very understanding and supportive. She listened patiently as I repeated my painful accounts of desertion and abandonment. She tactfully reminded me of my final triumph, and it wasn't long before I felt ready to return to my regular chores. Meanwhile, there was enough Mitchell infant and child care to keep me from being too constantly absorbed with my own predicament. Delighted by my presence at home, Hank took it for a vacation and worked me for all he was worth. As bad as I wanted to think my troubles were, I couldn't resist his insistence on playing. Being together in our nest was a healing process in itself.

E While the association was meeting, I was at home with our two small children. When Henry came home sick, I realized he was seriously worried about something. The doctor ruled out a physical cause and made him identify the source of his stress, so he finally described the whole mess to me. I was quite angry, of course, but not with Henry. I put my anger on hold and out of sight and dealt with his deep depression and sense of defeat. Eventually, we confronted the issue of whether we should stay or leave. "Why not put out some feelers and get back to the civilized East?" I asked. "Your best so-called friends don't really appreciate all the work you do. And God knows the salary is no incentive to stick around!" I was more annoyed about the way the board had treated my hard-working husband than if I myself had been the victim. I was more than willing to run away from it all.

Once the immediate pain had subsided, however, Henry and I determined not to think and pray about any move, at least for a little while. Surely God had not brought us all the way out west for just a two-year temporary duty. If God did have a short term in mind, there were no signals to tell us so. God had actually made this fiasco work on our behalf. In the eyes of his constituency, Henry ended up much stronger than before. Even so, we did pray, alone and together, asking, *Lord, what wilt thou have us to do?*

H Actually, it wasn't all prayer. Once I had returned to work, I realized I had already done what we used to call "kickin' butts and takin' names." There was no need to tuck tail and run now. It wasn't long before the two denominational sponsors gave me a raise in salary and pressured the General Baptist Association board to match their contributions. The work was now more rewarding in every way. Ella no longer felt I was outrageously put upon. Our trips together grew in number, and life in general was more abundant. We never sat down and made a formal decision; we just flowed together on our steady, happy course. I didn't leave the GBA for twelve more years, by which time I had absorbed three more positions.

In retrospect I marvel that neither of us ever took out our frustration on the other. In the words of the gospel song, I would "look back and wonder how I got over," except that I know God's providence always squeezes a blessing out of humanity's most demonic schemes. And I know, also, that I could take just about anything, given Ella's unswerving support and nourishing companionship.

Concerning this four-year period, from our arrival in 1945 to the birth of Elizabeth in 1949, I can say that God squeezed a blessing out of all our ups and downs, even the hassle with the board. It was no greater than the problem of not having a dependable car for covering my six-hundred-mile territory—a problem at home also. We had said we didn't want another child until we had reliable transportation.

One day in September 1948, we paid a visit to "Baby" Davis, an elderly lady living next to Beth Eden Church. She was fond of our little family, and we were fond of her. All of a sudden, Baby said, "Henry, is anything in the oven? According to your original schedule, another baby should be on the way." She knew I would be two months pregnant if the next child was to be two years younger than Muriel, as intended. I confessed. "Baby, we've had to revise our schedule. We haven't felt financially prepared to follow our former plans to the 'T.' But we aren't far behind, given the fact that we don't want them all born in July, like Hank." We told her we planned to make application for baby number three on Christmas Day.

My first labor pains came the morning of September 27, 1949, when I was on my way to the Codornices Village child care center. My day's work credit covered the other days when Hank and Muriel were there. I went across the street to the Evans Garage, to get Henry to drive me to the hospital. At the time, he was reboring and rebuilding a 1935 Hudson Terraplane. Covered with grease, he crawled from under the car and had to borrow Mr. Evans's family auto to rush me to the hospital.

H I washed off some of the grease, and we roared to Herrick Hospital in downtown Berkeley. As I waited to see if Ella was going to stay, a nurse came to say, "Mr. Mitchell, you are the father of another baby girl. She arrived in a hurry, without using the delivery room. She weighs seven pounds and thirteen ounces and has a mole on her forehead and freckles all over." I laughed at the freckles. My mother's family was full of them. My dream had been for a second boy before the second girl, but I thought I knew already that God would send a girl, and I was content with God's plan. They allowed me to see Ella for a moment, and then I returned to the garage and the grease. In two short days, Ella was back home with her family.

Three months later, we paid another visit to Baby Davis, taking all three children, including Liz. With a mischievous look in her eye, Sister Davis cackled, "When did you say that baby was born?"

"September twenty-seventh," I said.

"Eight ball in the corner pocket! You guys really call your shots, don't you?"

She had counted the nine months on her fingers from Christmas, our announced time of application; Liz had arrived forty-eight hours later. We pool shooters—as Baby would call us—hadn't realized how accurately on schedule Liz's birth was.

CHAPTER 6

Together in Tragedy:
A Murder and Its Aftermath

E (*Ella*) On Saturday, October 22, 1949, our sister Marty didn't arrive home from her job as a clerk in the Rose Waterman Drugstore in West Oakland. She had been working her way through college. On the side she had engaged in a typical Mitchell personal crusade, trying to help delinquent teenagers in an African-American neighborhood, the roughest in Oakland. She lived and worked there without fear. She was not working within a structured program, but she had a habit of forming close friendships and helping to steer at-risk youth in a constructive direction.

That night the police were called to the drugstore around midnight and found two bodies. The pharmacist, Robert Savage, and the clerk, Marjorie Wilson—our Marty—had been made to kneel before the safe. Then both were shot through the back of the head with a 45-caliber automatic pistol, from a range of twelve to eighteen inches.

When the police discovered the bodies, they notified Harold, Marty's husband, who in turn called me with the news at about 2 A.M. that Sunday morning. Stunned and weak from delivering Elizabeth three weeks earlier, I crossed the hall to tell Pops, who in his grogginess misunderstood and thought at first it was our Liz and not *his* only daughter who had died. When at last he heard me correctly, his heart broke, and he vented his grief and pain by pounding on the piano with his fists.

I managed to get in touch with Mom Mitchell, who had gone to Ohio upon the death of her sister Blanche. Then I tried to reach Henry in Merced where he was serving as interim pastor on weekends. Since the parsonage had no phone, I called a deacon, who walked the half block to rouse Henry and bring him to the phone.

"Henry, Harold called a few minutes ago to say that Marty was found murdered in the drugstore," I sobbed. "They don't have any details on how it happened or who did it."

"Oh, my God," he blurted out. "How is Pops taking it? Did you call Mom?" The questions poured from him, shattered as he was.

"How soon can you get here?" I asked.

"The two-thirty A.M. train just went by. I'll try to catch the earliest bus," he managed to tell me. "I'll call you from the bus station when I arrive."

H (*Henry*) I got into Oakland early the next morning, having cried the whole 135 miles. To me, Marty was both sister and daughter; I had often taken care of her when she was a baby and a toddler. I felt like an earthquake had hit me. But as soon as I arrived home and felt the pall that had descended on our household, I pulled myself together and concentrated on holding my family together as we grieved.

After Ella called me, she called my brothers, Louis and Elbert, in Sacramento. Then she went into shock, lapsing into a deep sleep. She awakened only briefly, when Elbert arrived with Louis and his wife, Janice, and again when they brought me in. Her sleep was induced by the phenobarbitol her doctor had prescribed that morning.

Three-week-old Liz received sedation through Ella's milk and slept around the clock; we had to pinch her to wake up enough to feed.

Our dear friends the Browns took care of the two older children, but Liz needed to stay with Ella. Harold left his apartment to be with his parents and took Stephanie with him. Friends from our church and Beth Eden brought food, cleaned the house, washed diapers, bathed the baby, answered the phone, and cared for every possible personal need.

Our housing project apartment was also filled with a continual flow of curiosity seekers passing for friends, drawn by the spectacular media coverage of what was a cold-blooded, senseless, gruesome murder. The radio stations and newspapers carried the gory details, reporting that both Marty and Robert Savage were White. Because of her light skin, it never occurred to the press to confirm Marty's racial identity. Her husband, Harold, was African-American also; it was Savage and his wife who were White. Marty's daughter, Stephanie Ruth, was eighteen months old, and Mrs. Savage had just given birth to their second daughter. Ella had been in the same maternity ward with Mrs. Savage three weeks earlier. When this poor young mother heard the news, she suffered a heart attack. She was utterly desolate, since her relatives were all back in Maryland and could offer their support only long distance.

One curious mourner, drawn to our home by the reports, unleashed one of the cruelest comments I ever heard. Seeing Liz sleeping by the bedroom door in her bassinette, this woman asked, "Whose baby is that?" When told the infant was ours, she blurted, "No, she isn't. Reverend Mitchell ain't never had no baby that black." It was all I could do to hold my peace and my fist, especially at such a tragic time—and especially with the newspapers reporting Marty as White. Meanwhile, friends quickly ushered the woman out the door. That barb pierced Ella and me to the heart, and we determined never to let Liz feel less than the highest self-esteem for her strikingly attractive appearance.

E Marty's misstated race and the disdain shown our beautiful baby were a bitter irony when the person later charged with Marty's murder was protected by his own Black community because Marty was mistaken by the media for White.

H Who murdered Marty and the pharmacist? The police investigation came agonizingly close to our own family. Marty's husband was a prime suspect. Harold was asleep when the murder occurred, but he couldn't prove it. It was known that Pops tried to call him late Saturday evening, and he hadn't answered. Homicide detectives took Harold and me into separate rooms and grilled us intensely. Our answers had to match, or Harold would have been arrested. This meant we had to stick to hard facts about what happened that evening—making it clear, for example, that Marty and Harold kept the telephone in a closet, so it wouldn't wake the baby—or a sound-asleep adult either.

It seemed unlikely to the detectives, but I *knew* Harold was a hard sleeper and wouldn't have heard Pops's phone call. I also knew he worked hard all that day in the open air with a group of boys, so he was very tired. This was why he didn't walk over to the drugstore to escort Marty home. It was such a weak-sounding tale, but changing would have made it worse, so Harold and I both stuck to the frail-sounding account of what really happened.

It was weeks before the police arrested a suspect in the killing, well known to Marty and Robert Savage. The accused man was already in jail, having been arrested for an unrelated robbery shortly after the murder occurred. His attorney phoned Pops's home and threatened to call him as a witness. Further suspicion cast on Harold would relieve the pressure on the suspect. Ella happened to answer the phone and refused to let the the attorney talk to Pops. Just hearing the cruel threat reduced poor invalid Pops to tears. They even tried to get Ella to influence Pops to volunteer to testify for them.

When I was called to the stand in the trial, the defense tried to get me to agree that Marty knew the defendant, and that even though he was in the drugstore he wasn't the killer. They asked rigged questions, to which I was allowed only yes-or-no answers. I was not permitted to debunk the alibi the attorneys were putting forth: that Marty had sent the defendant to get her some barbecued pork ribs, and thus he was not there at the time of the murder. Marty was brought up never to eat fresh pork; Mom was against pork on dietary grounds because she thought it was unsafe. The fact that Marty kept to this rule faithfully was not accepted in evidence. I was made to look like a fool, stymied and thwarted again and again by the yes-or-no rule, as I tried to tell the whole truth. It didn't help for me to know that the defense lawyers were avowed Communists. They were not just defending an accused murderer—they were using that trial to stir resentment among West Oaklanders, urging them to indignation at the way a Black man was being tried for murdering a woman they conveniently allowed the public to continue believing was White. The Communist Party had not yet been outlawed, and these lawyers were trying to recruit more members to their cause.

When I asked the prosecution why they remained silent and gave me no help, one of them replied, "The defense in a murder trial can do no wrong, but the prosecution has to walk a thin chalk line. We have to shun the very appearance of evil." In other words, they had to follow the strictest of constitutional rules, as I soon learned to my even greater sorrow.

The accused was convicted, but his lawyers appealed and the State Supreme Court ordered a retrial, based on two tiny technicalities. One was the prosecution's reference to the accused's method of operation in a robbery for which he had been previously convicted. As in Marty's case, he bought barbecued ribs first and then hid out for a couple of days afterward with the ribs as his food supply.

The other technicality was related to the prosecution's impeachment of its own witness. A teenage girl had seen the accused in the drugstore after the door was locked and the prosecution called her as a witness, even though they knew she had changed her testimony and said she was no longer certain she'd seen what she had said. The pressure to change came from her mother, her pastor, and her whole high school student body. They demonstrated against her, with placards and marching at her high school. She was a Black girl, and the whole community was against her for singing on a brother. The laws of loyalty in the 'hood prevailed. No doubt the defense lawyers helped stir all of this up. Nobody seemed to know or care that Marty was a loyal Black sister and a resident of that selfsame 'hood. Her ethnic identity was irrelevant to the case made by either side.

The impeached witness's original testimony when she was indicted and bound over for trial was the result of a slip of the tongue at a party. She never planned to tell what she saw, even though Marty had befriended her. She saw the murderer at the scene of the crime only because she was stopping by the drugstore to walk home with Marty, a woman who was not only a friend but a counselor trying to help her rebuild her life!

When I visited a place of business in the 'hood, the owner, a member of nearby Beth Eden Church, and supposedly a good friend of mine, hid a sign asking for donations to the accused murderer's defense fund. He didn't know I'd read the sign before he saw me enter, and I couldn't bring myself to confront him. I felt so ill I could have lost my breakfast right there in the store.

After the retrial was ordered, I wound up testifying in two more trials, both of which ended in hung juries. The memories of the key witnesses yielded more and more to pleas for loyalty to the 'hood and the race. Marty was continually and purposely misidentified as White, and the trial became "us against them." The issue wasn't Black vs.

White, it was a matter of the defense skillfully generating a polarization of the community, separating it by color and ignoring the justice that all citizens deserve.

It was a painfully frustrating situation. Here we were, a multigenerational family of radical advocates for racial justice all the way back to Grandpa H. H. Mitchell, yet we were oppressed in the name of that same justice. Refusing to pass for White, we Mitchells were and still are much more militant than most Blacks of any tint. Even in her native South, Ella was also a notorious rebel in matters of race and civil rights. But only our close friends gave us serious support.

The end of it all was that the man went free! What time he did serve was for a similar crime, another robbery that could also have ended in a death, and for which he was convicted. In this earlier robbery his gun jammed and the lives of the clerks were spared. Would to God that the gun had jammed at the drugstore that night with Robert Savage and Marty! Yet even though the defendant looked at me like I was dirt on the floor, I couldn't hate him. This spontaneous forgiveness suprised me, and I was comforted on reflection by the words of 1 John 3:14, "We know that we have passed from death unto life, because we love the brethren."

I couldn't muster the same forgiveness for his lawyers, even though I had once worked with one of them on a police brutality case. I arrived at the point of hating those lawyers with a passion. I had to give this up in time, of course, because the only one hurt was me, not the lawyers who created the injustice. Hatred is just unhealthy.

Although Ella and I were thinking and believing students of the Bible, in all our agony about the trials, we could only cling to a reflexive blind faith in providence. We dared not let the basics of our belief slip from our minds and hearts.

The impact of Marty's death itself finally hit me full force two months after her death, in December, when I was relaxing on Aunt

Arlene's porch in Columbus. Two-and-a-half-year-old Muriel had gone back to Ohio with Aunt Arlene after the funeral to help fill her void for a while. On my way back from a business trip, I was there to take her home. Joining me on the porch, Muriel wanted to know, "Why are you crying, Daddy?" That was when the dam burst.

Driving back to Califonia with Muriel, in our first brand-new car, a black 1949 Chevy, I managed to focus on the life before me once again. Muriel, a marvelous conversationalist, was a big help. Her curiosity and enthusiasm were a joy. Back home with Ella and Hank and Liz, now three months old, there was likewise added joy, especially now that we had a dependable new car to use in our travels together.

The tears still rise a little high every now and then, when I have to handle records in the family achives, as when Ella and I were moving the files or writing this book. I have to hold myself together, also, when I discuss the tragedy with Marty's thoughtful daughter, Stephanie, now herself the mother of Taj, a fine son in high school. One of our granddaugheters, also named Stepanie, is tall the way Marty was and possesses some of her great-aunt's mannerisms. The healing has largely taken place and there have been other great griefs to seize our attention, but Marty remains with me. I can hear her voice and see her face over a half century later.

CHAPTER 7

Together Time: Communication in Class, Church, and Family

E *(Ella)* Marty's death was the major heartbreak in our lives during those Berkeley years, but other, lesser traumas challenged us and also brought us closer together.

It had long been obvious that our popular young-adult choir at McGee Avenue Baptist Church far outclassed what was called the Senior Choir, composed of adult singers. We had a few voices who rightfully belonged with the seniors, and they were needed there, but those singers liked our music better. This left us a little vulnerable. It all came to a head when a clique of key people, some obviously very jealous, launched an attack on our choir and especially on me. They persuaded the congregation not just to enforce age restrictions but to disband the choir altogether. In its place they put a small choir made up of early teens, directed by a newly hired professional who was well paid and male, two things I was not. They might as well have kicked the rest of the singers out of the church. A whole generation of older youth was lost, not only to McGee Avenue Church but often to churchgoing itself.

I cried for days; I had never been so personally assaulted in my life. Yet I couldn't just walk away from this church. I had to stay there and worship with people who had hurt me, smiling in their faces every Sunday. This church was an active member of the association Henry worked for, and we dared not seem to be stirring up trouble.

Together Time: Communication in Class, Church, and Family

H *(Henry)* I was always somewhere else on Sundays, but I suffered at the thought of what Ella was going through. In a sense, I felt responsible for her having to keep taking abuse. Then it occurred to me that nobody would blame us for her leaving McGee if she were *hired* by another church. When I offered to find her a position on a large church staff somewhere, she was intrigued but doubted it could happen. The salaries of even the highest paid Black pastors did not allow for additional paid staff. However, Ella didn't realize how widely respected her skills were. Nor had she accurately gauged the racial climate in Berkeley and Oakland, which might have offered more opportunity than either of us suspected.

I went to see Grant Hanson, Director of Christian Education at the large White American Baptist church in downtown Oakland. After I explained how important it was to extricate Ella from her present situation, I made him a proposal. "Ella so desperately needs to escape that she'd work for very little. And if no salary is available, we'd gladly reimburse Oakland First Baptist from our tithes and offerings."

Grant Hanson's answer was reassuring. "You guys really are desperate, aren't you? But you don't have to do all that. Ella teaches at the Berkeley Baptist Divinity School; she'd be a welcome addition to anybody's staff. Now that I know she's available, I'll gladly take the ball from here."

It didn't take long for Ella to be officially hired as Director of Children's Work at First Baptist Church in Oakland. Our children accompanied her on Sunday mornings, and even though our official memberships were not moved, Ella was delivered from her suffering. She and I went so far as to sing with First Baptist's magnificent choir every Christmas, under the direction of John Wood. It was so rewarding that even now, at Christmas, we still sing the parts to "In the Bleak Midwinter," a beautiful, haunting carol we learned in that choir.

Beyond church and singing, I found new joy when the affable Hank was old enough to join me on some of my field trips, making me many unlikely friends. Former enemies, preachers who disliked my looks, my education, or my Northern (now American) Baptist ties, melted when Hank greeted them with a jovial "Hi Doc!" We two became great traveling buddies. He was always ready to leave in record time when I called from the office to say he could go with me. He took the long rides extremely well, keeping me alert with his endless questions about everything.

His most challenging question came on one of the rare trips he went on later. He was nine. I preached in Redwood City, and the Spirit was high. After I took my seat, the pastor said a few words, and the congregation burst forth in shouts.

We ate dinner with the congregation and were driving home when, out of the blue, Hank said, "Do you believe in that?"

"Believe in what?" I said.

"You know what I mean: what that preacher did after you stopped preaching. He *meant* to make those people do that."

"Those people were very sincere, and they believe in what they were doing."

"Yeah, but do *you* believe in doing what that preacher did?" he insisted.

"You don't see me doing it, but I respect what *they* believe," I managed to respond. But he hung in further until I agreed with his keen analysis that the pastor had consciously manipulated his congregation. Hank never ceased to press for the truth.

On my days at home, I was able to devote my full attention to Ella and our growing family. When I was home on weekends, we all went swimming in the salt-water pool in Richmond, six miles north of Berkeley. We frequented the swings, merry-go-rounds, and other equipment at nearby Kenney Park, as well as the other parks in town. We skated together, and, when Liz was three, Muriel five, and Hank seven, we all pitched in on the construction of our new house. We were always a busy bunch.

E Although I'd been training lay teachers for years, Berkeley Baptist Divinity School (now American Baptist Seminary of the West) was my first experience with graduate students. Henry and I gathered the kids and went off to Pacific Grove, the quietest town in California, for me to work on my curriculum and detail my lesson plans. It was an exciting enterprise, and I wanted to bring it off with real distinction. My first course was in Early Childhood Education, and the class of eighteen included only three women. It was a shock to see a front row of all men, several older than I and with more experience.

When I gave my opening lecture in January 1951, I spoke about the physical, social, mental, emotional, and spiritual needs of small children, elaborating on the pattern of Jesus' growth that the Gospel relates in Luke 2:52. When I came to the issue of how much physical space a child requires at various stages of development, I met with considerable resistance.

"How can you realistically say we ought to provide twenty-five square feet for every nursery child?" one of the men wanted to know. "We don't have that kind of money in our churches."

"We can't even do that for the ladies' parlor," another man declared.

"Well, gentlemen and ladies, we must realize that the smaller the child, the more space that child needs," I answered.

"Those theories aren't developed in the trenches where we have to do the real work," another student said.

"This isn't a farout theory," I told them. "Twenty-five square feet is a serious compromise already. The public schools provide forty-six square feet for the same age."

Citing these facts seemed to put their challenges to rest, and I felt as if I was accepted as their teacher for the rest of the semester. I was much more comfortable, after that first debate, and invited their questions. It was fun, because they were no longer resisting this young woman; they actually wanted to learn. They invited me to their churches and showed great respect for my advice. The preacher's kid from South Carolina via Union Seminary, with practice teaching at Riverside Church, had come a long way. My deep satisfaction has continued through the years; two men from that first class turned out to be national figures in Christian Education. I still enjoy fairly frequent encounters with people I taught during my eight years at Berkeley Baptist Divinity School.

H In fall 1952, Hank, Muriel, and even three-year-old Liz helped us stain the redwood siding of the home we built across Jones Street from Mom and Pops Mitchell. We moved there in February of 1953. Not only were the children good with a stain brush and other building chores, they had become quite articulate. In our evening "together time," they easily expressed their joys and worries and then offered up their prayers—unless, as was often the case, the younger ones had already fallen asleep on the floor, played out by the day's adventures. Our family sessions were a classic example of how a teacher can practice at home what she teaches at school. I assumed at first that Ella got the idea from a book.

E Actually our together time was the result of a goal I'd had for years. We Pearsons practiced something similar as I was growing up, a kind of daily family sharing. The only difference was that Papa always presided at the Pearson house, while the Mitchells passed the "chair" around. At eight, I was part of a family discussion of my sister Jess's plans for college. When I was sixteen, I had to research three possible colleges so the family could decide together which one was best for me. (As it turned out, the matter was settled when I received a full four-year scholarship from Talledega.)

For us Mitchells, together time was one of the keys to keeping the busy years of child-rearing happy and fulfilling. We set out the weekly chores and made real decisions about the trips we took, the music lessons we chose, and how we resolved sibling issues.

Our most significant decision came in February 1956, when we voted to adopt a brother. Hank, almost eleven, declared, "I don't think it's fair for me to be the only boy in the house most of the time. I need a little brother, just like Muriel has a little sister."

"I'm willing to give birth again, but I can't guarantee a little brother," I warned him.

Hank's face fell. "Well, skip it then. We don't need to risk having three girls and me *still* the only boy."

"I think you ought to just go ahead and have another baby," Muriel told us, "and if it's not a boy, that'll be okay. *God* decides who children will be, not us."

"I guess you're right," Hank conceded, "but I'll be praying for a boy."

Henry was committed to our having four children, just like the four siblings both of us had in our families. But the obstetrician who delivered Mu and Liz, Dr. Elsie Ross, advised me that it would be risky to bear another child, since I had a thromboid condition of the broad ligament. If I decided to have another baby, I'd have to be confined to bed for eight of the nine months. This would be a major disruption of my work, and I'd still experience a dangerous pregnancy.

We explained all this at together time the next Sunday evening. Hank was obviously relieved. "Can we adopt a brother now? We can pick what we want when we adopt, can't we?" We never had formal votes at together time but we always worked for consensus, and this time it was very enthusiastic: We would find ourselves a son and brother. We immediately built a double-decker bunk bed in the boys' bedroom of our new house and started shopping for an adoptee.

As we soon found out, adopting a child was easier said than done. Local agencies told us that because we had three children already, they were sending children to people who had none. An inquiry at a Mexican orphanage, made through a Hispanic pastor, brought up many technicalities and included the condition that we raise the child a Roman Catholic, which we did not feel comfortable doing.

Then we read an article in *Ebony* about racially mixed war orphans ("brown babies") from wartorn Germany and Korea, none of them welcome in the land of their birth and all in need of stable and loving homes. Through the California State Welfare Department we made application to the International Social Service for a boy, age two to six. The social worker was so impressed by our "together time" consensus, our picture album, the bunk bed we'd already built, and the published articles featuring our professional activities that she did something she said she never did. On our very first interview she showed us a case file and photo of a particular Korean child. His name was Kim—he was four, half Korean and half Black.

H "I'll let you see this case, but I'm sure he's too dark for your family," the social worker said. We wondered silently how a boy born of a Korean mother could be "too dark," no matter how dark his GI father may have been. We were also puzzled by the importance she seemed to give to color. When we asked why she was concerned, she confessed that most Black adoptive parents chose children lighter than themselves, not darker. We were saddened at that, but not surprised. Prejudice related to skin tone is a tragic sign of socially and culturally induced ethnic self-hatred. We couldn't have cared less about the child's color—we just wanted to know if he was a good match for the intelligence of our other three. The agency had no test of this child's smarts, but they did tell us he was rebellious and outspoken. "He's our boy!" I said. "He wouldn't fit into our bunch of Philadelphia lawyers if he were otherwise."

The social worker was deeply moved, even tearful. "I've never seen such a family!" she said to us. We hadn't seen such a family either, but we had a sense that God was putting this particular set of parents and children together.

E Why did I think God was helping us in this venture? To start with, when Kim was scheduled to arrive I was conveniently located in the state of Washington, teaching in a church-related lab school that ended in time for me to meet Kim at Sea-Tac Airport on July 27, 1956. I waited nearly two hours after his arrival, while he and maybe a dozen other adoptees were processed by U.S. Customs and the Immigration Service. The suspense was almost unbearable. Why were they taking so long? Was something seriously wrong with him? Was he giving them a hard time? Finally a worker brought out a child and called the name Mitchell.

I was not prepared for a crying boy of four and a half years, wearing mismatched rubber shoes (one much smaller than the other and much too tight). Cold as it was in Seattle that day, he was wearing only a T-shirt and cotton shorts, and he was covered with impetigo sores. He had every reason to cry angrily, and he did.

Kim and I spent his first American night in Seattle with the family of Hercules Anderson, an old friend of mine from Charleston. His wife, Carol, was Japanese, and their four boys looked like Kim, only healthy and happy. Kim was ill at ease even with them. He spoke no English. I had trouble bathing him because he'd never seen a bathtub before. He couldn't bear the softness of a bed. We had to make him a pallet on the floor.

Next morning Kim and I flew to Oakland, stopping first in Portland to pick up Muriel, who was visiting family friends, the Hashimotos. Muriel was fully prepared to play the role of supportive big sister to our terrified but wonderful new child. The trip home was much easier with Muriel's help. She gave Kim her undivided attention. Even with no English, our new child understood hugs and smiles.

We were met at the Oakland airport by Henry, Hank, Liz, and some newspaper reporters. (We had made the front page of the *Berkeley Gazette*.) Many people in our country were aware of the need to absorb these "orphaned" biracials, the persistent aftermath of wars and military occupations. Kim took in Oakland and Berkeley with a look of careful curiosity, studying his new sisters and brother and Dad and giving special attention to our new Plymouth station wagon. He was fascinated by all moving vehicles. One of the first things he learned to say was, "Look! Beeg trruck!"

In our first together time after his arrival, we listed various new job assignments now that Kim was a member of our household. Liz had the task of language teacher. We were advised not to learn Korean because he would adjust faster to his new home if we encouraged his quick child's brain to absorb English from the start. Hank had to deal with toilet training, baths, clothing, and caring for the room they shared. Muriel would focus on Kim's emotional needs and food, and we parents supported the whole operation. All three kids accepted the experience as an adventure, and Kim received almost constant attention.

Before the month was out we had 110 teenagers helping us to get Kim used to his new life. Our family had joined Henry at Camp Pinecroft, where he was dean of the high school session. It was good that so many were there to watch Kim. One day when his Chuggy-Popup toy engine rolled into the deep end of the pool, Kim jumped in to rescue it. Several campers went right in after him, so he hardly had time to flail around. He loved to hang out with the camp kids because they bought him soda pop and other goodies.

H Liz told us she was not jealous, but she did offer her near-seven-year-old opinion that we were spoiling her new brother with all this attention, including hers. I don't think we spoiled him. I think we just loved him. He needed a lot of that. And there's no denying that Kim enriched our lives as a family. His arrival was heralded across the nation in our 1956 Christmas card. On the front was a picture of our family and our dog. Next to the picture was printed the Christmas text from Isaiah 9:6, *"Unto us a son is given!"* One of Ella's grade school teachers didn't get the point of the quotation. She wrote back that the littlest one, Kim, was the spitting image of his mother at the same age—unaware that our new child had been "given" to us. We compared pictures, and actually this teacher was pretty close to the mark.

Kim was a cunning little rascal. He'd wake up before we did and wander over to some of our neighbors' houses, looking for breakfast. His foraging left the clear implication on our street that we wouldn't get up early to feed this poor hungry child. After eating breakfast with several of the neighbors up the block, including his grandparents across the street, he'd return to eat breakfast with us as if it were his first.

Having scrounged peelings in Korea, he ate as many meals as he could beg and stuffed his pockets with things like cornflakes. He ate his apples and oranges whole, without spitting out seeds or peels. During his prayers at our together time, he'd thank God for food half a dozen times. After he spent a day digging in the back yard, his gratitude for food at together time was replaced by a new prayer: "Thank you, God, for worms!" His offering moved us all, since we saw it as revealing just how very sincere he was in his praying.

Although Kim's sincerity later moved me to my first sure-enough shout the day I baptized him, he was a many-sided character and not always a sweet little boy. His hard fists kept neighborhood boys from abusing a spastic ten-year-old who lived in the next block. But he nearly drove his kindergarten teacher crazy when his baby bass voice commanded his schoolmates to disobey the teacher, and they followed their five-year-old leader's orders not to lie down for rest time. Mr. Graham, the Franklin School principal, predicted that we'd be sorry we ever sent to Korea for that child. But we viewed Kim's behavior in another way. This was a child who'd had to shift for himself at age three; he was only letting us see the survival skills he had used to stay alive. We had to understand where he had come from—in fact we were awed and impressed.

He had no concept of personal property, having grown to four and a half in a makeshift orphanage where everything belonged to everybody. He'd bring his friends to our deep freeze and give away all the family's Popsicles. He seemed generous to a fault, but he also enjoyed having the power to distribute food we all supposedly held in common.

Years later, in a sermon at Fort Campbell, Kentucky, I preached about Kim as a determined little child who had much to teach us. I was invited to this base on Martin Luther King Jr.'s birthday by Chaplain Herman Kemp, a former student of mine. As a dyed-in-the-wool pacifist, I faced quite a challenge speaking to military men and women. My sermon title reflected this challenge in the words of a Spiritual: "Do You Think I'll Make a Soldier?"

I told my military congregation about the time our family was driving with Kim in the rear of the station wagon, when we had to pass an army convoy, one unit at a time, on a two-lane road in South Carolina. When I pulled away from the lead jeep, Kim protested. He insisted three different times that I remain in sight of this slow-moving jeep, even though I was in a hurry. When I asked him why, he said, "I *like* that man!" The jeep driver looked all of seventeen, too young for Kim to have known him back in Korea. Kim looked almost scornful, so surprised that I didn't know the answer to my own question. He explained solemnly, in his still-heavy accent, "Soldiers that drive jeeps give candies and gum to litterl children." It was a powerful declaration.

I concluded the sermon with variations of what Kim told me: "Soldiers that drive weapons carriers help crippled people down the road. Soldiers that drive tanks find food for starving babies." My point was that whatever may be the necessarily violent goals of the military, every soldier is at heart a warm human being, one who can be loved by children all over the world. Ella told me that the commander of the post, the major general seated beside her, was in tears when I finished talking about Kim and his response to American soldiers. Memories of Kim as a little boy move me the same way even today.

CHAPTER 8

Extraordinary Times, Ordinary Times: Home and Holidays

E *(Ella)* Our trips from Berkeley across country were a kind of continued honeymoon, complete with children. The kids had their own turf in the back of the station wagon, and a good part of the time Henry and I could focus on each other. We developed a strange and deep affinity while on the road together, and even today we enjoy long rides together far more than words can explain. Our trips have included visits to family, friends, historical sites, natural wonders, and of course, the professional meetings that made the trips possible.

We often took others along. Marty's daughter, Stephanie, went east with us twice. In 1954, two sets of grandparents went along for the ride when we were eastbound. Henry had to build a rack for the top of the station wagon to carry all our luggage. Six adults sat in the regular seats, and four children played and slept on a mattress we made for the back of the wagon. I'm only now aware of how terribly dangerous that was. It was before seat belts were required for any age, and the impact of a sudden stop could have caused serious injury to a child who slid forward and hit the back seat. As it was, we made the trip in safety and with lots of fun. I have to feel it was providential protection that saw us over those thousands of miles, crowded as we were, singing hymns, playing games, being a family wherever the Spirit was sending us.

H *(Henry)* On the road and at home, we lived modestly. We furnished our home one piece at a time, from salvage warehouses, war surplus, and various dealers in recycled goods. I made it a point to find the very best deals on everything. Ella and I had to be creative, but the decor of our public housing apartment was rather neat, if we do say so. After we built our *Sunset Magazine* home, designed around three sides of a patio that had a loquat tree in it, we used the same furniture sources and some of the same pieces. God provided us with wonderful items, as long as we were not choosy about their brand names or the status of the dealers we bought them from.

When our old Thor washing machine broke down, we paid ten dollars for a much newer one from the stock of a junk dealer. We planned to use it for parts to fix the older machine, but all that turned out to be wrong with our ten-dollar washer was a nickel caught in the water pump. God, we believed, had something to do with our finding that nickel in an almost new machine.

E From earliest childhood I had been accustomed to living frugally. We frequently felt good about getting a deal in an often too-expensive world. Day-old raisin bread was still as delicious as it had been when I was a girl and my father brought it home to feed our family. We educated our children early that we ate whatever God provided. I agreed with Henry's firm stand against the luxury of allowing children to refuse to eat certain foods. However, if God happened to give us oysters, we didn't bother to insist that our children eat them, which left more of this delicacy for us.

Sometimes what God provided came from the San Joaquin Valley, when Henry brought in crates of peaches or boxes of grapes as he returned from his ministerial travels. We invested a little money in a canning vat and mason jars. All of us joined in the peeling and other chores. Henry knew how to boil and sterilize the jars, fill, and seal them. How pretty the peaches looked in the jar! It was fun, and we were proud of our season's worth of food. Later, when our whole family got to where we could often travel with Henry, we had an adventure picking delicious oranges right off the tree. When we went to live in Fresno, we planted our own oranges, lemons, grapefruit, and nectarines right in the parsonage yard. The tangerine tree was the only one that failed. I don't recall blaming that on God; what we lost in tangerines we received abundantly in sweet pink grapefruit.

H Ella and the kids had lots of new dresses, blouses, skirts, and shirts because Ella made them. But I wasn't left out. In September 1950, we stopped at a woolen mill as we passed through Worcester, Massachusetts, and bought a mill end of herringbone tweed. Ella couldn't find a man's coat pattern, so she and her sister Lurline adapted a bathrobe pattern. For a little more than fifteen dollars she made matching topcoats for Hank and me. He, of course, soon outgrew his coat, but I have mine and it still fits half a century later!

E Henry would take his vacation time at the close of professional meetings, and we would explore the United States. We went from coast to coast, and from Canada to Mexico at various times, in various cars, and we traveled the California coastline and mountains many times in connection with Henry's local engagements.

On one trip we emphasized Black colleges and Black achievements. When we drove through the spacious Black-owned homes of southwest Atlanta, our children's views of the South were radically changed. They wouldn't mind living here, they conceded. We had to remind them that it was not guaranteed that they would be among the Black Atlantans so fortunate. And of course they could not know that one day they would own homes and work and raise children in this same Atlanta.

Extraordinary Times, Ordinary Times: Home and Holidays

We visited the nation's capital in Washington D.C., Mount Rushmore in South Dakota, Mount Vernon in Virginia, the Grand Canyon in Arizona, Niagara Falls in New York, and a number of popular places on the West Coast, such as the great national parks. We attended World's Fairs in New York City and Seattle, where we all wore dresses and shirts from the same bright blue material, so we wouldn't lose sight of one another. We got caught in a storm in Missouri in 1954 with hailstones as large as Ping-Pong balls. One night after Ma Warren moved to Indianapolis, the kids were sleeping on her glassed-in front porch when a terrible thunderstorm arose. They awoke terrified to see great flashes of lightning the like of which they had never seen before. We didn't have such things on the West Coast. Panic-stricken, the children ran inside and slept the rest of the night under our bed.

In spite of all these adventures, the kids fussed a bit about not having spending change to jingle in their pockets. But they could never deny that God supplied their needs and gave them lots of travel besides. Once, when we were still in Berkeley and their complaints reached a new high, we offered to let them manage the money for a while. We put the bills and the deposit slips on the table, and offered to sign whatever checks they found it necessary to write. The two older teens did most of the work. We showed them how we gave a tithe off the top and how to prioritize the expenses: food, mortgage, utilities, car note, shoes, and clothing. They added up the bills and compared that sum to the total family income. Almost instantly they discovered that we had not been exaggerating what things cost or holding back any money.

"Mom, how do you cover all these bills? Unless this adding machine is wrong, we're way short of enough to cover," Hank called out anxiously one night.

"Why don't we stop drinking milk?" Muriel suggested, as she faced the shortfall. "For our cereal and cooking, we could use that powdered milk the government gives away."

It took only two months to convince them that we were money magicians. Oddly enough, they never considered giving up the tithe to the church. We hadn't lectured them on tithing, but they did know that we happily took our tithes right off the top. They must have gotten the impression that this kind of stewardship was the law of the universe.

Their anxiety was taking an unnecessary toll on them, Henry and I decided. They shouldn't have to worry about money at their age. It could undermine their sense of security. We took over managing the money again, and they were glad to give it up.

H Before our last Christmas in Berkeley, the children decided in together time to break from our rule that we didn't exchange presents. We had always said it was Jesus' birthday, not ours. We heaped gifts on the kids when their birthdays came, but they wanted to try a Christmas that resembled the one practiced by the rest of the world. We set aside the huge sum of $200 and divided into two groups, each to buy presents for the other. Ella had the two boys on her committee, and I had the two girls. We were to go shopping as teams.

On the first shopping expedition, we were put off and unnerved by the crush of the crowd of shoppers, not to mention the high prices for just about everything we might be interested in. The worst part was finding something any of us actually needed. As it turned out, nobody's gift brought all that much joy or was that useful. The crowning frustration was the most expensive gift, an exercise machine for Ella. She used it hardly a half dozen times. It sat idle in the garage, until we finally gave it away in Fresno. After that year, we heard no more calls from our children for a typical American gift-exchange Christmas.

|E| In the wake of that one attempt at a consumer Christmas, the children grew even more involved in the presents-for-Jesus projects. Their excitement in sending breeder rabbits to Ecuador (through Church World Service) made for a really gratifying Christmas holiday. The reports we received on the rapidly increasing rabbit population in one Ecuadoran village sustained their interest, rewarded their efforts, and lasted longer than any exercise machine for Mom. One year we sent blankets to an African country, learning in the process that blankets were needed because of high altitude. Through the John Milton Society we gave Braille storybooks for blind children. We sent clothes and shoes for children in flooded Mississippi. We baked cookies and hung them on a Christmas tree made from coat hangers for the children of our neighborhood. And we bought a heater for a missionary's car on a reservation in the colder foothills of northern California.

As the children grew and their interests broadened, we agreed to send a $500 check to the Southern Christian Leadership Conference. Whatever the project, we made our choice by family consensus during our together time. One Christmas holiday we went up to Auberry Indian Mission in the foothills near Fresno and brought to our home an orphaned teenager who had been recommended to us by American Baptist missionaries stationed there. Todd came from an abusive single-parent home, and his natural father must have been an African-American. He stayed with us for two weeks and took part in all the activities of our family and church. He ate heartily with our gang and listened carefully to our family prayer time. Although he didn't know the songs, he went caroling with the youth group, mouthing the words and smiling in spite of himself, enjoying being a part of a community of cheer. He felt needed and generous as he helped pass out the Christmas baskets. The young people took him to their hearts, as did other members of our church, and he was very happy. We were all tearful when he had to go back to Auberry, but I believe he carried with him the hope and goodwill of the holiday into the New Year.

Whatever gifts we gave had to be clearly useful. This was true of our gift to Kim on his first Christmas, 1956, when we made an exception to the rule against yuletide presents within the family. Kim received a pedal-pumped toy airplane that big brother Hank had won earlier that month on a children's television show he'd appeared on. Its virtue was that it built strength and coordination in this little fellow, who had never before had a wheel toy of his own. As the three older kids watched Kim's eyes, they knew far more joy than if the gift were theirs.

H The most enjoyable part of Christmas for Ella and me was the music. Songs brought us together in spirit and in couplehood. We had a collection of beautiful Christmas records, which we played on the fine equipment we had assembled. I had bought the kits for the hi-fi with the mad money I earned writing Christian Education materials. (I refused to use writing fees for essentials.) Every Christmas season our family sang, and years later, when our children were all in their teens, we finally achieved my dream of four-part singing grace at meals. It really moved me one afternoon to see Liz playing Handel's *Messiah* on the hi-fi and singing her way through the whole oratorio, reading alone from one of our copies of the music score. Now, years later, we have a compact disc player, and the Christmas music on TV gets better and better. The musical celebration of the birth of Jesus continues to bring us our highest joy of the season, but the choir at Oakland's First Baptist Church still stands out in our memory.

Ella and I also had our private duets, singing soprano and tenor, on the road or at home, when nobody was listening. As we did show tunes, we fancied ourselves sounding like Nelson Eddy and Jeanette MacDonald in the movies. But our deepest feelings of oneness as a couple came on hymns and spirituals, with a few gospels and classics thrown in. Our happiness wasn't because our rendition was so excellent, although we sometimes surprised ourselves when we were in good voice. The joy came from the way our singing released the deeper floodgates of feeling in us and blended our sounds into something beautiful.

Those seven years at Oakland First Baptist were wonderful years for me in many other ways. At home I had my husband and my family; at work I was fulfilled. I had ideal facilities, highly motivated trainees from both the church and the seminary, and a grateful church and parent group. Every Saturday church school was not just another baby-sitting project for shoppers at the nearby department stores; it was a child-teaching care program and actually a lab school that provided training for a second team of teachers. We used the same curriculum as the Sunday church school, and a few teachers were on both teams. Some of the children were there both days also. We had classes from kindergarten to junior high. It was very satisfying to have people following my instructions so carefully, and the affection they showed me at this virtually all-White church was in stark contrast to the way I had been treated at the church from which I had come.

Because the nearby community was practically all Catholic, we could not serve their children in our church buildings. But they gladly joined us when we moved our summer vacation church school to the parks and called the program Day Camp.

In addition, our children got caught up in various groups at the church and felt valued there. They frequently led worship and were asked to hold office. They even took part in the church's Every Member Canvass for tithes and pledges. Hank was baptized at First Baptist Church, making a youthful and sincere pledge of faith that moved us parents very much.

But this ideal situation began to fall apart when Hank and Muriel grew further into their teens. They still received unlimited acceptance in the youth activities of the church, but as the teenagers developed interests in the opposite sex they began to divide into cliques from which our two were quietly excluded for reasons of race. White parents had a demonic fear of interracial marriage and were avoiding cross-racial boy/girl ties even in the mid teens. Even though we don't recall Hank or Muriel complaining, Henry and I felt that if we stayed at that church, our teenagers' self-esteem would be whittled down to nothing.

The obvious solution was to get the heck out of there before our children's souls were scarred by the rejection of the very folks who had once seemed to love them so much. We didn't want to risk a return of my rejection at McGee Avenue years before. Had our providential run in Berkeley and Oakland come to and end? For the sake of our family and our shared calling to ministry, it was time to consider where we should go now.

H As we pondered how to spare our kids this sudden rejection, the Second Baptist Church of Fresno approached me with a call to be their pastor. Their pulpit committee knew that accepting their offer would cut my salary in half; the church's annual budget had never exceeded $10,000. And besides having so little money to offer, they had only a four-room parsonage for the six of us. But they couldn't think of anybody else they really wanted to call, and they thought they should at least ask me. I had been to Fresno many times, and the church members and I knew each other well. Their call had an added touch of providence because Grandpa Mitchell had served that same congregation in the middle 1920s.

I approached Ella, ready to support her if she felt this call asked too much of us. Did we want her to give up her seminary teaching in Berkeley and the home we had built with our own hands, not to mention our first decent salary, and try to stuff six people into a tiny parsonage in the Fresno heat?

Ella didn't answer my question. She had concerns of her own. "Do you feel like the Lord is leading you there? Is this something that appeals to your spirit, apart from any considerations of salary and such? Since when did I get the privilege of asking you to question a call from God?"

It was not hard for me to answer her. "It really does appeal to me, and I have a strong suspicion that God has arranged this call. But it would be a major risk for all of us, what with the size of our family and the needs we all have."

Ella didn't even have to ask for the usual time to pray about a decision. "You know very well I have always wanted to see you in a full-time pastorate," she told me. "And this has been your own long-time dream as well. This is the perfect time to move for the kids' sake. And since the Lord has always provided, I say let's go. Tell the pulpit committee that you will accept if the congregation's final vote is unanimous."

Ella was more willing than I was. I had halfway hoped I could use her for an excuse not to follow my own higher sense, and here she was running ahead of me. Once again, the wife I had prayed God to find for me was showing her scale of values. Going to Fresno wouldn't quite cause me the culture shock of that mission to Africa I'd felt I needed the right wife to undertake, but it sure would be a great adjustment.

Would the church build a new parsonage as soon as possible? (They had plenty of land for it.) What was their top salary offer? Would they cover my premiums in the American Baptist Ministers and Missionaries Board pension plan? The church's answers were backed merely by faith, but they were positive about achieving the new levels of budget the pastorate would require. This church had been seriously divided over its feelings toward my predecessor, but the very first vote to call me was almost unanimous. With God providing that kind of rare unanimity in a Baptist congregation, and with Ella willing to give up so much, I couldn't fail to see the hand of God.

I gave three months' notice, and we moved to Fresno on July 1, 1959. At the end of our first three weeks, after 106-degree heat every single day, I asked Ella if she wanted to move back to naturally air-conditioned Berkeley.

"If it doesn't get any worse than this, I could stay here for the rest of my life," she told me. Her brow was moist, but she was not completely at the mercy of the weather, since we had a swamp cooler that pulled air through wet pads and took the edge off the heat. But even without the swamp cooler, I knew she meant every word. I slipped away from Ella and found myself crying a little. Here, again, was the exact attitude I had prayed for in a wife. How could I have ever wondered what her answer would be?

CHAPTER 9

Building Life Together:
Joined in Work and Love

H *(Henry)* "Ella, when that crew of volunteer movers from Second Baptist set our furniture down in that little parsonage, did you have even the vaguest notion of what our life in Fresno would be like? Our tiny house was on a street with no sidewalk, on a long lot with no garage. The full-width front porch had not been blessed by a paintbrush in years. It looked like we didn't have any prospects at all. What on earth were you thinking, in the face of all that?"

E *(Ella)* "I guess I hadn't even tried to envision our future. I only knew that our two teenagers would be safe from the emotional hazards they had recently encountered in Oakland, living with half-a-loaf racial integration. I knew that for the first five months the boys would be sleeping in the living room, but none of us dreaded it. We just looked forward to the day when we would move into a nice new parsonage with four bedrooms big enough to breathe in, just before Thanksgiving 1959."

H "I was worried about how you would take the abrupt drop in living space, to say nothing of the increase in temperature, as compared to the cool San Francisco Bay area. I watched you closely, not wanting to burden you with more than heat, and I admired how you showed no signs of either discomfort or frustration. The main difference I noticed was that we had to be very careful to keep our little four-room bungalow neat, what with the wear and tear of so many people in so little space."

E "It was hard to be mad at the weather after I learned how much the local grape growers needed the heat. I remember that you, with your farmer's way of thinking, were impressed by the fact that they needed very hot nights to put sugar in the raisin-grape crop. A comfortable summer could cost millions in lost income and sugarless raisins. And all the raisins we ever ate came from right there in Fresno County. Far more important than the weather for us was having all of us living and working together, seven days a week, for the very first time. What a joy it was!"

In the years after Fresno, our older children were spread to the far corners of the country in colleges and careers. This was our only experience of having their schools close by and Henry's work concentrated virtually at home. The church and the parsonage were located on the same three acres, and Henry even kept his office in the parsonage for the first few years.

Day after day we experienced the kind of day-long buildup of oneness we had previously enjoyed only occasionally. If our real values were in our family, as opposed to physical comforts and possessions, this was the time and place to enjoy our life together to the fullest. It would never again be possible. As I remember, we really enjoyed those years—together.

H I was very much at home with the bowling parties we had with the church's deacons and their wives. The deacons tended to be middle-aged, younger than the typical "elders," and they were serious bowlers, including the chairman, who was a physician. This group consisted not only of Dr. U. S. Curry and some schoolteachers and janitors, but several salvage specialists (we used to call them junkmen). It was a marvelous mix of humanity, much as it will be over in the glory land.

Architecturally, our church was Spanish in style, a copy of a Methodist church in northern California. I had drawn the modifications to the borrowed plans in 1952, when I was on my previous assignment. At the time I never dreamt I was drawing a building in which I would one day serve. The church was beautiful and appropriate for its three acres of land, but the floor plan left much to be desired because the cross-shaped sanctuary divided the congregation into three parts, with one arm of the cross yet to be built. If a crop duster on the cotton patch across the street had crashed into it, I would have called it "Holy Smoke" and built a more unifying sanctuary. I had some better architectural ideas, such as a semicircle with everybody in intimate closeness to each other and to the central pulpit and choir. But I kept this to myself. Things in general were too good for me to complain—especially since I had Ella close by.

E I wasn't at home in that new parsonage all the time, of course. The first year I studied and did my practice teaching at the Fresno State College lab school, less than half an hour away at the other end of Fresno. Given my experience in early childhood education, in my second semester I was asked to serve as a member of the demonstration team of kindergarten teachers, where I stayed for the next two years while I got a California public school credential. Although this lab school teaching was secular and not Christian education, the methods and criteria for evaluating student work were much the same. The space and equipment were excellent, and once again I was in charge, although technically I was still a student. The trainees were younger than my graduate-school students and parents had been, but the overall situation was not that different from the combination of the seminary and First Baptist Oakland that I'd experienced before. Once again I could apply the things I had learned at Union Seminary. For me it was also important that this Black preacher's daughter from South Carolina could be so highly respected in an almost all-White context. There were times when I wanted to pinch myself to be sure I wasn't dreaming, but I kept a straight face, as if this situation were what I'd experienced all my life.

After the lab school, I moved to teaching kindergarten half days for the Fresno County Sunset School. This put me on salary, and the school was less than ten minutes from home. I had my afternoons free for playing the organ at funerals, making home visits for the school, and working with Henry for the church. Sometimes Henry and I had lunch together at home or went shopping. I suppose most people wouldn't see much romance in grocery shopping, but we still get a big kick out of wandering together through the supermarket aisles. And we surely did have to buy lots of groceries for our big hungry family.

When the national Head Start Program got under way, I was also appointed one of the teachers to train staff. The course was eight weeks of intensive evening sessions, but again I enjoyed the fulfillment and the additional income for our family of teenagers—the expensive age.

While I was doing neighborhood visitation for Sunset School, I was bitten by a dog and ended up critically ill with a pulmonary embolism, a clot in the artery of the lung. I was on sick leave from October 1963 until May 1964. It was a terribly trying time. I lay motionless for days and weeks, waited on by Henry, the children, and visiting church members. They never complained: they even seemed to enjoy waiting on me. Although there was no pain, I felt discouraged at being so useless. I finally found a little solace in knitting.

One day the Reverend T. C. Wynn, a seasoned pastor from a nearby town, came to visit me. He sensed my problem and, in his own simple way, set about helping me by means of a story.

"Sister Mitchell," he told me, "once there was a missionary who had to make a long journey. It was through a dense forest, and he could neither ride a horse nor drive a car. He walked as best he could, but night overtook him when he was only halfway there. As he sat leaning against a tree, he had fearful visions of being breakfast for some animal the next morning. There was nothing he could do except, finally, to pray. When he had prayed for a while, he thought of a verse of scripture: 'Behold, he that keepeth Israel shall neither slumber nor sleep' (Psalm 121:4). With that the missionary suddenly felt relieved. He told God, 'Since you're not going to sleep anyway, there's no sense in both of us staying awake.' So he went to sleep and awakened refreshed the next day."

I shall never forget that story. This country preacher with gnarled hands and no formal training had accurately diagnosed my depression and its cause. I was afraid to trust God and family when I could earn none of their love with my own efforts. As soon as I realized this, I began to improve speedily. It was as if a load had been lifted from my shoulders. Now I could relax while God, family, and friends cared for me. Providence had sent me an unlikely expert in healing ministries to work alongside our wonderful family physician, Deacon U. S. Curry. In a few weeks I was just about fully recovered and once again able to embrace the life Henry and I and our family were building together.

H Ella and I did enjoy to the fullest our life together as a couple and a family. With the church's youth group, including our own children, we had swimming parties, snow trips, picnics, roasts, and trips, all within an hour's drive. This was the start of a rewarding relationship with the young people, and they soon came to hang at our house. We thoroughly enjoyed having them there.

I even did a stint as dean of the Baptist summer camp for the whole valley. This was a largely White group of some 120 high schoolers. Despite the general conservatism of the farm-dominated San Joaquin Valley, the camp board vigorously recruited me to be dean. In a broad-based version of the Mitchell family's together time, I introduced camper self-government, with interesting results, especially regarding the mandatory chapel services. When a couple skipped chapel to wander around in the National Forest, they were hauled into student court. "How do you plead?" Guilty, they answered. "How would you suggest that you be punished?" Long pause. Hearing no reply, the chair called on members of the court to suggest a sentence. A wag on the bench offered, "Let them be given two shovels and a wheelbarrow and assigned the task of removing the meadow muffins"—dropped by the cattle pastured on these federal lands in the spring and fall. The ten council members immediately and unanimously adopted the proposed sentence. After that, nobody else had the nerve to play hooky from chapel. I was given credit for running a tight ship, and yet I got to be quite popular with my White teenagers.

The great national parks nearby provided convenient adventures for our family. One Sunday, Ella and I took the family to public worship in Sequoia National Park. Giving his all in leading the worship was a young White Southern Baptist preacher. Suddenly, in the midst of his passionate sermon, he sensed that nobody was paying any attention, especially the children, who were jumping up and down in their seats. He finally realized they were looking behind him. When he turned around, a huge brown mother bear and her cub were ambling by hardly three feet in back of him. Church was over, as the children trooped after the bear. Our little ones went along too. So did Ella and I, sheepishly, leaving our places in the back row to make sure no one was harmed.

When the cold weather set in that first year, Ella and I found that almost nobody in the congregation had been to Sequoia, or even to Yosemite National Park, which was closer. I had the joy of exhibiting the abundant life on a toboggan sled, with three or four kids holding on behind me for dear life. Roaring down those hills was the most exciting thing any of them had ever done. And just think, they did it with their pastor and his family! It was more than a bit dangerous, but God was good, and nobody's neck was broken. They seemed to respect their pastor even as he relived a childhood spent playing in the snows of Ohio.

H Henry was alone in his enthusiasm for the snow. I had grown up in the City by the Sea, Charleston, South Carolina. I never saw it snow enough to remain on the ground until 1941, when I was twenty-four years old and had moved to New York. I'm still all but panic-stricken when Henry and I have to drive on ice, whether in California, Rochester, Richmond, or Russia.

Whether they were playing in the snow or worshiping in the summer heat, the people of our congregation were wonderfully inclusive, to their new pastoral family and to everyone else. They belied their reputation for being snooty. One only had to come and see the members who were on welfare and yet prominent in the congregation to realize this was a warm and wonderful collection of God's children. There were luxury cars in the parking lot on Sunday mornings, but there were some raggedy pickup trucks also. Because this town of 150,000 was an "agribusiness" center, it was short on middle-class people of all races. The majority seemed to be either rich ranchers and packing plant owners or laborers just scraping by. Nevertheless, at one point our congregation had seventeen schoolteachers (including me), three physicians, some social workers, an undertaker, and a pharmacist, along with many members on subsistence-level incomes. Our congregation also included distinguished domestic servants to the wealthy, notorious ex-winos, former track stars, and many brothers from the football team at Fresno State. In fact, our church's teams in the Fresno City Recreation League were known to win almost all the age-level championships several years in a row. And we drew many team members from the community, as well as from the church.

Athletes like Rafer Johnson of Olympic fame visited us occasionally, accompanying his mother, who lived fifteen miles down the road. And we drew a sizable delegation from the Fresno State College football team. One Sunday morning in 1965, after the service, Jimmy Stewart, the glue-fingered split end, brought us greetings from our daughter Muriel. He had seen her the night before, in Colorado, where she was in college. When I asked him how this could be, he replied, "We played there last night, and then we flew home." I was flabbergasted. Just imagine him and his fellow players being on a plane half the night, and then getting up and coming to church the next morning! It really pleased me to think that these young men were that excited about our worship at the Second Baptist Church of Fresno. I think they thought Henry was "taking care of business" and making the Bible really relevant to the issues of the day. They also liked his militancy in civic affairs, and they considered him approachable. For most of his life, Jimmy Stewart had called him Uncle Henry.

H Ella and I were especially happy with the music in our church. They sang all kinds of music surprisingly well, from gospels to spirituals to classics, under Maude Hunter's direction. We had great soloists and balanced male and female voices. Of course, I often sang with the basses. If singing in a choir is the best metaphor we have for what goes on in heaven, I can hardly wait.

Our organist, Frank Byrdwell, was an organ major at Fresno State.

His grandmother had been minister of music for my grandfather when he was pastor there in the 1920s. When Frank left, Ron Harmon, another student at Fresno State, moved from piano to organ, with Ella filling in the gaps for funerals and other special services.

E As a Christian Education person, I was especially happy we had a good youth choir and a talented director for it, Rosalind Andrews, another student at Fresno State. One of the teens she inspired to musical excellence was our daughter Liz, whose voice was first discovered by Roz. On her advice, Liz began receiving voice lessons much earlier than the usual starting age for young singers, and later she studied voice in Paris for two years.

I worked hard to prepare teams of teachers and to develop a Vacation Church School (VCS). In addition to the children from our church, we drew so many children from other churches and from all over the community that we ran out of space. All the while Henry and I were getting double for our effort, because our own children were benefiting. My kindergarten group "built" a cardboard church out of a refrigerator carton. The children cut door openings in the ends and painted stained glass windows on the sides. Their little faces lighted up as they sang with gusto, "I was glad when they said unto me, Let us go into the house of the Lord" (Psalm 122:1), while scrambling in and out of their own cardboard church. The Bible verse came alive for them in a way that made me very happy.

Henry's junior high class filmed a movie of a Bible story they wrote together and then produced. They used a slightly damaged but very fine 16-mm movie camera, gleaned from Deacon Brannon Murcherson's salvage yard. They chose the cast from among themselves and then acted out the story. The shortest boy in the class climbed a tree as Zaccheus, the short tax collector who sought to see Jesus over the crowd (Luke 19:1–4). The film made the Bible breathe.

H Another summer, my junior high class in the VCS studied (would you believe?) church history. We met in the living room of the new parsonage. They were delighted, for instance, to know the meaning of the fish symbol. They had seen it displayed on so many cars. *Ichthyus* is Greek for fish, and the Greek acronym stood for Jesus Christ, Son of God and Savior. The early Christians under persecution used it as a coded message or "protest witness."

When we moved to Black church history, they were fascinated by accounts of the underground church of the slaves, often called the "invisible institution." Slaves had to sneak away to worship. Masters feared they would plot rebellion if they were allowed to worship freely. The junior high kids were also intrigued by tales of Harriet Tubman leading slaves out of the South via the Underground Railroad. I told how she kept escapees from panicking and never lost a "passenger." I acted out how the freedom-seeking slaves had crawled in the dark to the very caves I had visited as a child near my Ohio home. I told of the cold, damp hiding places under stone floors in basements I had seen, and how a Black church in my mother's hometown in southern Ohio even took the name "Anti-Slavery Baptist Church" and was a station on the Underground Railroad. Harriet Tubman became as real a hero to them as any athlete or movie star, and I could see them grow in wisdom, stature, and self-esteem as young Black people.

One day I read them Charles H. Brooks's 1922 account from *Official History of the First African Baptist Church: Philadelphia, Pa.*, where my grandpa, the first H. H. Mitchell, had been ordained in the 1870s.

James Burrows was born a slave and lived in Northampton County, Virginia. He felt that he was called to preach, but his master refused to allow him the privilege. He then persuaded his master to permit him to come to Philadelphia to earn money to purchase his freedom. His master consented to this after Samuel Bivens [the father of Mother Stevens] and his cousin, John Bivens, who were freemen, placed themselves in bondage as security for the return of James Burrows, their minister. After working a year and saving the necessary amount to purchase his freedom, he prepared to return but was informed that there would be danger in doing so, as the famous Nat Turner insurrection had just broken out. He therefore sent the money, released his friends, and they returned to Philadelphia and assisted him in his work in this church.

Rev. Burrows had quite a successful pastorate from 1832 until 1844, and from a membership of 60 at the beginning he left 252.

Then I asked them to tell me what they had heard. All of a sudden they realized that two men had volunteered to go and serve as *slaves* for a year in Virginia so their new pastor could be released to serve the church and earn his liberty. One of the girls said, "They really wanted a pastor, and they loved him enough to be slaves! Wow!"

"They were taking an awful risk," I told them. "Suppose the master took the money and then refused to let the Bivens cousins go? Such things happened many times." As they entered into the drama of our ancestors, these twelve- and thirteen-year-olds were all but moved to tears.

Ella was presiding at the concluding Friday VCS service in 1960 when Liz, age ten, came forward and made a confession of faith. Forty-one others joined our daughter, well over half of them from other churches, but it was Liz who moved Ella to speechless emotion. Liz was embracing the work to which her mother's whole life was dedicated. I squeezed her hand to help her get herself back together.

Kim, eight years old, was not among those forty-two children. The following Sunday night, I was surprised to see him in the second pew for Sunday evening service. I glanced up at Ella at the organ, and she was surprised too. This was not like our son, and, furthermore, I had just left him watching TV at our house, on the other end of the block. When I asked if he had come for any special reason, his little-boy deep voice responded, "I'm going forward." He meant to become a confessing Christian, and without saying so, he wanted it fully understood that he was not following the crowd of kids from the Vacation Church School. For a serious Christian, Kim would do some strange things in later life, but there can be no question that at eight he was in dead earnest. And, like David in the Bible, he never escaped the influence of his early experience of God's spirit.

The children needed book smarts as well as spirit. With the co-sponsorship of other community groups, we held a "Homework Help Study Hall" in our church's dining room and everywhere else we could squeeze in a study group. We recruited public school teachers and other professionally trained volunteers to tutor our children. Others served as monitors to help keep order and distribute supplies. This was for me a most relevant and satisfying project, as I saw the grades of many of the students rise. Even the initially reluctant and suspicious public school administrators had to admit our kids' success.

I also grew more and more active in the American Baptists' program of Christian Education. I directed many laboratory schools for teachers of nursery and kindergarten children. This meant doing introductory lectures, guiding student teachers in lesson planning, and then doing my own demonstration teaching with children of the various age groups. After that I supervised and evaluated their practice teaching.

These labs reached up and down the West Coast and even to the American Baptist National Assembly at Green Lake, Wisconsin. The most memorable of these was in Phoenix, Arizona, when the two national staff persons came down sick and I had to direct the entire lab school for three days. This required lectures on the needs and characteristics of additional age groups, but by this time I had become a veteran and was confident about taking on this emergency responsibility. I was especially fulfilled by the comments of my trainees in nursery school education, who commented that my first lectures had prepared them well for their roles after I had to spend so much more time in other age groups.

One of my greatest satisfactions came from the racial implications of my work in the midst of the great civil rights revolution of the sixties and seventies. Nobody called special attention to me as a representative of my race. That allowed me to use my gifts where they were needed. And so I was quite sure that I was being called on for reasons unrelated to race. There was a scarcity of people specializing in early childhood, and I was almost alone at my level of expertise. The people I trained at the national level at Green Lake, for instance, were expected to train the student teachers in their regions. I was convinced that my teaching was making a more effective effort for equality of opportunity than any other way I could communicate.

Just before we moved to Fresno, I'd been elected to the Board of Education and Publication of the American Baptist Convention, responsible for publishing church school literature, and the co-sponsorship of regional directors of Christian Education. The late Dr. Samuel D. Proctor and I were the first African-Americans ever to serve on this board. I traveled east to meetings three or four times a year. If I ever had any question about being fully accepted or respected outside my race, it was answered in this context. I had been trained in largely White Union Seminary. My teaching at Berkeley occurred in a similar environment, and the lab schools where I taught had been in White churches. Yet it was not until I served in this national office that I finally surrendered my feelings of being less than fully accepted.

During the last four years of my fourteen-year tenure on the board,

I became president, heading the annual national convention meetings, including the session when the decision was made to move the offices from Philadelphia to Valley Forge and build the present denominational headquarters. At the laying of the cornerstone in 1961, I got goose pimples. It wasn't just the civil-rights implications of my role that moved me; it was the awesome awareness of the hand of God in my life. My only regret was that Henry and I couldn't be together in office. The American Baptists had a rule against both husband and wife serving in national offices at the same time.

At this time when racial issues were inflaming America, with Martin Luther King Jr. and other clergy struggling in lunchrooms and courts for equal rights, I rose—like Ella—through the structure of our Northern California Baptist Convention, to the office of president and then to the chairmanship of the executive board. I was the first Black to head the very same body for which I worked for fourteen years. I kept a steady face, but—like Ella—I had to pinch myself sometimes, especially since it was during my administration also that the most sweeping structural changes took place. We streamlined the work from two offices to one, at the risk of offending former power figures, but it came off well in the end.

The Northern California Convention covered a territory six hundred miles long, with over two hundred churches, so most presiding officers had always had to ask the name of those who made and seconded the motions. To everybody's amazement, their first "colored" president—me—never had to ask. I just sounded out the name and church of every single person who felt at home enough or had the nerve to offer or second a motion on the floor. I could tell that with every name, the delegates were in suspense, wondering when I was going to miss. The closest I came was to pause and then say the name just as it was being given to me by a colleague. I had traveled the length and breadth of the convention for fourteen years, before I left for the Fresno pastorate; no other president had ever had such preparation for the job.

I believe my role offered a powerful witness concerning the potential place of ethnic membership in a typical middle-class Protestant church body. We Black people were definitely not to be marginalized, and this regional convention has continued to involve people of color at every level ever since, participating in all its work.

E Let's not make this outside recognition seem too easy; it wasn't all sweetness and light. When our American Baptist Board of Education debated divesting ourselves of all our endowment's assets in South Africa, I had to appear neutral and calm. The issue of how best to combat South African apartheid became a matter of huge contention. The best up-front supporters of my undercover campaign were the two youngest women on the board. One was Carol Stassen, nineteen, the daughter of Harold Stassen, a former president of the convention and perennial candidate for the U.S. presidency. The other was Kathy Hannold, a college professor. Arrayed against us was an army of conservative White males, determined to maintain the status quo even if it permitted oppression in South Africa. We studied long and hard preparing our brief, and we finally won the vote. This was a most satisfying victory, for me as an African-American and for the female minority on the board, but it was not easy.

H Ella, with all her sweetness, could be rough-and-tumble on civil rights. She was presiding at a board meeting one day when a top staffer failed to recommend the promotion of Ted Jones, a very competent African-American educator. His immediate superior had moved on, and this staffer was using the usual ploy of reorganizing to abolish the post, rather than fill it with Ted Jones, the Black man who was in line for the appointment. After the meeting was adjourned, a furious President Ella flat-out charged board and staff with being racist. The day after that confrontation at Valley Forge, I was at a seminary board meeting on the West Coast when the same top staffer asked me, "Do you think Ella was right?" My answer was, "No, I don't *think* she was right. I *know* she was right!" Apparently he heard us loud and clear. "Reorganization" was quietly tabled two months later, and Dr. Theodore Jones was promoted as he was due.

Two years later this staffer and I drove down from Green Lake to Chicago. He was complaining that Dr. Jones had already resigned for a higher position at one of the nation's great universities. I was a "good boy" and held my tongue.

H Henry wasn't always that cool. At times he could show more fury than I ever did. Often he ended up in the newspaper or on television, always in somebody's face. This was the 1960s, there was a great civil rights revolution going on, and we had our own little uprising against local injustice right there in Fresno.

Shortly after we landed in Fresno, a young member of our church was jailed for responding to White gunfire in our 'hood. He had simply protested the terror by firing a gun into the air on the White side of the tracks. Whites were never arrested for shooting up our side of town; they even fired into a church member's car and came within four inches of killing someone. But when a Black youth reacted harmlessly to these provocations, Fresno law came down hard on him. Henry assembled his reports and pictures of the bullet holes in the car and marched up to the Fresno chief of police, waving his evidence and threatening to call in federal authorities. That was the beginning of a long and tense relationship between Henry and the police chief. The officials of the city confessed no wrongdoing. However, the whole police force was called in, one shift at a time, and retrained to treat all people as human beings. The Fresno police officials would never admit that they had aggravated racial tensions, but Henry was given private phone numbers he could use to reach the mayor and police chief at any hour, if he ever saw any more brutality or unequal treatment by police officers, of the Black minority or of anyone else, for that matter. I relished every minute of this and of Henry's other battles.

We spent weeks planning for a march and mass meeting to be held Monday evening, June 1, 1964, and featuring Martin Luther King Jr. in person. We hoped to fill the ball park for his speech. Wyatt Tee Walker was King's advance man, and on the day of the event he called to tell us that King had missed his plane out of Los Angeles. King arrived late, but not too late, in a chartered plane, and Henry and I met him on the tarmac and drove him to the start of the demonstration line.

Dr. King was visibly weary from his constant routine of civil rights campaigning, but his speech on America's sins and hopes was well received by the crowd. However, the turnout disappointed me. We had anticipated three times as many as the thousand or so who showed up. The general population, even the Black population, did not respond to our widespread publicity efforts, or the historical significance of King's appearance in our small city. This level of response was typical in metropolitan areas also, but more obvious in a smaller city like Fresno.

When Dr. King had to leave early from the reception after the rally and fly back to Los Angeles, probably nobody suspected that I would be his driver. I spirited him out of the kitchen door of the St. Mark United Methodist Church and into our car, parked very close by. I still feast on the memory of that time of uninterrupted conversation with him. We talked about his children and his crowded schedule, which took him away from them so much.

I couldn't help sympathizing with him as husband and father, and I appreciated his openness. But seeing how tired and tense he was, I turned on some restful music and let him close his eyes and relax the rest of our twenty-minute ride to the airport. History had come to our city. For me and for the thousand others who saw and heard Martin Luther King Jr. that night, history had a tired human face.

H I too relished every moment spent with Martin Luther King Jr., and I had the privilege several other times as well. I served on the board of the western affiliate of the Southern Christian Leadership Conference, which was the driving force behind the 1960s civil rights movement, and our paths crossed several other times. King gave the address at Ella's twentieth-anniversary class reunion and commencement at Talladega in 1959. Two years later, at my Lincoln University twentieth reunion, he was again the speaker, giving basically the same speech we heard at Talladega. Later that day, I saw him on the campus, surrrounded by a crowd. When he saw me on the fringe, he called out, "Mitchell, what in the world are you doing here, all the way from California?" I told him, of course, about my class reunion. I suspected what was on his mind. He knew I had heard that address several times before—and not just at Talladega. But how could a man so busy take time out to craft a new speech for as many as fourteen occasions in a week?

What King and others were seeking on the national level, many of us fought for in our local communities. My most rewarding experience on Fresno's social action front was the board of the War on Poverty, more formally known as the Fresno County Economic Opportunity Commission. My salary qualified me as a representative of the poor, and the group's poor Blacks and Latinos joined to elect me president. This came as a surprise to the town's power elite, who had never seen these ethnic minorities united. The town's rulers had expected to put in their hand-picked candidate and control the War on Poverty in their usual paternalistic way.

One night a committee of migrant farmworkers brought in a very creative proposal for funding. They wanted us to help them secure a master mechanic, a large garage, and tools, all of which would empower them to repair their own cars during the down season of winter, when they weren't working in the fields. They wanted us to help them help themselves. I thought it was a great idea, and so did the members of the commission.

But how could they present their plan when not one member of their delegation spoke English? The only Spanish speakers on the commission were an Armenian rancher and yours truly. I had learned the language as a high school student, back when I wanted to be an engineer in South America. God had later used my Spanish when I was a denominational staffer, and now it was being used to help these ingenious farmworkers. As the migrant workers presented their details, first the rancher and then I would translate for the commission. The applicants were overjoyed when the commission approved their application unanimously. *"Muchas gracias!"* We could see it in their eyes even more than we could hear it.

I was more deeply touched when the western regional director of the NAACP remarked with great feeling, "That was one of the prettiest pieces of presiding I ever saw." My joy would have been complete, if only the regional board at San Francisco had given final approval to their entrepreneurialism. The proposal was denied final funding because of fierce opposition from the auto mechanics' union, who saw this independent effort as a threat to its members' livelihood. Social justice never comes easy, even when everyone's intentions are good.

E When Henry ran for the school board, I went to almost all the candidate meetings and coffee klatches and managed to knit a three-piece suit in the process. In both his candidacies he had the same excellent campaign chairperson, and I admired his tough and passionate speeches. But he ran into powerful opposition from the public school establishment, with all its hundreds of teachers and their families, many of whom resented Henry for exposing how an elementary school student in our neighborhood had been punished unprofessionally. Henry made a low-key protest to the principal, who denied the incident ever happened. The whole administration accused Henry of being a troublemaker. It was a miracle that he received as many votes as he did. With the enthusiastic backing of the alliance of African-American clergy and the NAACP, he continued to make his mark on the actions of the board, even though he was not elected.

During those close-fought elections, I felt so sad for Hank. At the *Fresno Bee,* the local newspaper that had endorsed Henry, Hank was the first Black copy boy. The editors phoned me to tell me that Hank "died" when the voting returns showed some other candidate edging his daddy out of the ones to be elected. It was a bittersweet moment for Henry and me. But from where I sit now, I can see providential action in these defeats; they kept us from being nailed down in Fresno when it was finally time to move on. In Fresno and beyond, we would work to find ingenious means to try to do God's work together, in ways large and small.

CHAPTER 10

Church and Family Together:
A Ministry of Loving and Learning

H (*Henry*) We marvel that our children never did resent my seemingly ceaseless involvement in the community or Ella's devotion to her teaching. Acceptance of all this activity is not that common a response among preachers' kids. Many PKs are very sensitive to the pressures they are under, as well as their parents' absorption with things other than the family. The secret of our success seems to have been our unwillingness to have our lives sealed off from the children. The entire family shared one way or another in all our commitments, especially the youth ministry of the church. Although we did have to observe confidentiality in things like counseling, there was otherwise a kind of common ownership of all our church responsibilities. The house was always full of our children's friends, and I believe that the magnetic pull between Ella and me kept our kids contentedly within the orbit of the family.

Just as they monitored our togetherness in marriage, Hank, Muriel, Liz, and Kim were also keenly observant of some of our more confidential pastoral labors. They would see who came to the office for counseling and, when the folks left, our teenagers would smile mischievously and say something like, "I know you're not going to tell me, but didn't they come to . . . ?" Maybe it would be a threatened divorce, a baby due out of wedlock, or some other serious concern.

137

They would not have heard the conversation, but they knew the players and were shrewd enough to guess the issues. I'm just glad they also knew that these guesses were to be as confidential as my conversations. I never once heard of a leak of their all-too-accurate yet never confirmed opinions. They strictly followed the PK code.

E *(Ella)* Our children had been taught respect. Even with Kim, we followed the precept of respect for property—not that we were selfish, but we had to know that what we shared was freely given. What could be said of toys and clothing and money could be said of space. Our parsonage dared not be poorly kept, but the children's organized care of their rooms was not to please prying eyes. It was to make the best use of their own limited space and to respect each other's turf.

This became an unexpected asset in Fresno, after our family's young folks drew so many others that we had to use every inch of space for congregational programs in both the church (before we expanded it), and the parsonage. We held classes in our living room, the laundry room, the office, even the garage. There was a Mitchell attending nearly every class, so there could be no feeling that the congregation had invaded our privacy. The line between our church family and our nuclear family was at times deliciously dim, and many of the youth of that era are still close to all of us; our dinner table—like our hearts—continues to reserve places for friends who grew to feel like family.

This arrangement might seem to work against our having quality time as a family and as a couple, at home and on the road, but it only added to our togetherness and enriched the bond between Henry and me. For instance, our eyes would meet as we overheard little Liz giving advice to her friends that would be a credit to any adult. We dared not speak about what was happening because that would spoil it. But we would sneak away and discuss it. "Look at that girl. We never know when they are getting the message. Don't tell me God didn't put this team together." Our chatter was not typically romantic, but since it was often with a lump in the throat, it was our way of saying to each other, "I sure do love you and the things you do for this family!"

H The church, of course, is both family and institution, and we had to meet the challenge of fund-raising for the budget. A church that had never raised more than $10,000 or so in a year could be expected to oppose anything like systematic fund-raising, but from the start the members agreed to give it a try. The first year, we did all the surveys and drafted a tentative budget. It included the dream requests of every group in the church. Then we held a meeting with free discussion and hopes. Bud Gaston, the church clerk, expressed the question in many minds almost unanimously: "What if the budget vote fails?" It didn't. The congregation adopted the goal: $22,000. When all the pledges were in, they totaled much more than that, and the actual receipts approached $18,000. As the congregation learned how to pledge realistically, the amount we collected rose every year. And I was never made to wonder if the members resented the portion of the church's annual income allocated to pastoral support.

E A year later, at another church business meeting, a couple of faithful sisters were concerned that they were no longer allowed to prepare meals and sell tickets. To them our new budget had not only done away with impulse-giving and begging; it had robbed them of their way of ministry. (Many others read their concern as denial of the privilege they had had of taking home a lot of leftover goodies that should have been used for larger servings on the plates of the dinners that they sold.)

The issue came to a head when Deacon Louis McNary, the superintendent of the church school, rose to testify. "I've been in the church all my life," he said. "And I have never given as much to the Lord's work as I have this year. But I have never enjoyed it so much either. I gladly give through the one offering, and that's the end of it. I don't have to deal with ticket sellers all over the church grounds. I move that we reaffirm the budget and pledges. I refuse to go back to Egypt!" There was applause, and the motion was seconded and overwhelmingly carried. There was a tear in my eye. Henry and I were too close for me not to know that his heart would have been broken if the congregation had voted to revert to its former practice of unsystematic support.

H In many matters, especially those involving money, pastors and boards often engage in a running battle for power. One of the most satisfying aspects of my work at Second was that I had to endure no such friction. I even have very pleasant memories of the two times I was rebuked by my deacons or trustees. Part of what makes the memories pleasant is how each one connected me further with Ella and taught me more about my own African-American heritage.

On the first Sunday in each month I used to take a couple of deacons with me as I brought communion to the sick and shut-in members. We went from house to house, rest home to hospital, until all had been served. One Sunday afternoon we made fourteen stops. That's when I was served with my first reprimand. "Rev, this is the last time we do it this way," one of the deacons said. "We have just sat in the car and enjoyed the ride and poured the communion and passed it, and we are tired. You have driven and parked and counseled and prayed—and now you have to go preach at the evening service. You must be half dead already."

I had to admit they were right. They carried their complaint to the next meeting of the board of deacons, and the vote for a new plan was unanimous. I was to visit no more than half the shut-in list, with a partner, and two assigned deacons would take the other half. We would alternate the halves, and I would visit every home with a shut-in member every two months. I liked the new system, especially since my partner was Ella.

When we visited parishioners in the hospitals, Ella and I got to kiss every time we rode the elevator. More than one of our fellow passengers was moved to suspicion when the man in the clerical collar kissed the lady right in front of everybody. Ella liked these Sundays too; they reminded her of visits she made with Papa Pearson. Sometimes she and I would find ourselves leading an impromptu and very moving worship service, as when we visited Sister Wicks and she sent for all her children and grandchildren to join with us as we prayed. When we served the communion in that home, the Spirit was high among us.

When we visited families who had just lost a loved one, consoling the mourners and planning the funeral, Ella was much more fulfilled than she dared admit at the time. She hadn't yet confessed that she was called to the pastoral ministry. But anybody could see she was born for what she was doing. Her comforting voice was a great asset as she collected data for the obituary, along with favorite hymns and scripture passages for the order of service—to say nothing of the singing and playing she offered. One elderly saint in our flock wanted to be assured that Ella's voice would read the scripture at her funeral.

My second official rebuke came from both deacons and trustees, who were displeased with the way I applied my opinion that all of us possessed equality before God. They resented the fact that I allowed people, especially young people, to call me by my first name. They saw it as gross disrespect and insisted on calling me "Reverend Mitchell." One night I had a difference of opinion with the treasurer, Hattie Allen, and at one point she lashed back at me with obvious contempt, addressing me as "Henry." Later, after the meeting was over, the chairman of the finance committee, funeral director Feltus Sterling, called me aside. "Reverend Mitchell, did you see what we've been telling you about this first-name business? That woman wasn't using your name as a sign of closeness; she was putting you down. First-name stuff may work on the other side of town, but over here on our side, the culture doesn't permit it. We struggled long and hard to gain respect as Black men and women, and we demand it for you. Aren't you the respected scholar who is always telling us to take our culture seriously?"

I saw his point. "You're right," I told Brother Sterling. "You may be sure that at my next church I'll start out on the right foot and carefully respect our race's culture."

Way back when I was a student, I had not always been so aware of the importance of my own culture. In fact, there was a time when I didn't know what it was, or if African-Americans even had one. I was awakened by no less a personage than the great theologian Paul Tillich. In his seminary class on symbolism, he assigned us the task of surveying the building and the worship of the churches where each of us worked. We were to report on all the symbols we could find.

I was worried, and I spoke to Professor Tillich after class. "I'm sorry I can't do this assignment, Professor. You see, I am a Negro, and I work in a Negro church. We have none of these thousands of years of tradition, and we have no symbolism. We have stained-glass windows that were put there by the previous congregation, but we don't pay those windows any attention."

Professor Tillich took a deep breath and said something I'll never forget. "Mr. Mitchell, *every* church and *every* race has both tradition and symbolism. Everything you do and all the ways you worship have symbolic significance. It's not just in the stained glass. Now, you go back to that church and write it all down and bring it in here."

Taken aback, and also intrigued, I returned to Concord Baptist

Church in Brooklyn with fresh eyes and ears. I saw meanings I had overlooked all my life. There was the significance of the pastor's late entrance into the service. Dr. Adams was implying, without conscious intent, that the preacher was central to this worship and all that preceded his arrival was insignificant. Another symbol was the way people treated those who shouted. Close observation convinced me that the tender care they received during their religious ecstasy told them they were holy, not sick. The list was long and embarrassing to have missed the first time around, but it was a turning point in my life and ministry. Paul Tillich was pleased. He gave me an A.

The culture, manners, and mores of our Fresno congregation were inevitably complicated, human, and full of joy and challenge. For example, Sister Hattie Allen could be disrespectful of Henry when she was upset, as in the board meeting, but she was a good-hearted soul and a faithful teacher and departmental superintendent. When Liz complained about one of our teachers, she helped us respond.

"Dad, when we were promoted to Mrs. Mack's class, we had ten kids almost every Sunday," Liz reminded us. "Now we are down to four, and the only reason I haven't left is because you are my father."

It was plain that this ineffective teacher had to be relieved of her class. Henry and I went to see Mrs. Allen, to let her know what we had to do.

"Reverend, don't you do that," she urged. "Let *me* get my hands dirty with this firing. She's my friend, but I'll take the risk. You still have to be her pastor when it's over."

It was a noble gesture on her part. Later, after we had moved on from Fresno, she was one of those who called several times to tell us how much she missed us.

Our culture was around us in every way at Second Baptist Church. It was changing us even as we were changing some of the church's ways and helping it to grow. One lady made a memorable comment while Henry was working on his master's degree in linguistics at Fresno State College (now University). "Reverend, when you went back to school for another master's degree, I said, 'O Lord, what are we going to do when he gets through with that? We can barely understand him now.' But Reverend, you surprised me. You're really letting the Lord use you. Praise the Lord!" We feasted on that comment for days and days.

H Little did that lady dream that I would quote her through the years, and in a couple of my books besides. What she saw as my finally loosening up and letting God use me was actually the fact that I had learned more about African-American culture and idiom. Frankly, I didn't sound like a White preacher to her anymore.

Another comical but good-hearted comment came from an octogenarian sister one really hot Sunday. It was so uncomfortable that after I baptized five candidates I stayed in the pool and preached from there. It was much cooler, and besides, Ella and I hoped that a reforming alcoholic would come forward and make a confession of faith. She did, and so I baptized someone for a second time in the same service. But even with the drama of a conversion like that, this older sister was alarmed.

"Don't ever let him stay in the pool and preach like that again," she warned Ella. "It will take away his manhood!"

The Sunday I baptized our children from the Vacation Church School, there was also a cultural element. There seems to be an unwritten law that the order of baptism is: shortest to tallest female, then shortest to tallest male. Liz was the shortest girl, Kim was the shortest boy. I didn't want to appear to show my children preference by taking them first, so I started with the tallest male and worked my way down. Nobody complained about my reversal of the order, but several people let me know they had noticed it.

I I shared in much of Henry's work in church and community, long before I admitted I was called to pastoral ministry and accepted ordination. This meant I also shared in his ministry to those in sorrow. My most memorable experience of grief started with a phone call early one morning. James Hunt and his family had been returning home from the Fresno County Fair when the driver of another car didn't realize a stop sign had been knocked over, ran the intersection, and hit the Hunts' station wagon broadside. Mr. Hunt, his wife Isabel, and their seven children were rushed to Fresno County General Hospital. Mr. Hunt died not long after they arrived.

Although the Hunts were not in our congregation, the hospital chaplain was calling us because he felt he was not up to the task of giving such bad news to Isabel, who was critically injured. One of her daughters, Ervietta, lay in the next hospital bed, also on the critical list. By the time Henry and I arrived at the hospital, Alvin, one of their twin twelve-year-olds, had also died. We gathered up our faltering courage and walked up each side of the mother's bed, to tell her the news we were morally and legally required to give, for without it there was no authorization to deal with the remains of the deceased.

I took one of her hands and Henry took the other, and she joined us as we recited the Twenty-third Psalm. After we had prayer, Henry told her what had happened. To my utter amazement she took the news with unusual calm and fortitude. She worried over the condition of the other children, after which we agreed to come back when she was a little stronger. We helped her arrange the double funeral, which she was unable to attend. Her pastor at the church in Fowler was away on vacation, so Henry officiated. With heavy heart I joined the family, buoyed up enough to help by Isabel's own faith and bravery.

H Mrs. Isabel Hunt went on to rear and support her remaining six children single-handedly. They moved to Fresno and joined our church, and we have been an extended family ever since. She trained as a beautician and then became a nurse, earning a college degree. Her children grew up to be achievers like their mother. When the 1996 Olympics came to Atlanta, she came to stay with us Mitchells because the head coach of the United States Track and Field Team was Ervin Hunt, the twin son who survived that accident. He is also head track coach at the University of California at Berkeley. As Olympics coach, he took a stand on principle, despite heavy pressure from the media, and refused to put Carl Lewis on the relay team, because he had not attended practice and his time was slow. I was so proud of him I hardly knew what to do. In earlier years, I had baptized him and married him to Jacqueline Richardson, another of our Second Baptist young people. I had also married his sister Ervietta, a high school home economics teacher, to Eugene Marzette, who is now a minister. They were later members of my parish in Santa Monica. We are in close touch with this family, our bond born of tragedy and cemented by our mutual ministry in faith and hope.

F For both Henry and me, our whole Fresno experience was a matter of God working things together for good. How could we have known ahead of time that accepting that great reduction in salary would only open the door for blessings to come from amazing sources in and out of the congregation? Our parsonage yard and the members' yards supplied unlimited grapefruit, lemons, oranges, and nuts. Cooked food came to the parsonage from everybody's kitchen. Sister Julia Kirk brought me some of the finest hand-me-down clothing anybody ever wore. Barber Edith Carter refused to accept pay for Henry's haircuts. Deacon Charlie Williams insisted on cleaning our clothes without charge. Trustee Melvin Combs fixed our cars for little more than the cost of the parts at wholesale. Trustee Willie Brown, M.D., and Deacon U. S. Curry, M.D., gave us superior health care. We have never been so well cared for in all our lives. Years later, Hank still consulted Dr. Curry, and our adult daughters still call Dr. Brown for second opinions. In the summer of 1972, Dr. Curry closed his office for nearly two months and volunteered to serve as tour physician to the Martin Luther King Fellows, whose studies we directed in West Africa.

Our children fared well in Fresno. Hank was president of the Edison High student body and made high scores on the SAT. He was given a scholarship to the University of Redlands in southern California. Muriel was chief justice of the Edison High supreme court, presiding over such controversies as the strange hairstyles forbidden by the school administration. (The school had opposed Hank's mustache his senior year, but that was before her term of office.) Muriel was also a lifeguard and a member of the school's figure-swimming team. She received a substantial scholarship to Colorado Women's College in Denver. For his part, Kim served at Carver Elementary School as a teachers' assistant with small children. In this setting he learned more about things like reading and had a better attitude toward school than he had ever had before. Already he loved small children.

H One morning I opened an envelope and found a catalog for an expensive New England prep school for girls. Liz had sent for it. She was rightfully disenchanted, first with the school in our 'hood and then with the spiffy junior high school she had transferred to across town. She was probing other options, unaware that my whole salary would hardly cover her tuition at a private boarding school. When I told her this, she was willing to forget the idea. But I reminded her that her purpose was good and she should keep her dream alive, pray, and see what God might do.

Two days later I stopped by my parents' home in Berkeley, 185 miles away. Mom told me that Maude Powell, an old friend who taught home economics at Ohio State, had moved to Berkeley and, as an active

Quaker, was recruiting minority students for the newly organized John Woolman School, located in the Sierra foothhills.

This school had one faculty member for every three of its forty-five students. These teachers were dollar-a-year Quaker retirees with distinguished records. Life there was simple, with students cutting wood to keep their cabins warm. Some of them were sons and daughters of U.S. senators and movie stars, but all were equally required to work, learning to bake bread, feed chickens, and milk cows.

I seized the phone, called Dr. Powell, and in ten minutes had a $2,000 scholarship for Liz. We would have to raise the remaining $200. I cried and shouted almost all the three-and-half-hour drive home. When I told Liz and Ella, their faces broke open in joy. Liz couldn't wait to get to Woolman, and we all drove up with her. The arrangement was made so suddenly that none of us had even seen the school before Liz enrolled.

The gift Liz received that day—the unexpected blessing—represents in a way our whole seven years at Second Baptist Church. The providence of God was awesome. Ella and I did encounter some dark days of illness and grief while we were there, but some of the warmest and most wonderful memories of our lives are of Fresno.

CHAPTER 11

Together in Turmoil

E *(Ella)* We left Fresno on July 2, 1966. Our new church was Calvary Baptist in Santa Monica. We had heavily mixed feelings at leaving so many dear friends, but I was completely at peace about the move. It wasn't because we were going to more pleasant weather, and certainly not to more peaceful church relations. It was just that Henry and I both sensed the same leading. God didn't speak to either one of us only or alone, making one the messenger to the other. God spoke to both of us, and we considered the move starting from the same point. That point may have come in part from our common reading of our Fresno work as having reached a plateau. True, Henry had been offered the post of deputy city manager for human relations, but that was *after* we felt led to accept Santa Monica. Looking back, we were very glad we had not been faced with the temptation to accept what would have been a well-paid but very high-pressure post, loaded with unreasonable expectations.

H *(Henry)* The Calvary Baptist Church of Santa Monica had been in great turmoil since the death of Pastor W. P. Carter. He had been a strong and beloved leader for many years, but there was no established person or official body to take his role. Nor were there any congregational bylaws by which to govern their decision-making or resolve their conflicts. The congregation chose sides in an argument over how to pay the late pastor's burial expenses, and the opposing factions continued to battle on all other matters. They fought often in court, encouraged and aided by a shrewd and expensive lawyer. The election calling me was held under court supervision, with a team of election experts from the National Labor Relations Board in charge. Our decision to go there would not have been final without the large majority I received in that vote, since I was not the candidate favored by the five-man board of trustees who now wielded all powers of the church corporation—of course, with the help of the lawyer and in the absence of bylaws to limit their authority.

We Baptists hold that pastoral elections are not political contests based on democratic rules. Elections are traditionally supposed to be fairly conducted canvasses to see what each person voting senses to be the guidance of the Holy Spirit. One votes what she or he sees as divine guidance, not personal preference. We sensed the guidance of God in the results of this election, and so did the jubilant majority. In fact, a large caravan of them drove to Fresno to be present at my last service of worship there. They may also have wanted to be sure I was leaving.

We were happy to be so wanted and welcome, and nobody gave us an inkling of the fierceness of Henry's small but powerful opposition. I don't think our joyous welcome party had any idea that the election hadn't settled all disputes. They had every reason to assume that under the new pastor their congregational wars would be over. I was impressed with the tremendous concern the new parishioners showed for me and the family. They were prepared to go to any lengths to make us as comfortable as possible in the transition. Even the children joined us in the sense that this was where we were supposed to be at this point in time. It may have seemed a risky decision, but we were in it together and with no fears of the unknown. To add to our blessings, we were able to rent my sister Lurline's lovely large home in Los Angeles, just ten or twelve minutes by freeway from the church.

H I had a third but much smaller influence in my thinking. Somewhere near the middle of my twenty-one years in northern California I had casually told God that when my days as a traveling staff person were over, I would enjoy serving either of two churches I had seen in the Los Angeles metropolitan area. One was Friendship Baptist Church in Pasadena, and the other was Calvary Baptist Church in Santa Monica. In later years, I had an opportunity to be a candidate at the first, and I actually did get called to the second. Little did I know that Dr. W. P. Carter, the late pastor at Calvary, had actually suggested choosing me as his successor. I'm not sure how serious he was about my following him, and my own prayer could hardly be called fervent. It was answered "yes" nevertheless, although most of my three years there were stormy. Of course, storms are not automatically tragedies, and our life during that time was exciting and adventuresome in many respects, even with the many trials in church and family. Yet I have learned to be more careful what I ask God to give me. It just might be granted.

In retrospect I see a church full of good-hearted people who lacked skills in conflict resolution and communication. They were not highly educated, for the most part, although they lived quite well. Many worked in the wealthy homes of Beverly Hills. When I accepted the call to Calvary, I thought I was providentially equipped with the legal experience and spiritual insights to heal the divisions in the church. I misjudged the situation terribly.

I like to think that my early interest in Calvary was not ifluenced by its size or beautiful new building. At that time, I saw it as a small, quiet, suburban, family-centered church with great potential for ministries. I had not yet served in Fresno, so the fact that Calvary was larger and in a major metropolitan area was not a factor then. By the time Calvary became a real option, it had lost a great deal of its earlier appeal. Ella and I saw the church at Santa Monica as a providential call only.

E The ashes of the Watts riots had hardly cooled, but Santa Monica was miles away and supposedly very peaceful. I had no idea that Henry would be promptly and officially removed from the pastorate there by the legal maneuvers of four trustees. Even this didn't bother us too deeply, however. Henry preached first on the front steps of the church and then was excluded from the entire church premises by court order. We comforted the church members who cried in the courtroom, but we never shed a tear ourselves. Somehow we were convinced that we as a family were still in God's care, in spite of apparent defeats.

The strong majority of the members were with us in our bid to win Henry the pastorate he had been called to. They formed a group called Concerned Members of Calvary, led by a dedicated layman and successful businessman named Lloyd Allen. We urged them to attend the regular services at Calvary at least once every month. They were advised to give an offering of record (by check), even if it was only a dollar. It had to be clear that this was not a church split and that they all remained members in good and regular standing at Calvary.

They saw to it that we were never in any kind of material need. We worshiped with them every Sunday, but at various evening hours. We met first in the Philomathean Club's hall, and then for five months in the local Seventh-Day Adventist church. Many pastors in the Los Angeles area were in sympathy with Henry, because of what they saw as bitter persecution, so he was invited to preach often for them at the Sunday morning hour. In our thinking, Los Angeles also included our large and lovely residence, far better than the tiny parsonage in Santa

Ermine, Papa, Jessica, and
Mama Pearson before Ella
was born, around 1916.

Ella, age twelve months.

In the yard at 93 Beaufain
Street, Charleston, 1935,
just out of high school.

Ella in New York City
in the summer of 1943.

The Mitchell family in 1925:
Mother Bertha and Father
Orlando with Henry, Elbert,
and Louis.

At age nine, Henry posed for a
street photographer who sold
this picture to his parents.

The Reverend Dr. Henry H. Mitchell Sr., Henry's Grandpa at seventy-two in 1924, as Henry knew him.

The Mitchell children, about 1941: Elbert, Henry, Louis, and Marjorie.

Henry and Ella on our wedding day, August 12, 1944,
with most of the wedding party.

Here we are in
Oakland, 1945.

At age two, Hank
loved this stunt.

Hank traveled with his dad
in the car that his daddy
rebuilt later as a sedan.

Muriel and Hank on their
tricycles in Berkeley, 1949.

Ella P. plus three—Hank,
Liz, and Muriel in 1949.

"The Team" posing at home
in the Cordinices Village
apartment in 1951.

We posed in front of our first new car in 1951.
Ella made all the topcoats for the family.

At church camp in
northern California
in 1953, with our
famous Mitchell tent.

In our home in 1956. We even laid
the quarry tile on the raised hearth
when we built the house in 1953.

Kim, around 1954. This photo
was sent to us from Korea
before we adopted him.

Liz and Kim in 1957, about
a year after Kim's arrival

The whole family
in the Fresno
parsonage yard,
1963.

That's Henry on Rev. Dr. Martin Luther King Jr.'s right,
marching toward Ratcliffe Stadium in 1964.

Liz, Mama Pearson, Ella, Henry, Mother Mitchell, Ken
(in his Penn Military Academy uniform), and Muriel at
Covina Theological Seminary in 1966 when Henry was
awarded an honorary doctor of divinity degree.

Christmas 1970 at our home in Rochester.

Hank at age ten.

Hank's graduation picture at
Fresno-Edison High in 1963.

Hank in photography class at the
University of Rochester, 1971.

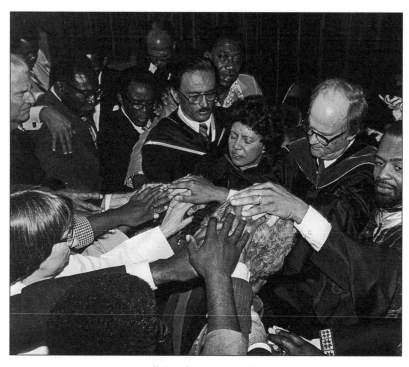

Ella's ordination in 1978.

In Cleveland, Ohio, 1980.

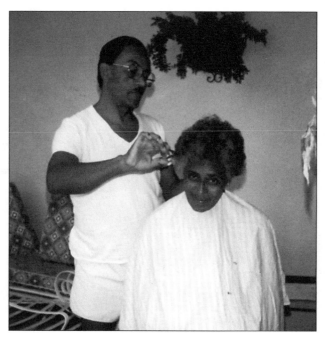

We've cut each other's hair for many years.
Here we are in Bermuda, 1989.

The Mitchell tribe in Atlanta, 1992,
with children and grandchildren.

The Mitchell Brothers—
Henry, Elbert, and Louis—in 1990.

The Pearson Sisters—Lurline, Ermine,
Ella, and Jessica—in 1994.

We almost always dress alike,
even for "swim and gym."

For our fiftieth wedding anniversary in 1994, the family spent a
week together at "Wild Dunes" near Charleston, South Carolina.

We've always loved to kiss with the slightest excuse,
especially on elevators because that's where we met.

Monica from which we were excluded by the action of the trustees. Henry alleged that the living room was large enough for touch football. To sum up, we have never been more comfortable or felt more loved and supported by so many people at any one time. The fierce opposition of the four ruling trustees actually didn't crystalize until after we moved to Santa Monica. But we as a family certainly sustained no losses at their hands.

H What many of my pastor friends expected to be my embarrassment at being without a church was swept away by the love that was poured out to us. I don't think it occurred to any of us to envy Reverend Benford, the puppet interim pastor whom the four trustees placed over the Sunday services. After that first stormy year in Santa Monica, Liz even left Woolman School to live with us and spend her senior year at the school that television made famous, L.A. High.

We lived in faith for almost six months before we saw a providential break in our strange position. The break came after a series of blunders by Reverend Benford, culminating in a divided response by the four ruling trustees. Without previous consultation, Reverend Benford added to the Order of Service a "Consecrated Dime" offering. After several Sundays, the trustees requested a report as to why this was done and what was happening to the receipts. When they were told, "It's none of your business what I do with this offering," two trustees pointed out that this was outright insubordination. "We are the trustees of this corporation, and we can fire you if you don't respond," they told him. The two senior trustees were too proud to admit that their choice had been so wrong, so they supported the rascal. The vote of the fifth duly elected trustee, Virgil Brown, was the only way to break the tie and make good on the threat to fire the interim pastor. (Up to this point, Brown had been ignored, because he supported me.)

On Friday, December 16, 1966, the two trustees in favor of the firing paid me a visit at our home in L.A. They simply wanted me to ask Trustee Brown to come to a meeting and vote to oust the interim they had so unwisely appointed. As Trustee W. T. Calvin put it, "Reverend, we realize that if you were to accommodate us in this matter, there would be some conditions to be met. We are prepared to meet those conditions." Trustee Jim Buckman heartily agreed. It sounded for all the world like politics, and it was. But it was also providential, with these two trustees being used by God to rescue a congregation from turmoil.

My condition, of course, was that they should offer me the non-Baptist-like appointment as interim pastor, but they put more than that into the bargain. I was to go through the motions of a vote by the congregation to confirm my interim appointment. At the end of a year, I was to stand for full election as "permanent pastor." This election was to demonstrate to the world that they had acted properly in setting aside the first election. The second election was contingent upon a traditional Baptist requirement of a three-fourths majority vote of the congregation. In their unspoken opinion, I was highly unlikely to get such a majority, but Ella and I thought differently. We figured the Lord had brought us too far to be leaving us at this juncture. We also felt certain that the strong majority's earlier support would not change. We prayed and trusted and refused to be political or strategize.

E With strong hope of an impending solution, and no fear that the three majority trustees would enforce the old injunction against Henry's setting foot on the church property, we decided to attend Calvary Baptist Church on Christmas Sunday morning. We were fully aware that our attendance would put Henry, technically, in contempt of court. But Hank and Muriel were home from college, and the others were already there. All four were gung ho for some civil disobedience.

We had been sweet and docile long enough. We would still be non-violent, of course, just engaging in powerful demonstration.

I must confess that this maneuver appealed to something deep down in my soul, too. I had demonstrated against segregation in Alabama in my college days in the 1930s. My special concern for justice seemed out of character in the eyes of many, but underneath my soft voice there has always been a burning commitment. This march into Calvary Baptist Church was just my cup of tea.

The uniformed and armed guards at the door of Calvary told Henry, "You can't go in there. There is an injunction legally barring you from these premises." Henry kept walking and replied, "This is *God's* house, and unless I am physically restrained we will all be worshiping here this morning."

Once God was introduced into the debate, the guards were noticeably shaken. One of them finally burst out with "But you are not allowed in the pulpit!"

"We are just here to worship. Who said anything about going into the pulpit?" Henry asked. With that we marched in and took our seats about two-thirds of the way from the front. Our pew was just under the balcony, and we six Mitchells filled it up. All eyes were on us. We seemed welcome and returned people's smiles as we sat down. We really felt good about the supposed risk we had taken. Nobody was scared but the guards, and our gang recalled their great demonstration with pleasure for years afterward.

Reverend Benford was noticeably nervous. He left the pulpit at least a dozen times, presumably to visit the rest room in his office. His sermon, "I'm Dreaming of a Right Christmas," never touched a text or returned to his title. Clearly, he sensed he was on his way out.

H It was a strange service, hardly worthy of the word *worship*. The music was very good, but the people were tense and inattentive. We could not truthfully say we felt the presence of God in that place. We did, however, feel strongly the providence of God. If the guards were afraid to throw me out, and the phony interim was driven to the toilet, salvation could not be far away. It was the sort of "trial and tribulation" we would savor for the rest of our lives. If the guards had drawn their guns and made some hostile moves, we can't imagine what the result might have been. But as it was, if this was the "dangers, toils, and snares" that "Amazing Grace" mentions, we had more than our share of grace to take us through.

I was finally escorted into the pulpit on Sunday, January 29, 1967. I preached from Philippians 3:13, on "Forgetting the Things That Are Behind." In this hour of joy, however, I could not forget my predecessor as contracted interim. He was still in the tiny parsonage, bedfast from a heart attack. The deacons and trustees agreed with me that it would be fitting to take up a "Love Offering." It would be divided between Reverend Benford and the family of a Los Angeles pastor who had died because of a heart condition and had no insurance.

I insisted that the chairman of the trustees, J. Allen Reese, should at least accompany me to deliver Benford's share of the offering, well over $100. After all, he had been one of the two who voted against terminating this interim pastor. Yet he was quite reluctant and embarrassed. He offered no explanation as to why. I kept pressing him, and he finally conceded. "Okay, Rev, if you insist." It was almost as if he had never even known Benford. We drove to the parsonage and had a word of prayer, and then gave the envelope with the offering as received. Brother Reese said as little as possible and got away just as soon as he could.

This was the closest I ever came to trying in any way to punish any of my former opponents. In fact, I bent over backward to be reconciled with them. Mrs. Laura Lee, my opposition's capable strategist and unofficial leader, became one of our very closest friends. Even at the height of the struggle, it was she who had said, "Reverend, I have nothing against you personally. So far as I can see, you are a fine Christian and a capable pastor. It's just the group that supports you that I feel I must oppose." Her husband, Emerson, had the same sentiment.

If Trustee Reese had known then what we all know now, his attitude toward my immediate installation might have been different. In fact, one could wish that he and his fellow supporter of the interim had lived to see the fate of their original candidate for the pastorate. He was sentenced to life imprisonment for the murder of one of the deacons of the church from which these Santa Monica trustees had wished to call him.

At the bottom of their tragic comedy of errors was the fact that these four trustees were fascinated with the awesome power their attorney discovered them to have. Many of their backers were sincere and deeply spiritual in their opposition, but these corporate officers made no attempt even to appear to be led by the Spirit. Whatever satisfaction they received from their maneuvers had to be limited to the infantile fun of playing with the church's power buttons. Their recreation was extremely costly and hard to resist, but it was brought to a sudden and final end. We saw the hand of God as granting freedom to all mortals, but setting the limits to which they may go as they choose to torment those who sincerely seek to do the will of God.

When I ponder the providential blessing that God squeezes out of human tests like these, I see myself learning more in this experience than I ever learned in any formal study, even for the doctorate. And our family as well as the congregation felt blessed also with a vibrant kind of new trust and understanding of the Christian walk together.

CHAPTER 12

Together Still and Glad Regardless

E *(Ella)* The support of L.A. pastors extended to finding me an instant position. Dr. Thomas Kilgore, senior pastor at Second Baptist Church, had a Teen Post program that needed a director. Although my training and experience had been centered on children, he wanted to help me find a job, and he was sure I could direct the staff in this daring venture in the heart of the 'hood. Our program consisted of game-room activities, basketball and other teams, field trips, teen jobs, homework help, and counseling. Our teens were about half Hispanic and half African-American. We had very few discipline problems, but when I had to go one-on-one with teenagers I found them little different from my kindergartners. They listened when not yelled at, and they couldn't resist an adult's genuine warm acceptance.

One experience involved a thirteen-year-old Hispanic boy who had been expelled from school for truancy. We learned this when he came to the Post to hang out before school was dismissed. He was a member of a gang and seemed compelled to assert himself before his peers. Already out of school, he needed to belong somewhere. However, his bodacious front melted when he sensed that I was really interested in him and anxious to help. When we agreed that school would be fun if he could do the work, he accepted our homework help and was soon back with his classmates.

My brief stay there culminated in a summer carnival in the church

158

parking lot, with booths and concessions by a wide variety of groups from both in and out of our community. The ethnic and national flavors represented made for an intriguing collage. It was one of the few times in the program year when the cultural groups interacted, and the reason was joyous rather than tragic. I didn't enjoy saying goodbye to my Teen Post friends, but I was glad to get back into my specialty, early childhood education.

My next assignment was as child development supervisor for ten sites of the Head Start program sponsored by the graduate chapter of my old sorority, Delta Sigma Theta. I worked from Santa Monica to Los Angeles and down to Willowbrook and Paramount. It took two weeks for me to cover my beat, at one site per day, besides evening meetings with parents and staff.

One day as I visited a classroom in Willowbrook, about lunchtime, a teacher from a nearby trailer came to borrow some equipment. A three-year-old boy rose up and ordered her back to her room, calling her a most profane name. When the child's teacher prepared to wash his mouth out with soap, I felt led to restrain her. The child was only repeating what he heard at home. I advised her to counsel with the child's parents, urging them to be careful about what words the child was allowed to hear. There was never a dull day on that job.

After Head Start, my final two years were spent in teaching early childhood education at Compton College, south of Los Angeles. I taught weekday classes, preparing teachers for child care facilities, and supervised their field work in various agencies. This was an exciting challenge and very fulfilling for me. My Head Start work in Fresno and Los Angeles had prepared me for it, and the students responded with enthusiasm.

Our new program prospered, and a bungalow classroom had to be brought on campus to accommodate a newly developed demonstration program. This on-site laboratory school proved so popular that we were permitted to take it into the community. The public schools and the public housing authority gave us space to provide labs for an innovative program for improving parenting skills. The sewing teacher, Fran Washington, made the site a model of home decoration, in addition to showing parents how to stretch their resources by making garments for their children. Kathleen Huff, the food services teacher, worked out the menus for the daily lunches, as well as family meals for the participating parents. My part was to help the parents understand their children's needs and train them.

The parents were so receptive to our program that many wanted to continue their studies in the two-year program at Compton. Then one of the parents, with an AA diploma from Compton, went on to get a degree in early childhood education at Long Beach State College. This one success story made our outreach efforts in the community worthwhile. Years later, this student was employed at Compton College as lead teacher in early childhood education.

One of our parents solicited enough free yardage from a local merchant to decorate the bare windows in their housing project units. Another parent solicited enough free milk for the nursery lunches for a six-month stretch. The enthusiastic response did much to bond the college with the community and the community with itself. This project was one of the most gratifying efforts of my entire sixty years of service. The quality of life in the 'hoods of urban America is definitely not hopeless; it just needs relevant and willing hearts and hands.

With my work at Compton, there was still time to help at Calvary, after Henry was made interim pastor. I sang in a choir Henry organized to replace the departed gospel chorus. (They were among the folk so opposed to his election that they started a new church.) I led Bible studies in several of the women's circle meetings and planned and directed the evening Vacation Church School in August. The youth were so pleased with it they didn't want to stop at the end of two weeks. We finally settled on a year-long Wednesday evening session, before youth choir rehearsal. We were once again in a happy union of church family and personal family.

H *(Henry)* My second election, as provided for in the interim contract, was held within a year, with equipment borrowed from the L.A. County Elections Commission. That night Ella and I sat in our car, on the church parking lot, waiting to hear the results. Meanwhile, a good friend from Los Angeles, Dan Jones, came to the car and announced that he was there to find out if I won the election. "If Calvary releases you, the pulpit committee of the Good Shepherd Baptist Church in Los Angeles is waiting to recommend you to their people." We were amazed. "Just look at God!" I had never seen such an ingenious hedge against anxiety.

As it turned out, instead of getting the required 75 percent of the vote, I received 85 percent. Most of the group originally opposed to me had already moved out when I became interim. They had organized a split and called as pastor a former associate at Calvary. The members that remained surrounded us with love, and our two years of turmoil came to an end.

E We moved from Los Angeles to a comfortable three-bedroom apartment in Santa Monica. I continued at Compton, leaving early in the morning to get in a swim before my nine o'clock class. I conducted workshops for churches' workers with children and preached all over southern California for Women's Sundays.

The supposedly hard days were over. We were settling in a larger church, with a larger salary, in a much larger metropolitan area than Fresno. It was time to focus on our family and the needs of our teenagers. In our third year at Calvary, the extended family feeling grew to be genuine and churchwide. One spring Sunday a sister was dropped off at the curb in front of the church by her wealthy White employers. They promptly drove away, presumably because they thought this Black church could be depended upon to give their employee, homesick for her family in Ohio, a feeling of belonging and emotional support. They were right. Henry and I met her as she came warily up the steps, and by noon that day she had members competing to take her into their hearts and homes. She had plenty of invitations for her day off and joined Henry and me in our new "Inspirational Choir." Together we all sang in mutual praise, everything from Spirituals and Gospels to simple anthems.

H Once again we were blessed with the best of music, with our excellent "Cathedral Choir" directed by Dave Weston. One Sunday during Lent, 1968, I was planning to preach from Isaiah 53:4, "Surely He hath borne our griefs and carried our sorrows." I started to read the scripture lesson and then stopped and said, "No. Let's just sing it." With that, I stepped back into the bass section, and the full choir burst forth with the same passage, as set to music in Handel's *Messiah*. It was such a moving, awesome moment of worship that I still get goose bumps when I recall it.

Every Good Friday, we sang Du Bois's "Seven Last Words," complete with costumes, orchestra, scenery, and lighting effects. The whole city looked forward to it and crowded the sanctuary. It was a most satisfying answer to my dreams of how God should be praised in a congregation. I had the same feeling when this choir did their amazing renditions of Gospels and Spirituals.

E One of our most memorable services was during Black History Month, when we focused on Black business and professional people. Reading the scripture lesson that day was my god-sister's husband, the actor Ossie Davis. The passage was a little-known story in Judges

(20:12–16), in which seven hundred left-handed sharpshooters could "sling stones at an hairbreadth, and not miss." Henry's sermon, "Handicapped Heroes," was about Benjaminites who overcame injuries to their right hands, refused to "draw their pensions," and went back to the battlefront to use their left hands. The sermon was focused on motivating Black self-esteem and ambition to overcome the many handicaps faced by Blacks. However, the members are likely to remember Ossie's reading far more than the sermon. The worshipful way he read it was unforgettable. (Ruby Dee and her daughter LaVerne were members of Calvary while she was in town filming *Peyton Place*. Ossie was there on his regular visits to his family.)

H Unlike the ample talent pool in music, there simply were not enough adults with skills and time for drawing in and developing the teenagers. With Kim in our own family, I was forced to face the huge need we had for youth work. As was the case in Fresno, I was drafted to teach a class of youth in the Vacation Church School for two weeks in August, which was continued on Wednesday evenings, by demand. The high schoolers were out one night per week, and that night out was well spent.

Our discussions were lively and relevant to their real needs. They were less interested in boy-girl relations than in issues of race and identity in a hostile society—issues that consumed more and more attention in the tumultous 1960s era of civil rights advocacy and racial and social discord. When I invited the striking garbage workers of Santa Monica to meet at Calvary after they had been kicked out of another auditorium, some of my congregants resisted. They didn't want "those rowdy men" in the church. Our youth endorsed the position I took, and we developed biblical arguments to support our position. We didn't just read Amos 5:24, "Let judgment run down as waters, and righteousness as a mighty stream," we shouted it as we took the role of prophets for Santa Monica. We had as many as seventy-five gathered to take part in programs they themselves planned. Furthermore, since they sang in the choir, they attended Sunday worship in large numbers also.

One Sunday I was spurred by our youth dialogue to preach a sermon called "Hypocrites Anonymous." The text came from Ezekiel 3:15 and focused on the obligation to sit where others sit before we condemn them. I admitted how hypocritical most adults appeared to be in the eyes of the day's young people. A cheer went up in the forty-plus youth choir behind me. Then I turned around and asked, "How many of you would tell the truth if I asked you where you were last night at twelve o'clock?" They got the point; they too were hypocrites, failing to live up to the very ideals they demanded of others.

We faced our most serious youth problems as we worked in the Western Baptist State Convention's youth camp, at Thousand Pines. I was dean of the camp, and Lloyd Allen and Ella were among the volunteer counselors. About the third day of camp, Lloyd said to me, "Reverend Mitchell, my boys don't go to sleep at night. I used to think it was just persistent playfulness, but long after they get quiet, they are still not really sleeping. These boys are emotionally disturbed, and nobody is doing anything to help them. They are from very fine families, but they can't relax enough to go to sleep." I was stunned. I am still stunned, because we have not been able to help significantly, either in camp or afterward. We dedicated ourselves to help our own teenager. But in the larger world, we only preached and taught at a level that still needs the specifics of careful research and creative program development. If I had to designate my one area of greatest concern and deepest frustation, it would be ministry to youth. It's not enough just to be their popular minister and model, or even that they enjoy hanging out and singing at the church.

Together Still and Glad Regardless

Once some representatives of the American Cancer Society and UCLA Medical School came over to our church in Santa Monica to urge us to send African-American women for the free cancer tests offered on campus. Their clinic was only about two miles away, and yet the death rate for cancer among our women was alarmingly high. The Cancer Society people couldn't imagine why our women simply declined to come and get the free exams.

We tried to explain the problem. It was too hard to park near the clinic and impossible to reach by public transportation. Besides, it was in a congested area of campus turf, often seen as alien and not hospitable. White male doctors would probably be doing the invasive procedures. Contrary to popular stereotypes, these women were extremely modest, even puritanical. A radically new approach was needed, if our sisters were to be encouraged to take a test that was necessary but scary.

H "The first thing you have to do is to move the clinic to our neighborhood," I told the testers. "The clinic has to be easily accessible and conveniently scheduled, like on a Saturday morning." They all but declared these terms to be impossible, to which I retorted, "I thought you wanted to save lives. If Saturdays off are more sacred than human lives, and if equipment is impossible to transport over here, we don't need to waste any more time talking." The cancer crusaders were shocked, but they allowed that they might be able to move some equipment after all.

My other conditions seemed even more outrageous to them, but they knew my reply ahead of time, so they just swallowed my demands in silence. "We will need an all-female staff of doctors, and if they could be Black doctors that would be even better." The delegation gulped and waited for the final blow. "And the person in charge of each treatment room will be a sister from the church here. They may

165

be nurse's aides or even custodians at the hospital, but at *our* clinic they are in charge. They will recruit the people the doctors are to see and fill up their schedules with their friends. The women we examine will put their confidence directly in the sisters in charge and only indirectly in the staff 'under' them."

The cancer people were aghast at first, but the longer they thought about it, the more sense my conditions made. They finally agreed, and we set the date. Our Women's Society was pleased to have such a relevant missionary project and went right to work.

Penny Powers, a ward clerk at UCLA Hospital and a former president of the Women's Society at Calvary, was appointed clinic chairperson. The sisters in charge filled their rooms' appointment schedules and had examined ninety-nine women as the clinic's closing time drew near. They insisted on having a hundred. Everybody in sight had been examined except Bernice Cole, who had come by to pick up her parents, trustee Virgil Brown and wife. Bernice was a hospital clerk and had recently had a complete cancer scan, which had shown nothing amiss. However, she consented to be examined again and become number one hundred. Her test came back positive! It was the only positive test result for the day. Because of the warning from this test, she is still alive and well. I still get lumps in my throat, when I remember the day her report came back and she was immediately placed under treatment, and I rejoice at God's workings.

Henry and I were quite experienced at marrying people, with my organ-playing matching his sonorous pronouncements. Two weddings especially made my heart proud. The bride in one of them was Sandra Jackson, sister of Maynard Jackson, later mayor of Atlanta. Sandra's grandpa was the nationally famous grand master of the Prince Hall Masons of Georgia. Many of our deacons at Calvary were Prince Hall Masons and greatly impressed when Sandra joined the church.

The groom had a very different background. He was a Mexican national who spoke no English, and since both the bride and the minister spoke Spanish, Henry conducted the whole wedding in that language. The only other language was the Latin of Liz's singing of Schubert's "Ave Maria."

H One day a Hispanic mother stopped by the church office to see if her daughter could be married in our large and impressive sanctuary. The prospective groom was of German descent. "We'd be delighted to have the wedding here," I told her, "but there are two things which perhaps you should know. One is that I require premarital counseling. The other is the fact that this church's members for the most part do not look like me. This is a predominantly Black congregation, but it's God's house, and you are more than welcome." The mother assured me that this made no difference to them, and the whole family began attending Calvary, even before the wedding.

They loved the way the ceremony was carried out, and soon they became full members. One Sunday, the new husband, Grant Keller, came forward and asked to join the church by confession of faith and baptism. Then, on Friday afternoon two weeks later, Grant called almost in tears. "Reverend Mitchell, I can't be there to be baptized Sunday! I just got orders to report to Lemoore Naval Air Base early Sunday morning. And I don't want to go to Vietnam without being baptized." He sounded desperate.

I was so glad I could set him at ease. "Grant, God knows you really wanted to be baptized, and people are saved without the water when they can't get to it. Remember what Jesus told the thief on the cross? '*This* day shalt thou be with me in paradise.' But you can actually be baptized if you want to be. What are you doing tomorrow morning?" He apparently felt he had to remind me that tomorrow was Saturday, not Sunday, so there was no hope for him before he flew off to the war zone. "Grant, don't you know that this church is ours, and we open it up any time we feel called to?" I told him. "And we pay our water and gas bills, so we can fill and heat the baptismal pool any time we wish. We'll see you here tomorrow morning at eleven o'clock."

The chairman of the deacons, Melvin Forbes, joined me in mobilizing the church's phone network of people, including Velma Latimore, Ida Dooley, Amy Buckman, Weltha Bolton, Grace Bryant, and Eloise Sykes, to invite the members to witness the baptism. The usual deacons were there to help. Saturday morning or no, 110 members showed up. Grant and his family arrived on time, and he was baptized, prayed for, and sent off with joy such as I have never seen at any other baptism. The tears flowed, the hugs abounded, and Grant had to know that he was dearly loved by this mostly African-American congregation. When Grant came back from overseas, he joined the choir, and he and his wife gave their first son the middle name of Mitchell.

I am reluctant to mention just one notable exception to this beautiful support. My final legal hassle with Trustee W. T. Calvin came when he served me with one last summons just before we left Santa Monica. He was challenging the validity of the annual election of officers, from which he had been excluded. He didn't succeed, but a year or so after we moved to our next place of calling, Rochester, New York, we received a call from Mrs. Laura Lee, humbly and sincerely asking me to be sure to visit our mutual friend Calvin on my next trip west. It seemed a bit odd, since Calvin had made one last unsuccessful effort in court to upset the church's annual election just before we left. He was now completely out of power, smarting, and surviving on dialysis, so our only possible guess was that he wanted to reconcile with us as he prepared for eternity.

I arrived at Calvin's home in Los Angeles, all set to hear his confession and freely offer my forgiveness. It was a rare opportunity, and I could hardly wait to hear what he had to say. He greeted me with his usual combination of pompous formality and warmth. He had lost a little weight but appeared to be holding his own. He didn't seem nearly as close to the end as I had thought, so I was not at all prepared for what I heard. This former trustee soon made plain his real reason for the urgent invitation. He wished to enlist my help in his fight to oust my successor!

Would this poor fellow ever change? I left his home, greatly disappointed and sorely grieved that Calvary Baptist Church still endured turmoil. My sadness was aggravated by the fact that I had spent a whole year helping the congregation draft and understand a set of by-laws designed to protect both pastor and members from the kind of power plays that had victimized all of us and cost the church upward of $100,000.

However, these evidences of struggle were not Calvary's main activity. They were just the most spectacular. The members as a whole grew spiritually, and many wounds of division had healed before we left.

An important evidence of the healing was the monthly allotment voted for the care of Pastor W. P. Carter's widow. Henry's original opposition had also been hers, and the very thought of any kind of pension for her had been lost in the fray over funeral expenses. When the smoke of battle had settled and the church's finances stablized, Henry thought it was time to consider a monthly grant for her, since there had been no pension plan carried by the church when her husband was pastor. Henry knew it could be a volatile issue, but thinking of how well I, his own wife, was insured by the church, he felt compelled to raise the issue. I was a bit embarrassed by this inequality, and we kept the discussion on the level of spiritual guidance and equal justice. It was a real joy to see the church vote unanimously to grant Mrs. Blanche Carter a monthly pension. It seemed the Bible studies I had led and the sermons Henry had preached were not in vain.

After such experiences of healing and growth, it was hard to leave Santa Monica, but we heard another summons, to teach at the Colgate Rochester Divinity School in Rochester, New York. It would be a new life for the two of us, and full of unfamiliar challenges. The pain of departure was eased by our twenty-fifth wedding anniversary celebration. This silver anniversary was observed at Calvary Baptist Church, and it also became the occasion of our farewell party.

H We took the worship part of the anniversary seriously. We updated the original vows, keeping as much as possible of the poetic language in the first ceremony. I didn't shed tears this time, but I looked just as deeply into Ella's eyes as I recited the vows of renewal from memory. Ella was radiant as she said her part. We used Ella's same rings and she wore her original wedding dress, even though it was now too large. I had not been nearly so impressed by her beauty when we married. It brought to mind one of my favorite verses: "Seek ye first the kingdom of God, and his righteousness: and all these things shall be added unto you." Her striking attractiveness as she glided down the aisle was one of these "things," and it moved me deeply to see it.

The Reverend Drs. Elliott J. Mason and Floyd Massey presided over the ceremony, helping us to sense the wonder of twenty-five years of love and peace. We had grown a great deal, and we vowed, at ages of half a century, to keep growing together. Our second vows were spoken with all sincerity: "I Ella/Henry continue to take thee Henry/Ella as my wedded husband/wife, and I do promise and covenant before God and these witnesses to be thy faithful and patient spouse, in sickness and in health, in plenty and in want, in joy and in sorrow, as long as we both shall live." We would have used my same ring, but my finger had swollen from a softball injury. The "new" ring Ella gave me had been in her family for over a hundred years. The initials of her ancestor are still inside this thick old-fashioned heirloom.

Of those present at the original wedding, there was Ella's sister Lurline and Mama Pearson. Lurline, her husband Wendell, and the Mason and Massey wives stood as our attendants. Winnie Collier Day, daughter of the Colliers who drove us to our reception, came all the way from Ohio. Over the twenty-five years, Mama Pearson's attitude toward me had changed radically. A recent widow, she was yet beaming, proud as could be of her son-in-law and this loving, lasting marriage.

E The anniversary/farewell reception was planned and executed by members in the congregation who managed similar affairs professionally for folks in Beverly Hills. They gave it all they had, and it was a tearful and wonderful occasion. The decorations, refreshments, and lavish silver gifts would make one wonder why anybody would ever leave such a loving group voluntarily. And in a way we would never leave them; not only would we frequently return to southern California, but the people we met and loved at Calvary would be forever part of our spiritual family. We will never forget the warmth with which we were surrounded, both in the midst of crushing legal defeats and in peaceful times.

CHAPTER 13

Together as a Family:
Challenge and Renewal

H *(Henry)* Someone is bound to wonder about the impact of all these shifts and conflicts on our lives as a family. The civil disobedience at Calvary was enjoyment for them, but so was the rest of our life together. No matter what my situation in the churches, when all four children were home there was always an explosion of fun and frolic. We sang our four-part harmony and caught up on one another's happenings. Each one of the four managed to live out her or his own personality, wih the love and affirmation of the rest of us.

While we were still in Fresno, Hank demonstrated against General Maxwell Taylor in San Francisco, and we had to visit him in jail during his Christmas vacation from Reed College. In Santa Monica he would show up from time to time with his schoolmates, driving down from Oregon in a vintage DeSoto with very low mileage, which we bought at a bargain for his transportation. He was a jolly sort, with his friends and his guitar, but he was serious as a heart attack about peace and justice. Hank had already moved east when Pops died, December 15, 1966. After my new pact with two of the ruling trustees at Calvary, I could now deal with this bereavement. Pops had died in his sleep, and it was a merciful relief from nineteen years of gradual deterioration, ending with his body bent into a fetal position. His mind was still clear, and he had recently been placed in a rest home because Mom could no longer care for him. He had far outlived the physicians in Columbus and Berkeley who had given him only six weeks to six months. And even then he didn't die of the cancer they had diagnosed; he was drowned painlessly and accidentally when he inhaled his own fluids.

Our whole family was present at the memorial service. Hank flew in from New York and Muriel from Denver. The rest of us drove up from southern California. After the service in the McGee Avenue Baptist Church in Berkeley, all six of us returned to Los Angeles to celebrate a sad but hopeful Christmas. One of our family's two most pleasant memories of Santa Monica was of the Calvary choir rehearsal Pops attended in our house in Los Angeles less than two weeks before he died. He had dearly loved choir music and was very happy that night. The other memory, of course, was our civil disobedience at Calvary that Christmas Sunday.

E *(Ella)* Muriel was not at all behind the rest of the family, either in independence of thought or in willingness to take unpopular stands. Without any consultation with us, she decided to study at an African university for her junior year of college. When every country she sought to study in became unstable with coups and such, she registered at Dillard University in New Orleans, assuming at the time that Henry would be joining the faculty. As it turned out, he didn't go, but she stayed and finished her college work there with honors. The transfer cost her an extra year.

H One night at a National Baptist Convention in New Orleans, I heard Dillard's choir. Afterward, I greeted Professor Hall, the director, and his wife. When I told them of my daughter at Dillard, Mrs. Hall must have thought she was tattling when she reported, "Oh, yes, I know her, Dr. Mitchell. She's that radical transfer student." Mrs. Hall looked shocked when I smiled pleasantly in approval. After all, I was Muriel's late-1930s-radical-student father, and I was proud of her. We hadn't directly taught her to buck the crowd, but we had taught her to think for herself. She had learned well that part of the Mitchell family curriculum.

E An interesting series of events in Elizabeth's life illustrates this tradition. In 1952, on one of our trips from northern California, I was busy teaching a lab school at Pacific Palisades. Henry took the children to eat at a restaurant in Santa Monica. The chef was a high school classmate of Henry's named George Boone. When the waitress asked Henry to order, he deferred to the kids, even for their choice of salad dressing. When Liz's turn came, the waitress was looking to Henry for an answer when this three-year-old piped up with her own specific brand of dressing, "Milani's 1890!" We always encouraged the children to think for themselves, and she was learning the lesson well.

One day in 1965, while she was a student at John Woolman School, we received a call from the principal reporting that Liz had disappeared. We were terrified. The next day, her picture appeared on the front page of the *San Francisco Chronicle*. She and two classmates were seated in the middle of the gridiron at the University of California in Berkeley. She was the spokesperson for the group, and they were demonstrating against the Vietnam War, along with thousands of others. Being clearly younger than the rest, the Woolman group was singled out by the reporter. "We're here as a matter of high principle," Liz declared. Despite all the worry she and her friends caused us, we had trouble summoning up the determination to scold her. It was indeed a matter of high principle, and our daughter was thinking for herself.

H With Kim's independent thinking, things worked out differently. He lived in Santa Monica before we did, boarding weekdays with a generous surrogate mother, Mrs. Alta Butler, and her husband, so he could attend the school of his choice, the highly rated Santa Monica High School. One evening we were called to Santa Monica Hospital, where we found him with a foot dangling awkwardly from the gurney. His ankle had a compound fracture from an attempted slide into second base. The cast covered his entire leg. "Do I have to keep this whole cast on my leg?" he inquired. "If you want to get well, you will," I assured him. "I know how active you like to be, but for now you'll have to keep still. Does it hurt a lot?" "No," he answered. "The medicine takes care of that, but I hate having to stay so still."

When we were sure he was on the mend, we went to Boston for the American Baptist Convention. When we returned, Kim was back in the hospital. He had become impatient with inactivity. Thinking for himself, and without consulting the doctor, he cut the cast off down to the knee. This caused him to dislocate the metal pin in his ankle, and now he had to be fitted with another full-length cast.

When I went to the hospital to take him home, the clerk said there was no record of a Kim Mitchell. I ran to his room and back to report that he was very much there. The clerk cried, "He? I thought you were looking for a daughter." That was the end of the name Kim. With some surplus cash from double insurance coverage, we offered Kim the option of a legal name change, and he took it gladly. From then on, he was Kenneth Mitchell. And for years to come, the same sort of impatience he showed with his cast would lead him into trouble and leave us shaken.

Ken was always a generous-hearted fellow, with a touch of the showoff, and for a long time he had a bit of a temper. One day he promised some schoolmates a ride in a high-powered Dodge Charger we were keeping for a friend during her overseas trip. He took the keys from our dresser and went to get the car. When the owner of the garage called our house to get our okay to open the garage for Ken, we weren't at home. Ken got mad, and she called the police. Ken fled.

When we got back to Santa Monica, the police had taken him into custody while he was at a football game. When we visited Ken, he was angry and withdrawn. "You guys don't care about me." "Oh, yes, we do," I said, "or we wouldn't be here. We came to take you home, if you're ready to listen and stay out of trouble." "Don't bother," he replied. It was apparent that ten years of hidden and gross misunderstanding of our love and care had boiled over. It was to take ten years more before we got to the bottom of his mistaken reading of his standing in the family. He had actually received from us far more than we gave the other siblings, including two cars, because he was the only one at home. But at age eight, because he didn't get a pair of new shoes when the others did, he had thought the exact reverse. We were unable to get past his angry defenses. We had to seek help.

E At this point I was completely frustrated. My ways with children and youth just didn't work with Ken. I felt utterly helpless and depended on Henry to handle this one. He needed help too, so we called on "Ish," William Ingram, the director of a Los Angeles County juvenile detention camp, who was close to both Henry and me. Ken was released to the three of us, and we drove up to look over Ish's camp. Ken had to choose between incarceration and a strict promise of obedience and cooperation with us.

The camp was a fine place, as juvenile detention camps go, but its bunks and dining hall had no privacy, and the lifestyle was rugged. It was desolate compared to the comforts to which Ken was accustomed. He saw no way out, so he agreed to be obedient.

It wasn't very long before he warmed up a bit, and we started talking again. In the chats that followed, it was plain that he was uncomfortable and embarrassed about going back to school after the incident. Like his sister Liz, he would love to go to a private boarding school. It turned out that he fancied Penn Military Academy near Apple

Valley, in the mountains up above San Bernardino. At this school, students learned to fly airplanes, and he could continue his earlier flight training received in Santa Monica. His second semester of his second year of high school was spent there, before we moved on to Rochester. But we had an earlier concern with Ken that should be shared.

One day when we were visiting sister Una Singleton, she told us that her neighbor's daughter was pregnant and the father was our son Kim. A few other people knew it already, but here we were faced with a pregnancy of some two months, with no warning and no plans. We went next door immediately to visit the girl's mother. She was greatly upset, but she was glad to talk with us. I was a bundle of nerves, so I let Henry do most of the talking. After we had discussed how all this had come about, we assured her that we would do our best to assist in every way. There would be no effort to hide from the issue or escape responsibility.

When we discussed our prospective grandchild at home, there was a certain pain, but it was not a matter of embarrassment or personal shame for us. It was readily agreed that we would provide for hospital expenses and later support, but there was no fear that our congregation would be critical and cruel. Most of them were middle class, true enough, but not class-conscious and snooty. We trusted them to be genuinely sympathetic, and we were not disappointed.

H At the time of the birth—a fine baby boy—Kim was fifteen and the mother fourteen. The child was conceived while we still lived in Los Angeles. They wanted to get married, but her mother rightly ruled that they were much too young and immature to be married. When the baby was three months old, his parents insisted that he have the blessing of a dedication in public worship. They figured their son deserved all the benedictions and benefits of any other child. Ella and I readily agreed with them. I was their pastor, as well as the baby's grandfather, and we felt that we had no right to deny their urgent request, regardless of the possible embarrassment.

The other grandmother agreed also, but we all knew there were some serious questions to be answered. Would our embrace of our grandson encourage other young peole to believe they could bear babies without consequence? By what names could the unmarried parents be called in the ceremony? Who would be the godparents? The answers were not long in coming.

In the first place, we decided the focus would be on the baby, not the parents. This was the baby's admission into the family of the church. There would be none of the usual promises made by mature mothers and fathers. These young parents were not yet prepared to make such pledges. In the ceremony, they would be referred to by first names only, as opposed to using their family surnames.

Henry and I and the girl's mother pledged to serve as godparents and covenanted to continue rearing both generations of children. We wanted the child's service of dedication to be just as deeply worshipful as any other service. As it turned out, it may have been more so. Henry barely managed to speak over the lump in his throat and the tears in his voice. The grandmothers' tears joined his, and so did many from the congregation. Instead of drawing criticism from the audience, we seemed to have brought a kind of healing. For we were saying, Yes, God and the church of Jesus Christ receive and bless all children, regardless of their conditions of birth and the traditional attitudes of society.

After the service the teenage parents were embraced by many and made to know that they too still belonged in the family of God's people. The child's worth as a person was witnessed to by the fondness all of us had for him, and I still treasure the pictures Hank took.

Our first grandchild was later adopted by his stepfather, but we will always cherish the brief season when he was in our lives and both church and family were blessed by his presence.

H After I pronounced the benediction, Ella and I went to the door to shake hands with the worshipers. When I thought everyone had left, I happened to see a member still seated near the front and bent over crying so hard she was speechless. When she got herself together, she said, "Thank you, pastor. That was the most beautiful service I ever saw in any church." "Thank *you*," I responded. "You don't know how much it means to have you say that." She added, "Well, you can't know what it would have meant to me to have had my pastor do what you did when my boy was born. They actually put me out of the church, and I have carried a heavy burden until this day." Even though her son had become a nationally famous athlete and then a business executive, it took our honesty before God and the church, and the congregation's ready acceptance, to finally heal her wound.

As we went on to Rochester, we hoped and prayed that during our three years of service together in Santa Monica many other wounds were healed as well.

CHAPTER 14

Together in Tragedy:
Trauma and Loss

H *(Henry)* As had been the case at Fresno, a highly improbable agreement between opposing sides made the call to Colgate Rochester Divinity School seem providentially arranged. In those 1960s days of Black student militance and White faculty resistance, the agreement by both sides on my name as Martin Luther King Professor of Black Church Studies was a miracle. I couldn't get away from the conviction that I was supposed to go, since there seemed to be nobody else who could draw the support of both students and faculty. I believed I could easily be replaced at Calvary Baptist Church in Santa Monica, and I felt that the task of legal structure and stabilization had been accomplished.

The student uprising came about to demand a whole new approach to training African-American pastors to practice in their own culture. Typical seminaries, both Black and White, had curricula designed to reach White middle-class Anglo-Saxon Protestants. My own training had been on that basis. Many seminaries were now beginning to be aware of the need, but there were almost no scholars with degrees preparing them to teach a curriculum focused on practice in a Black-culture church and community. How could one have a Ph.D. in Black Church Studies when all the supposedly standard degree programs, unbeknown to the schools, were in *White* church studies? Besides, Black Church Studies seemed to them to be a single subject or discipline, while White church studies included all the traditional departments and courses.

I had no doctorate in anything at the time, but I had been published in the *Christian Century* on Black theological curricula, and my book *Black Preaching* (still in print) was en route to J. B. Lippincott Company in Philadelphia. No one could say the standards were lowered by my appointment. And once again I had the strange memory of a 1944 wish expressed to God that when I reached the age of fifty I might begin teaching at a seminary. The request wasn't pressed, and I had all but given up the idea, since I hadn't bothered to earn a doctorate. Nevertheless, I began teaching at Colgate Rochester almost to the day of my fiftieth birthday!

It no doubt seems strange for us to leave Santa Monica after having put out the fire, so to speak, only to go to a seminary where the Black students had made demands and closed the school, in order to get what they considered just and good for theological education. But here again was the deep sense of being called, not to comfort but to creative labor.

E (*Ella*) I was attending a meeting of the American Baptist Churches' general board, in Valley Forge, when I heard of the lockout at Colgate Rochester by the Black students. Most of my colleagues thought it was terrible, because, as they said, "We are giving them so much already." I was quietly pleased, since I was familiar with the issue: a White-culture education to serve a Black-culture church. When I was finally asked what I thought about it, I said, "I'm only sorry it took these drastic methods to get a seminary to do what many secular institutions have done already." I didn't tell them that Henry had served as a consultant to this and many other seminaries, urging them to do exactly what was being demanded, only with greater haste.

Back home in Santa Monica I was soon confronted with the call for

Henry to be one of the main answers in this tense situation. I found it hard to insist on curriculum changes and then refuse to implement them, especially since the valid new trend in Black Studies had so few courses and faculty members who dealt with religion and the Black Church.

H I attended a series of conferences at Colgate Rochester Divinity School and, while there, picked a house to buy. After that I served as a consultant to the World Council of Churches' Conference on Racism in London, England, May 19–22. Then came the novel experience of flying back over the North Pole, starting at 6 P.M. in London, and landing at 6:45 P.M. the same day in Los Angeles. The next day I received an honorary Doctor of Divinity degree from the California Baptist Theological Seminary at Covina (later moved to Berkeley and then renamed American Baptist Seminary of the West). Many members from Calvary were there. My mom and Ella's mama were there. Muriel came from Caltech in Pasadena, where she had spent a semester, and Liz was home from Talladega. Ken came from Penn Military Academy, looking sharp in his uniform. It was another amazing part of the unforgettable sendoff we received.

E Henry and I flew to Rochester on July 7, after a farewell round of breakfasts, lunches, and dinners, in homes as well as restaurants. The cancer clinic testing occurred during these last days, as well as our wedding anniversary and farewell. The girls drove our small car to Muriel's commencment at Dillard University in New Orleans, and went by Talladega College in Alabama to leave Liz's things. We had learned the previous year that Liz's room was the same one I had forty years earlier. Our dear friend, Colgate Rochester student, and concert pianist/conductor Charles Walker drove our larger car direct to Rochester, loaded with presents.

Ken flew east from his academy and joined the girls for the drive up to Rochester. At least for the rest of the summer, we had everyone but Hank—now living in Manhattan—under our new roof. Our stored furniture was moved into our new home at 7 Highland Parkway, next to seminary property and at the foot of the steep hill on which the buildings sat. The side of the hill next to us was covered with trees, and the other was a huge steep lawn, excellent for sledding in the winter. It was a beautiful campus, overlooking the whole city of Rochester and across from the famous lilac gardens.

The house was large and comfortable, renewing the dream we had in Durham, of a teacher's home where students were welcome even to the refrigerator. I could mother my own brood that summer and then be host mother to our Black seminary students in the fall. Henry and I saw the students as part of a model extended family, parallel to the family structure of the Black churches. We parents of the clan served a popular spiced tea on cold evenings and fed whoever showed up hungry. I loved every minute of it.

I declined a full-time appointment to teach teenage pupils with learning disabilities, although I enjoyed the days I subbed for them. It was a gift I didn't know I had, but I wanted to be able to decline invitations to substitute-teach on snowy days. At the State University at Brockport, and at Monroe Community College, I taught a course in "Social Distance and the Learning Process." The American Baptist board meetings and some local committee meetings helped to keep me busy. In fact, I was elected president of Church Women United my second year there. My professional life was not as focused as it had been in California, but I had enough to keep me occupied.

When the chairman of the radical Black caucus at the University of Rochester came down with emotional exhaustion and the university clinic could offer him no place to recuperate, he asked to stay at our house. I felt honored that he thought we could help him, and we had plenty of room. In three weeks he was back to his old self and had missed almost none of his classes. Another guest seeking healing came from the staff at Kodak. She stayed much longer, but much of her time with us was because she was reluctant to leave.

Although Henry would earn his Th.D. later, he was already a full professor with tenure, just two months before his fiftieth birthday. He did his best to justify this rare honor, working night and day to develop courses in his new discipline of Black Church Studies. He taught course after course for which there were no precedents, requiring him not only to define studies of everything from Biblical Hermeneutics (interpretation), Black Church History, Pastoral Care, and Church Administration to Homiletics (methods of preaching in Black pulpit tradition). He had to create materials where there was little or no bibliography. At last it was possible for a clergyperson to get a professional degree that would prepare him for ministry in the African-American culture rather than the White middle class. But venturing into such unmapped academic terrain was going to make Henry's life difficult, especially in a politically and racially charged seminary of the 1960s. Henry did some of his hardest and most valuable work in his new incarnation as a Black Church scholar.

H In Rochester, Ken entered the public schools again and once again set his heart on driving a car, this time one he expected to own. It was no wild dream, since he was so talented. He had a night job processing checks on a computer at a major bank, and he earned very good wages for a high school kid. He was so good at it he did his work in half the normal time and then slept the rest of his night shift. The bank finally saw this on the computer record and cut his hours to fit. Given his temper, he became disgusted and quit. He was fired from his next job, a security officer, because of an accident driving a forklift.

Without money to buy a car, and feeling like a failure, Ken ultimately erupted in rage.

E The week before Ken was to graduate from Monroe High in Rochester, a counselor called me and begged, "Please come and take him out of here!" He was on a wild rampage, screaming and disrupting the school, in connection with a political demonstration on campus. It had something to do with his ethnic mix, but I never was able to get to the bottom of it.

Henry was in Virginia, speaking at the Hampton Ministers Conference, so I went to the school to pick him up. He was acting strangely sullen and withdrawn all the way home, and this worried me. When he started banging things with a nightstick and threw the reel-to-reel tape deck into the television, I was terrified. I ran out the back door and up the hill, to get help from someone at the seminary. By the time the groundskeeper arrived at our house, Ken had broken all the glass in sight: TVs, mirrors, windows. He was on the front porch shooting a gun. A neighbor called the police, and I got back to the house in time to see the police take Ken into custody.

Seminary student guards were placed at the house, and I was given refuge in the home of Prof. and Mrs. Devadutt, a few doors down the street. Henry rushed home to join me, and we began getting our home back together. We were mystified at what had spurred Ken into such violence and more than a little upset. After batteries of tests could find no drugs or alcohol and nothing wrong with Ken psychologically, and since we decided not to press charges, he was once again released to us.

We probed as best we could, getting no blatant disrespect, but getting no answers either. Ken was sullen. It was pretty clear he had no better notion than we as to why he had destroyed some of his most treasured possessions. Our best guess is that his explosion was the packed-in frustration of failing to keep a job and buy the high-powered sports car he had promised himself.

H Ken entered Talladega College in the fall, and after starts there and at other colleges he finally finished a B.A. degree in Florida. He had been elected student body president at Fresno City College, and to *Who's Who in American Colleges and Universities* at Florida Memorial College in Miami. Throughout this strange pattern of starts and stops, he seemed to be searching for his real self. Even when Ken's behavior left us angry and in pain, we knew we couldn't give up on him. Here was a kid whose early treatment as a foundling and orphan could explain all the scrapes he'd ever been in. Mr. Graham, the principal at Franklin Elementary in Berkeley, where Ken caused several crises, told us that we would be sorry we ever sent for him. Mr. Graham was greatly mistaken. Even as we stood amid piles of broken glass, we knew our love for him could never be shattered.

E In the spring of 1971, I flew from St. Paul, Minnesota, to join Henry for engagements in Newark and New York and visit Hank at his East 96th Street apartment. After studies at the University of Redlands in California and Reed College in Portland, Oregon, he had gone to New York and worked for a while as an assistant to his "Uncle" Ossie Davis, who was directing a movie, *Cotton Comes to Harlem*. Later, at McCann-Erickson, Inc., the advertising agency, Hank helped produce such ad campaigns as Coca Cola's "It's the Real Thing" and Nabisco's "Dr. Seuss's Horton Hears a Who," a children's ad.

The Saturday we arrived at Hank's apartment, we found him ill and unable to keep anything in his stomach. He was limited to herb teas and cream soups, but even these were too much for his digestive system. The doctor assumed his sickness to be a lengthy case of intestinal flu. When we saw how weak and pale he was, we were seriously worried. He had never looked like this. We insisted that he travel back to Rochester with us Sunday night so we could care for him. He helped us drive, but we soon saw that his steering was at times dangerously inaccurate. He never ran off the road, but he would weave within the lane. On every curve, Henry and I clutched each other's hands in fear for our lives. It would have hurt his pride to give up the steering wheel, but we could see that his sight was failing. We would have insisted on taking the wheel back immediately, but we knew how sensitive he was about his driving, as we too often compared him with careful, flight-trained Ken. This wasn't flu. We knew something was seriously wrong with our firstborn. I felt nervous and on the verge of tears during the entire three-and-a-half-hour drive to Rochester.

H The next morning, Monday, Dr. Bertram Boddie, a family friend, had us take Hank to Genesee Hospital for a workup. Later that day, when the reports from the blood tests had come in, Bert called me at my office at the seminary.

"Henry, I hate to have to tell you this, but Hank is in the worst stages of acute myeloblastic leukemia," he said. "I would advise you and Ella to spend as much time with him as possible."

I sat there stunned.

"He might live as long as three days to three weeks, but his blood supply is hardly any better than dishwater," Dr. Boddie continued. "The resident hematologist in this hospital is scheduled to go to Canada for a series of lectures. But we have a very fine hematologist, Dr. John M. Bennett, here on leave from Harvard. He'll take the case. We'll give it everything we've got."

I felt like I had been kicked in the stomach. This was the last thing I expected to hear about the son I prayed for. I was too numb to release tears or cry aloud. I went through a few quiet, fierce convulsions before I finally pulled myself together for the dreaded task of telling Ella.

E I knew something was dreadful the moment I heard Henry on the telephone. His choked voice blurted out, "Ella, I've got the worst possible news. Bert just called to say Hank has been diagnosed as having leukemia. I'm on my way home right now."

I was so shocked I didn't even hang up the phone. When Henry came through the door, I was sitting in a chair in the kitchen, unable to move, staring into space. Henry tried to comfort me, but he was in about as bad a shape as I was. Our firstborn was near death. Our answer to all those dreams and prayers was about to leave us. I heard Henry make noises I had never heard before.

When he saw the phone receiver on the floor, he hung it up just in time to receive another call from Dr. Boddie. He wanted us to pick Hank up at Genesee Hospital and take him over to Highland Hospital for treatment. We kicked into action and raced over to Genesee. Highland Hospital was hardly three blocks from our house, and easily accessible even if we were walking. We were glad for that much, at least, as we began our vigil.

H We felt a bit of relief when we picked Hank up at Genesee Hospital. He was gaunt and pale, but still active and jovially articulate. The doctors hadn't told Hank just how serious his case was, so he spent the ride to Highland Hospital worrying about our worrying. After he was settled in the hospital's intensive care unit, he casually pushed his intravenous pole away from the bed and out into the hall, strolling around as if he were at a fine resort. Even when nurses offered to bathe him, he insisted on doing it himself, intravenous pole and all. When Muriel and Liz rushed in from Atlanta and Boston, he greeted them amicably, as if they weren't there for anything life-threatening. He didn't seem to realize how seriously ill he was, even when so many of his colleagues from McCann flew all the way to Rochester to give him blood.

Ella and I could not escape the truth. We had no access to oblivion. Our every moment was dominated by the awful awareness of his condition. Minutes dragged into hours, and hours seemed like days, as we waited for the last-ditch treatments to begin. We barely ate; our sleep was fitful and shallow at best. We had never had to deal with so terrible a prospect as the death of a child, and we were emotionally wiped out—not just disconsolate, destroyed.

E Not only did we have to keep going, but we had to manage other people's reactions to Hank's illness, which weren't always positive or helpful. Henry and I were absolutely outraged when Susan, a former Reed College schoolmate of Hank's, flew to Rochester uninvited. Hank had given her a place to recuperate from an abortion, and she had stayed on as his self-appointed Manhattan housemate. Now, unbeknown to us and with no authority whatever, she ordered Dr. Bennett to release Hank—whom she called "Mose"—to New York's Sloan-Kettering Cancer Center. She ignored his objections that even the flight to New York might be fatal and was completely insensitive to Dr. Bennett's great reluctance to sign the medical release. Without our knowledge or consent, she charged our AMEX account with first-class tickets on American Airlines for all four of us to fly to New York City. (I can't imagine where she got our account number.) She took the authority to reserve a bed and engage doctors at Sloan-Kettering. In the midst of my enormous grief, what I most resented was this White woman calling our Hank "Mose." It was not a title of endearment; it was a bigoted stereotype and a put-down born of her superior attitude. She thought we poor Negroes needed her to take command of our lives.

We canceled all her arrangements and begged Dr. Bennett to readmit Hank to the hospital. Henry then went home and threatened to beat the living daylights out of Susan if she ever again dared speak a word to Dr. Bennett. This tongue-lashing was peppered with the ample vocabulary of profanity he had picked up from the 'hood in his youth. Terror-stricken, she rushed over to the hospital to tell Hank. His response was simply, "That's not typical of my dad. You must have deserved it." Susan retreated.

At that same time, Mama Pearson was visiting us in Rochester, having come with her pastor for the Presbyterian General Assembly. She was still recovering from a heart attack, so we didn't dare risk shocking her with the news that Hank was terminally ill. We did take her to visit him just before she returned to Charleston, and they had a short but warm and affectionate time together. It hurt me so much to be the only one of the three of us who knew that this would be the last time grandmother and grandson would see each other.

H To compound our trying days, I was having some strange coronary symptoms, including sharp pains in the chest one morning when I ran up the hill to my office. I was able to function, but the severity of that one day's pain kept us on constant alert. Our doctor found no problems in my cardiograms, but warned that such symptoms always mean *something*. For all Ella and I knew, I was at risk for that first massive heart attack that ends the lives of so many men my age.

In addition to being worried about Hank and uncertain of my own strength, I had the profound frustration of watching helplessly while Ella grieved. She didn't scream or cry aloud; it might have been better if she had. She just quietly shed tears all the time, so that her eyes were dangerously red and burning. When she went to an eye specialist, he examined her and said, "Whenever there is major stress, it attacks the weakest part of your body." For Ella, that was her eyes. The drops he prescribed helped a little, but there were no drops for her heart.

As a young man I had asked God for a wife and a son whom I could help to make happy. Their happiness was what I wanted most in life. I wanted desperately to find some way to comfort them, but I couldn't.

I became aware that many marriages probably suffer because of the frustration of being powerless to comfort and console. The frustration can work in reverse and embitter a husband or wife. A grieving spouse can blame the other for the tragedy. Thus they wind up with divorce instead of mutual healing and consolation. Even if I had to endure losing Hank, I didn't want to lose Ella too. I made sure we prayed together. Often we just sat in tears and patted each other. I learned to let my tears flow freely in sorrow, for the first time since childhood. I had never been able to hold back my tears of joy—I couldn't at our wedding—but it was a harder thing to allow my grief to show.

We didn't try to cheer each other up or exchange pat answers or false hopes. Returning from seeing our cheerful terminal son in the hospital, we just clung quietly and tenaciously to each other. We believed in God's providence. We knew God sets limits on how much we may be tested. We were just present for each other. It lent a kind of tragic beauty to life.

Besides all this, I spent hours just staring blankly into space. My staring and my tears took a toll on my eyes. It was a destructive, desolate escape, my soaring into nothingness. When Hank caught me doing it, he would quickly snap me out of it with his amazingly good spirits. Hank always talked as if he expected to be the one to beat the odds. He could not avoid knowing he had leukemia, but his attitude was always positive, even toward the end, when he knew the doctors could offer him no more hope for recovery.

To keep our minds focused elsewhere, there was already the fact that I was teaching courses in the practice of ministry in the African-American culture. Nobody had ever taught such courses before, and I was constantly digging to organize and produce them. There were virtually no textbooks. This very fact justified a study tour to look at our religious roots in West Africa. We could never understand ourselves if we made the mistake of thinking that our culture was only the best we could do to imitate the dominant culture. The books we would write would save others from having to see our roots to believe in the value of our heritage.

Our trip in 1971 was to prepare us for directing our funded doctoral study tour for the following year. Before we knew of Hank's illness, we had planned to leave July 2, 1971, with a study group from another school. We didn't dare ask Hank if we should go, since we didn't know how much he knew or accepted about his condition.

Dr. Bennett advised us to keep our plans for the African tour in place. "Go ahead with all the required immunization shots," he told us. "If our chemotherapy succeeds, and Hank goes into remission, you can go ahead with the trip. If he passes, it will be far enough ahead of your departure for you to need the trip for healing." If Hank did go into remission, Muriel and Liz could serve as Hank's caregivers. To our unspeakable delight, Dr. Bennett declared Hank to be in remission on June 29. We took his advice and flew out of New York four days later.

Once our feet were on African soil for the first time, we were engulfed in African history and culture. We studied under African lecturers and visited villages, learning all we could about the culture of Nigeria and Ghana. At night we plotted a tentative itinerary and program to submit to Kofi Opoku, the director for our own African study tour for the following summer. We were more at peace than we had been since early May. We didn't know how long Hank's remission would last, but we exercised our right to hope it would be for many years. We faithfully followed his request and gathered for him samples of soil from what he affirmed as his motherland. In a sense, we were on an expedition for him, and we returned home with small jars of dirt from towns in Ghana and Nigeria.

I learned a great deal about the way children are reared in West Africa. The whole culture seemed centered on preparing them for life. Even while they danced and sang, they were having to memorize important proverbs and stories. Their toys were significantly different from ours, and for the better. For instance, boys enjoyed dolls, even going so far as to strap them on their backs, and male gender roles were more humane and less macho than ours. I did a research paper on this and received graduate credit. Though I didn't plan it at the time, I ended up doing my doctoral dissertation on the oral tradition in African and African-American culture.

H Back in Rochester we knew from our car's odometer that Hank and his sisters had made many trips and enjoyed themselves. We were glad about that. For Hank's next trip we put the air fare from my expense account into the gas tank and drove with Ken and Hank to Glorieta, New Mexico. I went there for a speaking engagement. Hank had really wanted us to make this trip together when we returned from Africa. It would be a rerun of our joyful family expeditions and a healing change from both our busy schedules and our weeks of anxiety over Hank's condition.

Our chauffeurs would be Hank and Ken. They both loved to drive, and they seemed to enjoy each other immensely. Their endless chatter and humor were great entertainment for us. Ken was no longer Hank's tiny little brother, but he admired Hank and copied his mannerisms. Ken had never been so funny as he was now under Hank's influence. He relaxed and showed a new maturity in the way he carried himself.

E The trip was another honeymoon for Henry and me, with the scenic grandeur lifting our spirits and drawing us closer as we traveled over the days and miles. Hank's spirits were especially high as he headed west into the sunset with a steering wheel in his hand. He and Ken got out and kissed the ground every time we entered a new state.

H My conference lectures on the African roots of Black-American religion were radical scholarship for the day. But these Southern Baptists were very receptive, and I felt encouraged as a scholar when they published my lectures in a magazine and a book.

Soon after we left the Grand Canyon, we broke a U-joint on our four-year-old Chrysler. When we considered a new car in Santa Monica, Hank objected to our choice. "Why do you want black? That thing looks too much like a funeral car." We backed off. With the condition he was in, we were prepared to do anything he wanted.

E A few days later, we stopped in Fresno, for Hank to check with our old family physician, Dr. Curry. While we were there, he picked out a high-powered, gold-colored Chrysler 300. Since we had left Ken to live for a while in Santa Monica, Hank was pleased to be able to drive his chosen "racing" sedan most of the way back to Rochester. His happiness was good medicine.

After we returned to Rochester on September 2, Hank's condition began to deteriorate. It was touch and go until November, when it was officially confirmed that he was no longer in remission. In plain words, all hope for his recovery was gone. Henry and I were devastated, but we showed little of it, both to help Hank and because Hank's own activity was so good for our morale. He bravely remained enrolled in a photography class at the University of Rochester and drove himself to class, whether from home or hospital. Hank and Henry sang bass in the Charles Walker Chorale, along with Liz and me in the soprano section. We would watch the expression on Hank's face as he sang and then compare notes when we got home. At times, he looked as if he were in another world. Whatever his expression, we were happy to be singing together.

Hank avoided sitting beside Henry in rehearsals and concerts, because he may have sensed the deep emotion his dad felt about their singing together. Henry had irrepressibly tearful visions of singing bass with him again in the heavenly choir. He still has this problem sometimes, when singing along with recordings of fine choral music. He hid it from me then, and he still tries to hide it.

H Ella's restlessness in the middle of the night would awaken me, and then the wet pillow would tell the story. All we could do was to hug each other, saying nothing but affirming our togetherness in grief. Sometimes we managed to choke out a brief prayer, and other times we would lift our scratchy voices in Hank's favorite hymn, "Joyful, Joyful, We Adore Thee." The main value of our comforting efforts was the way we would get it out. It was healing to give each other permission to release deep feelings.

When Hank became so weak he had to drop out of his classes, Ella was foolishly concerned about how his transcript would look. My sad comment was, "So far as I have heard, there are no academic transcripts in heaven."

I was called to Highland Hospital late Saturday night, January 22, 1972. Hank had had a rare spell of mild delirium. Since he kept calling my name, the nurses thought I could help calm him down. We talked awhile, and he did relax to some extent. He wanted me to take him home, and I did. Once he was settled in his bed, we thought he would go to sleep. To our surprise, he still kept calling for me. "Daddy! Daddy!" he called. Ella and I didn't know the cause of his outcries, but we tried to help as best we could. We lost a lot of sleep that night and shed a lot of helpless tears.

The next morning I arose and scurried off to Aenon Baptist Church, where I was scheduled to preach. I looked forward to the experience of preaching there among my friends and Pastor Greer. In the pulpit, I suddenly realized my mouth was moving, but my voice was so low even I couldn't hear it. When I tried to speak louder, nothing happened. I had strength enough to stand there, but I was too weak to speak. I had barely started my sermon, but I had to leave the pulpit. My head began to swim a little.

Pastor Greer helped me to the study at the rear of the sanctuary. Ella quickly left her front pew and joined us to see what the trouble was. As I sprawled on a chair, I heard her say, "Pastor Greer, I can finish the sermon." He was greatly relieved, as he said, "I'm so glad, 'cause I know I couldn't do it." I passed her my notes, and she went sraight to the pulpit. Even though women were not known to frequent that pulpit, Pastor Greer was willing to forget his rules, given the emergency. While these arrangements were being made, the congregation sang. I didn't have the strength to join them, of course. In fact, I was suddenly aware of some pain beneath my arm. It wasn't flu after all, as I had thought; it was angina—heart trouble. When Ella wasn't looking my way from the pulpit, I sneaked out through the side of the sanctuary, to the early-detection heart clinic at St. Mary's Hospital, just a block away. The oxygen they gave me was very reassuring, and to have this clinic so handy made it seem as if God was at work on my behalf.

E This same troubled period started for me when Henry handed me his sermon notes and I had to mount the pulpit in a dress I considered too short to preach in. Even worse, the whole pulpit desk was made of clear plastic. I did feel better, however, when I looked back and saw that Pastor Greer had left Henry and joined me in the pulpit. He appeared to be relieved to have me finish the sermon. When I realized that Henry wasn't with Pastor Greer or in the ofice, I felt a bolt of fear. When I learned later that Henry was ill, I was chagrined to re-

alize that at a time like this I had been so concerned about a short
dress and a see-through pulpit.

When the service was over, I discovered Henry had been rushed to
nearby St. Mary's Hospital by two clergy assistants and was already in
the coronary care unit breathing oxygen. At the same time, Hank was
worried that we had not come back home and was frantically phoning
around to locate us. Every time I tried to reach him, the line was busy.
Why I didn't just go home, I don't know, except that under my calm
exterior I was facing the imminent and untimely death of two loved
ones at once. Hank finally found us about 5 P.M., when I had to tell
him that it looked like his father had had a silent myocardial infarc-
tion—silent because it didn't show up on the cardiograms. Later that
evening, Hank returned to Highland Hospital.

One of the most heart-wrenching episodes of my entire life was
pushing Hank in his Highland Hospital wheelchair to visit his father
in St. Mary's. At the time, it appeared possible that neither of them was
long for this world, and seeing them together was almost more than I
could bear. Henry had already poured out a lot of his tears for Hank.
He was consoled a little just to see his beloved son and to know he was
strong enough to make the visit, and his pale face reflected surprise
and joy as they embraced.

In contrast, the grief Hank was suffering seemed intense and un-
mitigated. We can never know what was going through his mind; we
can only guess what was behind his terribly pained countenance that
day. Perhaps it was "Poor Dad, he's checking out before any of us has
had a chance to repay any of the stuff he has so freely poured out for
us. I'm not sure I've ever told him how much I admire him and how
thankful I am." Or maybe it was "We've really come to a deep understanding now, but I hope the worries I caused when I was so far out
didn't add to the stress that brought this on." And possibly "He seemed
tough at times, but he was a marshmallow underneath." Hank had an

amazing capacity to be jovial about his own serious illness, but he was not able to face his father's apparently serious illness with the same attitude.

To everybody's surprise, Henry was moved from coronary care on Wednesday and released outright the next day. He continued his recovery at home. He even held classes in our living room, which was just down the hill from the seminary.

H The next month we had a family gathering for Muriel's wedding in Atlanta, where she had been living and working. Her husband was Spurgeon Smith, a gifted Morehouse College student expelled in his senior year for radical demonstrations. (We hardly noticed this; it was similar to Rochester.) Hank played the guitar, Liz sang, and I officiated at the wedding ceremony. By this time Hank was unable to walk. He had to be chair-lifted onto the plane for his flight with Liz back to Rochester. Ella and I left for Barbados, where I was to continue recovering from my heart problem.

E Henry had been doing Martin Luther King birthday speeches in Pittsburgh, Pennsylvania, and Oakland, California. He flew to New York City for our last concert with Hank on January 16, 1972, in Carnegie Hall. Hank, Liz, and I went down from Rochester on the chartered bus. Sunday morning, we had a rehearsal with the Rochester Philharmonic Orchestra, which accompanied us. The program celebrated Martin Luther King Jr.'s birthday, and we performed the "Requiem for Brother Martin." It was composed by Charles Walker, a recent graduate of Colgate Rochester and now pastor of a church in Philadelphia. Hank's godmother, my cousin Emily Gibbes, had recently completed her tour of service as a missionary in Kenya. She joined us at the hotel and was there for the concert and our stay in New York City.

H As we worried over Hank, faculty politics back on the Rochester campus added to our burden. Our trip to Africa was for credit toward the doctorate-in-ministry degree for our students, and the president and I had not obtained faculty approval before accepting the foundation grant that underwrote the program. The faculty were amazed and dubious that we could deliver so much for $112, 000. (We did get another $70,000 from the foundation before the degree program was over.) In addition, our academic integrity was under attack, because at the time there were no precedents for what we were attempting. In other words, there was a move to force us to cancel the trip.

The next week I worked night and day to prepare my defense against this attack on the Martin Luther King Jr. Program. We fully intended to take our twenty Fellows to study our African religious roots. It was at the end of that week, Sunday morning, that I wound up almost fainting as I tried to preach in Aenon Baptist Church.

Soon after we returned to Rochester, Hank did a videotape for Dr. Bennett's fourth-year medical school class. At dinner that night, Hank reported, "Dr. Bennett asked me to make this video of how it feels to know you're dying. I couldn't refuse him. I did pretty good at first, but toward the end I broke down and cried. Doggone it. I couldn't help myself."

His comment took our breath away. It was the first time he had said anything to us that implied he knew he was dying. It was also the last. We assured him that he seemed to have borne it far better than we, most of the time, and we were glad he let it out rather than holding it in. Later, Dr. Bennett offered us the videotape of Hank's presentation, but we have never felt strong enough to play it.

E Help came from everywhere, as we faced our son's impending death. Henry's brother Louis and his wife, Janice, and family came from King of Prussia, Pennsylvania, and we had a cookout on our lawn. Stephanie Wilson, then a Pan-Am flight attendant and Henry's late sister Marty's only child, went with us to Niagara Falls. Later Ruby Dee Davis and her children came from New Rochelle and spent a whole day with Hank in the hospital. Our close friends Andy C. and Ruth Lewter came from Amityville, New York.

"What time is it?" Hank asked Andy, from his hospital bed. Andy replied, "Don't you have a watch?"

Hank responded with obvious regret, "No, I don't."

Andy took off his expensive watch and placed it on Hank's wrist, insisting over Hank's protest that he keep it. After Hank's death, we returned the watch to Andy, despite his objections. But we might as well have kept it; it never ran again. It stopped at the time Hank died, and no watchmaker has been able to get it to run since.

H Since the beginning of his illness, I kept trying to give back to Hank the railroad watch we had bought on credit during his summer job on the Southern Pacific Railroad years before. I had repossessed it when he walked away from his job and I had to make the payments. Now he was too proud to take it back. For him, my gesture was loaded with pity and brought back bad memories. It was much easier to accept Andy's watch than the one I had taken from him nearly a decade before. That same watch is now an heirloom, in use in the family, and I feel like crying every time I think about it. That watch reminds me of the regrets I feel about my earlier bond with Hank.

Hank was past twenty-one when he let me know how deeply I had hurt him when I stopped throwing him balls for batting practice back in Berkeley in 1951. The project yard where we played had grown too small for how hard he could hit. Hank lost balls in heavy traffic and broke windows. The closest city park was too far away for the thirty minutes of playtime we usually shared. But Hank at six was too young to appreciate those problems and too timid to insist that I keep on pitching, somehow, someplace. He only knew himself to be suddenly robbed of his greatest joy. Even before this time, he had traveled with me all over northern California on business, so frequently that people asked where he was as soon as I arrived. It was almost as if they thought he was on the payroll and was obligated at age four to show up whenever I did. When he reached six, the law required that he go to school—but in his child mind he read this change in our relationship as a kind of rejection. Later on, we took lots of trips together as a family, but he never forgot or surrendered his early claim to monopolize his daddy, on the road for hours and days. No more batting practice with his father, no more travel alongside him—the strain of those losses, unexpressed, tainted the rest of his childhood and haunted his youth, too.

I didn't know it was there until the two of us corresponded during his spring 1964 semester abroad, when he was a freshman at Redlands. Based in Salzburg, Austria, he traveled many places, including Prague, where he visited the home of Franz Kafka, the existentialist author and master of the theme of alienation. Kafka's profound alienation from his father brought Hank's own sense of alienation into his consciousness. One of Hank's long letters, which I have since misplaced, said something of the parallels between our relationship and Kafka's with his father, as well as the places where, thank God, we were different. With all his loyalty and devotion he could not avoid seeing his beloved father as rigidly judgmental, at times, not just strong in character. After I read Hank's letter, I was driven to reread Kafka and write my son, trying to understand what he was feeling. To the very end of his life, Hank kept my two-page, single-spaced, crowded letter of response in his box of most treasured belongings.

I have just been through the soul-shattering experience of [re]reading some of Kafka's letters to his father. . . . I have a terrible feeling of guilt about having been insensitively responsible in part for giving you the feeling you seem to have about authority. . . . It came to me very clearly that I had been drawing hatred for reality and facts [authority] because I was using them as a tool. . . . The facts couldn't get through because they were being used to make strong and impregnable a person who was not sure he could be strong otherwise. And in the process of so wielding the facts I could hardly expect to be dearly loved.

Our transatlantic correspondence brought more healing than I dared expect or dream. We were at a safe distance from each other, and Kafka was our catalyst. Once I had seen the error of my seeming rigidity, although unintentional, I swore off it. Our communication flowed easily after that. Hank was very gracious about not using my words against me, and he felt liberated to confess some errors of his own.

Our rapport blossomed when he found Ella and me to be in sympathy with his politically radical causes, even if not always his tactics. As we waited to be called in a court hearing on one of his acts of civil disobedience, he told us proudly of how one fellow radical had said to him, "Man, your dad is more radical than we are. Did you hear him giving us hell for not sticking to our stand and proudly pleading guilty to civil disobedience? He was asking us, 'What kind of protest message is that?'"

It was an unspeakable comfort to know that we were deeply united in spirit long before the end came. And I often speculate what might have been the wonderful result of our bond had he lived.

We were in Berkeley at Mother Mitchell's house when Henry's brother Elbert and Mom's pastor, James Stewart, brought us the news that Hank had passed. Muriel, Liz, and Ken had been at his bedside in

Rochester. He had asked for some of his favorite music, had a candle lighted, and went to sleep. Muriel, a lifeguard, had tried her best to revive him, but he was gone home. He was pronounced dead on arrival at the hospital.

We flew back to Rochester immediately, with the airline's special in-flight courtesy for the grieving. It was thoughtful of the flight attendants, and the blankets kept us warm, but they didn't bring sleep. Our own attempts to help each other through conversation were just about as useless.

"I wish I had stayed in Rochester instead of joining you," I told Henry. "But Hank insisted that I come out and take care of you. 'I'll be all right,' he said. 'Dad needs you more, after all those places he's been speaking this week. Muriel, Liz, and Ken are here. They can take care of me.'"

"Well, I'm real glad you came," Henry said. "You support me so much more than I show. But I do know how you feel. If I had known what I know now, I wouldn't have left in the first place. But maybe it was better for both of us not to have to watch Hank slip away."

"That's for sure. At least my last memories will be of our lively son, our firstborn, rather than the house where he doesn't live anymore. I shudder just to think of looking at him now."

Henry was anticipating a problem he quickly tried to fix. "Darling, we do need to see him before the cremation. It's important that we do the grief work of parting. If we don't, it'll trouble us later on."

I didn't get the point at first. "But Henry, I want to remember him as he was in real life." I began to cry, and Henry gave up for the time being. Then we started pulling together some tentative plans for the funeral. Finally we dropped off to sleep for the rest of the flight.

H The girls supported my position quite strongly, that we all should behold Hank one more time. So Ella agreed, and we went to the morgue to do the work of parting with Hank's now-vacated human house.

This setting was cold and damp and forbidding. His body, too, was cold, but there was a smile on his face we will always remember. Ella cut off a lock of his dark, curly hair and put it in her purse.

E I am glad I saw his remains. I was losing so much. I craved one tiny memento of this child, grown tall and talented, caring and compassionate, only to be snuffed out at age twenty-six. He was a kind, sensitive, loving human being who wanted everybody to enjoy abundant life.

H I kept thinking back to the vision I had as a bachelor: the dream that turned into the even more beautiful reality of Ella, with Hank in her arms, in the third pew. I have to remember, though, that he never did belong to us. He was only loaned to us for a season. Now, as he lives in memory, we often recall his advice to us, with wisdom far beyond his twenty-six years.

E He told me one day to leave his bedside and go for a long drive. "Think back," he said, "over the Berkeley days, when you were teaching at the divinity school, and you were your own woman. You can't live through Dad. Or me. Whether we live or die, you need a life of your own." These words will buoy and spur me for years to come.

H Hank was painfully aware of the increasing resistance I was facing from my own Black students at the seminary, plus various problems I was having with the faculty. Hank was as typical a rebel of his generation as any, but he never sided with the students who were breaking my heart, going on strike against my teaching plan, with its call for numerous quizzes. They didn't know the quizzes they struck against were requested by the previous class, because there was so much new material and they would get behind if not regularly monitored. "Go back to California, where the weather and the people are warmer than this cold place," he told us.

He was unusually sensitive to how we were taking his illness. One day toward the end, as we stood by his bed trying to mask our grief, he put on his smile of faith and quiet mischief and ministered to us.

"Didn't you guys tell me all my life that God works in *everything* for good? You're not going to give up on it now, are you?"

He knew he had called us back to our basics, and his smile now mirrored the joy of a kind of triumph. To harbor and articulate such faith was a blessing both to him and to us. It's still blessing us. He marched unflinching and without self-pity right up to the very gates of death. Hank didn't want to be our single exception to this great principle of God's providence. He knew we would have to trust God on the basis of all the other experiences that had eventually ended in good. But he knew that even in the face of this tragic loss, for us to surrender that faith after all these years together would be unthinkable.

The whole community ministered to us, including friends we didn't even know we had. Among our known friends was Howard Thurman, world-famous preacher, author, and mystic. He was on the Rochester campus, his alma mater, to do some lectures. At this point he was a true pastor to Ella and me. From him and many others we gathered the strength we needed to go through those days with a measure of serenity, a testimony of unshaken faith such as Hank would have desired.

We held a memorial service in the chapel at Colgate Rochester Divinity School, with the eulogy by Charles Walker. Liz and Ella and I sang lustily with the Walker Chorale from where we were seated, with the relatives and friends who had come from coast to coast to celebrate Hank's life and give us their support. Leotis Belk of the faculty

wrote and led students in an antiphonal reading, from the four corners
of the chapel, of seven verses from our beloved chapter, Romans 8. It
included our favorite twenty-eighth verse:

*And we know that all things work together for good to them that
love God, to them who are the called according to his purpose.*

Hank would have loved it. He would also have enjoyed the remarks
by Edward Wheeler, a CRDS student, and Ron Harmon, a local medical student. Ron was the one with whom Hank had worked cutting
grapes in Fresno County, who had served as organist at Second Baptist
Church. Hank would have loved the artwork on the Order of Service,
done in his own exact style by his cousin Schery Mitchell, a Howard
University medical student. Somewhat to our own surprise, Ella and
I were able truly to enter into this very appropriate celebration of
Hank's unusual life. The only real tension was hidden; it was how
tightly we clutched each other's hands during the entire service.

E There was another memorial service, at the McGee Avenue Baptist Church in Berkeley, where, when he was three years old, our Hank
had helped Pastor Wilson break ground for the present building. The
current pastor, "Uncle" Jim Stewart, gave the eulogy, with participa-
tion by Hank's local contemporaries. There was the Youth Choir from
"Uncle" J. Alfred Smith's Allen Temple Baptist Church, and comments
by Craig and J. Alfred Smith Jr., Ken Stewart, and Chris Combs. Frank
Byrdwell, originally from Second Baptist, Fresno, sang a solo. Grandma
Bertha Mitchell, strong in the faith, sat with us as we once again celebrated Hank's life. Less than a year later, Mom would slip away, her
ashes joining those of Pops in a crypt near Hank's, in the Chapel of the
Chimes in Oakland, California.

As we sing together as a family now, we still sense his presence and
seem to hear his melodious baritone voice. We know he would have

joined heartily as we sang at both memorial services Charles Albert Tindley's hymn of trust and faith.

> Trials dark on every hand. And we cannot understand
> All the ways that God would lead us to that Blessed Promised Land,
> But He guides us with His eye, and we'll follow 'til we die,
> For we'll understand it better by and by.

> *Chorus:*
> By and by, when the morning comes,
> All the saints of God are gathered home,
> We will tell the story how we've overcome,
> For we'll understand it better by and by.

CHAPTER 15

Together When Troubled:
Wonders in the Wilderness

E *(Ella)* The grief of parting with Hank was assuaged somewhat by the flow of work on projects to which Henry and I were deeply committed. We were permitted little time just to sit and grieve, after the first major outpouring of tears. Henry was still considered an invalid and at risk, but my health was good, and I was happy to carry a larger share of the detail work at hand.

H *(Henry)* My main labor in addition to teaching Black Church Studies was to direct the seminary's Martin Luther King Jr. Fellows Program. This project was funded by the Irwin Sweeney Miller Foundation to produce books in an area for which there were no seminary-level texts: the professional practice of ministry among African-American–culture congregations. It meant the Fellows were designing study materials where there had never been any, with the expectation that my students' dissertations later would become textbooks for future courses.

I had to help select and confirm twenty Fellows, representing a variety of age groups, denominations, seminaries, and geographical areas. For this first year I also had to arrange an African itinerary for the Fellows, with transportation, food and lodging, and lectures. We were to be on the road in Africa for five weeks, with daily studies and lectures.

I received authorization to appoint a deputy director, Ella, and an African operations director, Professor Kofi Asare Opoku of the Institute of African Studies at the University of Ghana. These two seemed to have inexhaustible capacities for supportive work. They made it possible for this "invalid" to work without any recurrence of cardiac incidents, not even while we were overseas. Ella was quite watchful of my condition.

I was especially pleased with three further appointments to our study-tour faculty and staff, from outside the seminary. One was Elliott J. Mason, a Ph.D. in New Testament studies. Imagine our surprise when he turned out to be a cousin to Dr. James A. Joseph, the director of our funding foundation. Mason could help lay the basis for doctoral work in Black Church Studies because he was a highly successful pastor in the culture.

My only female colleague at the outset, Dr. Thelma Davidson Adair, was a graduate professor in education, a Presbyterian pastor's wife, and the first female African-American to serve as moderator of the Presbyterian Church, U.S.A. She brought great research expertise to the program, as well as a contagious, radiant interest in the necessary scholarly writing.

Our volunteer tour physician, U. S. Curry, M.D., had chaired our deacon board at Second Baptist Church of Fresno. He intended to ensure that his invalid ex-pastor made it over and back. He was a resource also to two diabetics on the tour, and, as the son and brother of pastors, his presence and perspective were invaluable.

Other faculty included Professor Leotis S. Belk of the CRDS faculty, various faculty members of African universities, and, later, Sister Francesca Thompson, Ph.D. Other consultants were Charles Hopson,

Communications, Clark College, Atlanta; Father Clarence Joseph Rivers, National Office of Black Catholics; Louis S. Smith, president of Operation Bootstrap in Los Angeles; and J. Lynwood Walker, Ph.D., director of Washington Pastoral Institute, Seattle, who was especially helpful with both curriculum and funding.

Once again we sensed a kind of divine arrangement beforehand, and I rejoiced in the way our program was adequately funded. With a supplemental grant, the total finally rose to something like $182,000, at a time when that was a very large amount.

I was glad at the way Henry just put things in my hands and let me do what I had to. He knew he could trust me to follow up on the innumerable details that he didn't enjoy even when he was well and healthy. My word was respected among a group of male master pastors who were often characterized as all chiefs and no Indians. It was a new and very challenging role for me, particularly since they weren't used to following female leadership. I enjoyed making the adjustment to a leading role in this tour group, which included nine spouses and two female board members who had accompanied us.

Day after day, Professor Opoku and I had to make arrangements for housing, food, and transportation as we went from place to place across West Africa. We coordinated class lectures and field trips during the intensive five weeks. I also paid the bills. It was demanding work, but fulfilling for both Henry and me. Henry was free to concentrate on the group process in the lectures and to serve as ceremonial chief, as we followed the protocol of visitation among the tribal groups.

After we returned from West Africa, I was also responsible for arranging where and how Henry was to spend his year of sick leave. I offered his services as scholar-in-residence to several schools and finally chose an institution now known as the Claremont School of Theology, some forty miles east of Los Angeles. It was a good place for

Henry to do his series of five lectures and, unexpectedly, to begin work for a Th.D. We moved there in September 1972 and took up residence in a student housing apartment, quite a different setup from the parsonages we had known.

H It was a gorgeous campus, at the feet of the Sierra Madre Mountains, among a cluster of high-ticket colleges in a very expensive village. A huge botanical garden bloomed next door, where I could take the walks prescribed for me. And there was a dining room where we could eat if we didn't wish to cook. It was like vacationing at a resort. We enjoyed each other's company with all these amenities and what seemed to us like a relaxed schedule. The students were all much younger than we, but we formed a few lasting ties among them, both Black and White.

Liz was in law school and living in Cambridge, Muriel was working in Atlanta, and Ken stayed and worked in Rochester. We were sharing an empty nest, but we turned out to be busier together than we had first planned.

E Soon after we arrived in Claremont, I was running the usual errands required to get my beloved heart patient Henry registered in a Th.D. program we hadn't originally planned. But more than I knew, I longed for a new and separate role for myself. "Why don't you register too?" one of the women in the registrar's office asked. "We've never had a Black woman earn a doctorate here. I'm sure the faculty would welcome the opportunity to claim you as an alumna."

I was a bit flustered. "But doesn't registration close on Friday? And it's already Tuesday afternoon. I don't have transcripts, and I have no money."

"If you'll get the transcripts, I'll see if I can get the funding," she said. "Nothing beats a trial but a failure. See what you can do."

She seemed excited at the prospect, so I called the seminary at Rochester immediately, managing to reach the CRDS president's office just before they closed for the day. They promised to put my transcripts (already assembled from Talladega, Union/Columbia, Fresno State, UCLA, and the University of Massachusetts) in the mail that same evening. My UCLA credits had been required when I taught at Compton College, and the U Mass credits were earned on our first West African tour.

In an era before FedEx or Express Mail, fax or E-mail, it was Special Delivery that brought my file to Claremont Thursday afternoon. My total credits beyond the M.A. were judged more than sufficient to allow registration for the D.Min.! I could hardly believe it. This had been a secret dream; I had wanted to register myself when I was registering Henry. Plenty of other (White) women were registering for D.Min.'s, but I didn't have the slightest notion I'd be able to pay the tuition.

A former schoolmate of mine at Union Seminary in New York, Dr. Paul Irwin, had just retired from his post as professor of Religious Education at Claremont. I was drafted to teach the introductory course the second semester, based on my degree and other credits, plus my eight years of teaching at Berkeley Baptist Divinity School in the 1950s. This paid my tuition.

I still pinch myself when I realize how Henry's illness not only opened the door for him but made it possible for me to do two years of graduate work and earn a Doctor of Ministry degree I had never expected. Hank was right when he perceived me as living through my husband and family in those years. I would never again be the retiring mother and wife I had become. I believe it was God who helped Hank speak those words. Doors opened then are still impressing on my heart that text about how God indeed works in everything for good.

In November, at the first lecture, I watched with growing unease as

Henry came close to experiencing the shortness of breath he had had at Aenon, but he soon recovered and finished very well. (We had a supply of oxygen nearby for the other four lectures, but he never needed it.)

To my amazement, two of Henry's lectures were published nationally on cassette. His lecture on the Black folk approach to the Bible was released as a tape by Thesis, Inc., a company that offered subscriptions to pastors, who could then keep up on their scholarly interests by listening as they drove about the parish. And his lecture on "Black Belief Systems as Serious Theology" was released by the School of Theology itself, to all the alumni. This lecture repeated Henry's New Mexico presentation on African Traditional Religion sources as very close to Old Testament themes. It went on to show how it was possible to be authentically African and be systematically orthodox Christian at the same time. Henry's good work was finding a national audience, and that made us both happy.

Claremont School of Theology later decided that Henry's five presentations would serve as his qualifying exams for the Th.D. Henry had insisted that he did not want a degree in White theology; he would agree to do whatever was to be considered his research, but only in Black religion. But who was there to examine the person who was one of only two or three scholars pioneering the new field of Black Church Studies? The solution came after the faculty opened the lectures to the student body and the community, who were invited not only to hear the lectures but to ask questions as well. None of the participants knew these were to become qualifying exams for Henry. Henry didn't know it either. The decision was made after seeing the success of the lectures. They covered a typical selection of five fields: biblical studies, theology, history, pastoral care, and homiletics. Henry might not have been so much at ease had he known his lectures were also his exams.

H Ella's academic wonder was hardly more unexpected than my own Th.D., accomplished in the one year I had requested for health leave, to wander west and not to die early. Two of my lectures and all my research papers were published immediately, and in 1975 Harper & Row published my dissertation, *Black Belief,* in which I sought to track the beliefs of West African Traditional Religion, in ideas like the justice of God, right into the mainstream of Black Christian faith, both in the church and in African-American street culture.

In February 1974, I was also selected to do the Lyman Beecher Lectures at Yale, which became *The Recovery of Preaching* (Harper & Row, 1977). In the lectures and the book, I traced African rhetoric and communication patterns in the highly effective Black Church preaching tradition. The rather unique style was *not* an unsuccessful attempt to imitate dignified and learned White preachers; it was a tenacious retention and adaptation of the much more effective African mode.

I did all this work in bed and still could not preach without shortness of breath. I felt so hopelessly invalid that I resigned my tenured full professorship at CRDS in 1974. However, my workload of MLK Fellows program continued, and during the 1974–75 academic year I read and responded to most of the dissertations of the nineteen Fellows who graduated in June 1975. Several Fellows even came to Claremont to work on their projects with my assistance. They were quite accomplished, and anyone familiar with the Black Church in America will know that the list of Fellows reads like a Who's Who in the African-American church. Suffice it to say that I am still awed that I was privileged by providence to make some contribution to their historically significant ministries. As MLK Fellow Sam McKinney often still says, "Henry, you had no idea what you were putting together with the King Fellows, did you?"

E Earlier, during the summer of 1971, I studied at Fordham University with Henry. During the summer of 1972 in West Africa with the King Fellows, I continued my studies informally, still unaware that I would ever use my findings for a degree at Claremont. At the same time, in Africa, Henry was keeping his eye open for materials related to the book he hoped to write on the African roots of Black belief. It came in mighty handy for his Th.D. dissertation. We interviewed children and adults on the huge corpus of traditional proverbs, and we seriously examined spirit possession and the way African Traditional Religion's heritage was passed on from generation to generation. When all of it fell into place in our doctoral projects, we were doubly thankful.

What we learned in Africa changed Henry and me profoundly. Already sensitized by the the 1960s Civil Rights movement and Hank's activism, we came to an understanding of ourselves as members of wide kinship groups, of the kind familiar in African society. This explained the "countrified" way that Henry and I kept track of a huge number of cousins, all of whom were part of our vast network. We had far better insight into the shouting in our churches because we saw its close similarity to African traditional spirit possession. We understood the way our culture venerates old folks and keeps them in church offices; we saw that veneration at work among Africans. We found that our folkways were from Africa and that they were highly sophisticated and functional. The fact that we did all this together kept us equally yoked and only increased our togetherness. What turned out to be our doctoral interests kept us side by side, both excited by the richness of what we were finding out.

H I had always wanted to write that book on Black belief. I had gotten angry for years every time I heard the widespread myth about Black Christianity spouted by so-called intellectuals: "Slaveholders gave Christianity to Blacks to keep them docile and make them willing to work harder to get their reward in heaven. Christianity is a White folks' religion." This is ignorant hogwash! My tracing of dozens of proverbs on the justice of God clearly established that Africans believed God was just, long before they ever saw a Bible or heard about Jesus. The "Law of Identical Harvest"—reaping what you sow (Galations 6:7,9)—was readily accepted by slaves because they already knew it. If Africans hadn't believed in this law of divine justice, and that it applied to slave masters, as they expressed it in spirituals, they would have lost all hope during the era of slavery. And if they had been dependent on masters to tell them about the doctrine of the justice of God, they never would have believed it, the way it would have been told.

Proverbs and praise names for God show that Africans possessed a complete set of traditional doctrines of God, Omnipotence, Omniscience, and Providence not unlike Old Testament doctrines. All our ancestors learned about on this side was Jesus and hell. They had a typical Old Testament faith system already, and they embraced Jesus on their own terms. Black Christian belief is a system whose roots are in Africa, not Europe.

E It was only natural for us to work together with our mutual education at home as we had done overseas. Henry and I each read half of the forty volumes of slave narratives then available, which had been recorded in the 1930s. Henry and I screened items for each other. Henry was looking for slave statements with theological substance, and I was looking for examples of how slave parents nurtured their children and trained them to deal with the rules and cruelties of slavery. This nose-to-the-grindstone arrangement drew us close together instead of driving us apart, as so much graduate study tends to do. One morning, I jumped up from my reading and screamed, "Henry!

Henry! Come here quick! Look at this!" I had found a slave's doctrine.

One-hundred-year-old Mary Reynolds of Texas recounted how Ol' Solomon, a White slave driver, would try to stop prayer meetings in the slaves' cabins. He would "beat on the wall with the stock of his whip. He'd say, 'I'll come in there and tear the hides off your backs.' . . . I know that Solomon is burnin' in hell today, and it pleasures me much to know it."

Henry was ecstatic. I found many other such statements of folk theology, and Henry did the same for my topic. But there was no sample quite so exciting as that first one. It was a powerful example of the belief in and function of the doctrine of the justice of God. It also brought outright fun and a fresh motivation to what is all too often the drudgery of research. I'm sure neither of us would have completed our work so soon had we not had the dynamic of trying to find research "gifts" for each other.

H I like to think it had another dimension, too: the promise of the presence of the Spirit where even two are gathered together. For us, the efforts of 1 + 1 equal much more than two. This is especially true when the "ones" are collaborating rather than working on unrelated projects.

Our daily labors occurred in a chaotic kitchen, our workplace. A ragged array of note cards was taped to all available wall space above the kitchen table and on the refrigerator. It may have looked messy, but it was well organized, and those cards were eventually assembled into a first draft we typed up and submitted to the faculty. No doubt the process was aided a bit by the fact that we always celebrated and kissed after we felt we had scored in some way, from the slave narratives or from other sources.

Unfortunately, Ella, with all her meticulous attention to detail, was short on self-confidence. She dreaded her qualifying exams, especially in Old Testament. Once her study mates and I could convince her that she was ready to take them, she passed them all with flying colors. When busloads of friends from Santa Monica came to her 1974 commencement, she was still in a state of wonderment that she had actually finished, had done so well, and was now Ella Pearson Mitchell, Doctor of Ministry. Her radiant, happy smile was often drenched in tears of joy, and I was deeply moved myself. It was another answer to that prayer about being able to help make a wife happy in a way consistent with my own calling. This was more than I would have had the sense to ask for in the way of togetherness.

I had received some serious criticism for not inviting some close friends to my commencement the year before. They sounded almost angry when they asked, "How's come you kept secret the fact that you were layin' up in bed doing a Th.D.? We're pitying poor, sick Henry and praying for him, and he's out there in Claremont running ahead of everybody." What they didn't know, and all but refused to believe, was the fact that I myself had no idea I would have passed exams and had my dissertation approved so soon. I had more advanced credits and language fluency than I knew, and, unlike any doctoral student I ever taught, I was allowed to perfect the final draft in a photo finish seventy-two hours before commencement. That kind of grace is not to be found at Claremont or anywhere else anymore. Photo finishes are a thing of the dim dark past. To justify those who so graciously held the gate open to the last minute, there is the fact that the document was soon published by a reputable press.

Attending my commencement, all the way from northern California, was another droll critic of my supposed illness and lack of gainful employment. My brother Elbert favored us with a walking prayer/monologue: "Lord, I'm willing to suffer in your service, just like my big brother, who only has two cars to drive. Lord, I'm ready to bear life-threatening illness and yet get only an earned doctor's degree, just like my brother. And, Lord, I'm willing to go to Africa once or twice a year and let you cover all the expenses, just like you did for my brother. I will look to these beautiful foothills, from whence cometh my inspiration." We all fell out laughing. Everything he mentioned was a blessed fact, however. Apart from my inability to preach and a few minor physical limitations, I realized I was actually living a quite abundant life.

In September of 1974, Charles Brooks, an A.M.E. student pastor, asked, "If you could build a Black Church Studies program in Rochester, why not develop one here?" When I didn't flatly refuse, he arranged for me to meet with retired A.M.E. Bishop Frederick Jordan, who convened the local Black Methodist bishops and other church leaders, and they all agreed to establish a center for Black Church Studies in the Los Angeles area. I was once again deeply involved in developing a new program.

Our early overtures to a number of funding sources failed. Then Douglas Fitch, a Black United Methodist pastor and Ph.D. candidate at Claremont, told us, "Forget the White folks and their money too. We've got credentials. Let's teach!" In a wave of enthusiasm, we all cheered and agreed. I readily promised to do all I could and began developing tentative class schedules and curriculum, for acceptance into the extension courses at nearby La Verne College, a school sponsored by the Church of the Brethren. It was exciting and very fulfilling, until I realized Doug Fitch had suddenly disappeared. He had accepted a position on the national staff of the United Methodist Church in Nashville. I was left holding the sack virtually single-handed. My sole helper was Harold A. Jackson, a candidate for the Ph.D. at Claremont, who helped negotiate the accreditation of the curriculum.

However, I wasn't really as alone as it seemed at first. Once again there were provisions I knew not of. In short, with a tiny Church of the Brethren grant but with speedily approved course syllabi and an amazingly qualified faculty with earned doctorates, we were in business almost overnight.

The Ecumenical Center for Black Church Studies was an undergraduate program for laity and clergy who wanted to improve their skills for service in the Black Church. I ended up as the program director and teacher of English and homiletics and pinch-hit as first-year teacher of the lab course in ecology, a course required for natural science. We had no access to a laboratory, so my main assignment was to give out five-gallon glass bottles. Each student had to fill the bottle with soil and plants, seal it and make it work as a self-sufficient ecosphere, and then understand and describe all the processes going on in that bottle. This made God-given use of all the science I studied so hard, back when I wanted to be an engineer. The college accepted the course with compliments for my creativity.

Everybody on the administrative staff served with meager pay, while all of us who taught were paid small fees as adjunct teachers at La Verne. Some of us also soon received pay from Los Angeles Southwest College for tuition-free introductory courses that were registered there and accepted in our La Verne curriculum. The initial tuition for studies at this church-related college was $25 per unit. It is many times that $25 today, nearly twenty-five years later.

We had the courses, the teachers, and the students, but we didn't have enough space. One pastor I approached suggested I visit now-Bishop Charles E. Blake and the West Angeles Church of God in Christ, on West Adams Boulevard. They had some free space in a building they had just bought, next to their sanctuary. I went to see Elder Blake, who seemed to know who I was. I told him what I needed and said we had no room for classrooms in the budget. Almost instantly, he responded, "We'd be happy to have you. Let me show you what might be a good space." We visited a two-bedroom apartment at the far end of the building, on the second floor. It was perfect. I could see as many as three classes operating at one time. When we returned to his office, he gave me the keys. Astounded, I asked, "Don't you need to consult the minister of Christian Education?"

I didn't know then that the space being given me was not needed by her programs when our center was in session, but that was really none of my business. "I'm pastor here. I'll take care of that," Elder Blake said firmly.

As I would find out later, Dorothy Webster Exume, the Christian Education director, soon came to Elder Blake's office with an anxious inquiry. "Charles, do you know where I can find a Black professor named Henry Mitchell? I met him when he led the MLK doctoral group in Haiti, before I left the mission. When I signed up for this Ph.D. program, while we were in East Africa last summer, I made him my mentor. But now I can't find him. He isn't in Rochester anymore, and I have to have his written consent to be my mentor by this week!"

"Look across the hall from your office," Elder Blake replied.

Dorothy assumed her pastor was kidding. "Look, Charles, this is desperate. I have too much invested in this to lose it over a technicality like a signature."

Elder Blake repeated what he had just said. Dorothy's request got even more urgent. Finally Pastor Blake, still very calm, said, "Dorothy, sit down and hear my story." He went on to tell her what had happened when I came to see him two days before. "Here's his phone number, if you want to call him and arrange to meet him there." Dorothy was stunned. How do you express sufficient joy in response to that rapid an answer to prayer?

Needless to say, I felt some joy too. It was awesome enough just to get free space, with free utilities and janitorial service thrown in. But it moves me deeply even now to recall how the hand of God custom-tailors blessings for all concerned. When I reflect on Bishop Blake's ministry, as it is now expands into a new fifty-million-dollar church facility, I can only rejoice in the knowledge that he truly deserves it, if anybody ever did.

E To assure our mature student body that the standard introductory courses weren't just academic and intimidating, we taught each one along with its counterpart in ministry. You didn't have to put blind trust in the relevance of your education when you took Psychology 101 in tandem with Pastoral Care. Sociology 101 was paired with Church and Urban Problems, and English Composition required the writing of sermons instead of essays, with the evaluation also performed in Homiletics. I liked the way this was put together, and I still think this is how it ought to be done. I recall with wonder the fact that La Verne College (now University) was flexible enough to see the value of this approach and bypass the red tape so typical of curriculum design among many faculties. Twenty-five years later, we are still looking for another faculty that is willing to be this relevant to the needs of its students.

La Verne had a "quality control" system, to see if the teachers' performance in class matched the course syllabi. On short notice, academic monitors would visit classes, as they did Mrs. Craggett's senior seminar on classical literature as a resource for biblical preaching. One day her students had to report on the Grand Inquisitor in Dostoyevsky's *Brothers Karamazov*. The monitor that day was utterly astounded when James Perkins, a post office electronic technician, handed in a paper written entirely in poetry and printed by computer. It was more than excellent! The academic monitor had never seen anything like it even in graduate school.

In classes like World Religions, Preaching, and Introduction to the Old Testament, La Verne soon learned that our adult students who had no college degrees were often blessed with more than ordinary gifts. An automotive research employee, Richard Hayes, produced on his computer an Old Testament time line so complete and accurate (it went the length of the wall) that we asked him to hide it. If he hadn't, no other student would ever have had to study at all for that same assignment.

H In 1987, thirteen years after this meagerly funded, struggling institution began, we were amazed by the total degrees earned by persons studying there for all or part of their work. There were thirty-four bachelor's degrees in religion from the University of La Verne. Students at the American Baptist Seminary of the West (moved from Covina to Berkeley) had earned twelve Master of Ministerial Arts degrees and thirteen Masters of Divinity. Six Doctor of Ministry graduates at Claremont School of Theology had done work at the Center, and one Ph.D. graduate at the Union of Experimental Colleges and Universities in Cincinnati had written her dissertation under a Center mentor. At the 1995 commencement of the Interdenominational Theology Center in Atlanta, a student with a B.A. from the Center and La Verne, Stephen Johnson, graduated magna cum laude and won the preaching prize. He said he had learned to write and to study after he enrolled at the Center, with special thanks to Mrs. Craggett.

CHAPTER 16

Together in Maturity

E *(Ella)* From 1974 to 1982, while we were engaged in our amazing Center, our children were spread across the country, involved in their own studies and careers. Muriel was in Atlanta and had been married in 1972. Her daughter Stephanie was born the next year. Muriel worked in various aspects of education and in Atlanta City government: consumer affairs, community affairs, and then urban redevelopment.

Liz studied at Northeastern University Law School in Boston, and then at Emory, before joining Jimmy Carter's staff in 1976. She followed him to the White House and worked in scheduling and appointments. In the fall of 1978, she left the White House to study music in Paris.

Ken worked in Rochester before going to Fresno City College in the mid seventies. When Liz was moving from Georgia to Washington, D.C., with President Jimmy Carter, Ken met us all at the president's inauguration. He was the official representative of Fresno City College. Our whole family was there, and Ken moved Henry to tears when he insisted on sharing his expense money with his father, who at the time was not fully employed.

His big heart showed again when he called to ask, "Dad, what is your fee for public lectures on Black History?" Since he hadn't bothered to tell us of his high office, we had no notion that he had the authority to contract for his father to come. It was interesting to note his scarcely concealed pride when he handed Henry a check for his fee and expenses before they even went into the student assembly for the lecture. Ken completed his college work at Florida Memorial College in Miami in 1981 and began a specialty in telephone installations, to which he has returned.

After Mama died in 1978, the quiet sense of resistance to my ordination began to fade. I was not consciously thinking it through, but I was definitely recovering a life of my own, as Hank had advised so wisely. I was getting more and more invitations to preach and coming back into my own in responsibilities like the Human Relations Commission of the City of Claremont. One Sunday in the spring of 1978 I was confronted in my spirit with a compelling drive to confess my call. I had no power to resist. I had to go to the front of the church, much as a new convert does. When Pastor Mason asked why I had come forward, I said between sobs, "I feel called to be ordained to the teaching ministry."

"We have no such ordination," he replied. "Is there some special minstry of education to which you feel called?"

"Well, I feel called to be ordained, whatever it is." I had finally arrived at the will to be ordained without any subtle female limitations. I would be a minister, period, like all the rest. My frequently blessed preaching would no longer bear the stigma of my being only a licentiate, en route to full status but not yet there.

H (Henry) Before she left for Paris, Liz flew to Oakland to sing at Ella's ordination, held at the Allen Temple Baptist Church, Sunday, October 1, 1978. Ella had finally come around to facing the fact that she was as much called to the pastoral ministry as I was, regardless of resistance from the clergy and the culture. She had been scheduled to be ordained in Los Angeles, September 30, but it was called off a month before. Dr. J. Alfred Smith, my "younger brother" by spiritual adoption, was standing beside me in San Francisco when I received the phone call telling of the cancellation. On the spot, he scheduled Ella's ordination at Allen Temple. It was to be only twenty-four hours after the original schedule, and the only other difference was the need to transport our family and friends from Los Angeles up to Oakland.

Pastor Smith preached the ordination sermon for Josie Kuhlman, a returned missionary, and Ella. The laying on of hands was the most moving one I ever witnessed, including my own. I was unaware of why at the time, but I am sure now that it was because of my intense identification with Ella, first felt when she was pregnant with Hank. I was feeling the joy of her final acceptance as if it were mine. It was a belated but powerfully impressive certification of Ella's standing before God and the church.

E Liz went on from Oakland to study voice in Paris for two years. Her studies ended when Arthur John Clement went to Paris in April 1980 and convinced her to return to the States and marry him in October. I went to Paris to help her pack and return. Art the fifth was born August 30, 1981.

Everywhere we went, we all carried Hank in our hearts. In July of 1977 we went to West Africa with the whole family, including Muriel's Stephanie, born March 25, 1973, and our extended family members Lillian Jones and her daughter Michelle. We toured for two weeks, taking in Liberia, Ivory Coast, Ghana, Togo, and Nigeria. We were determined that our children should not wait as long as we did to gain the benefits of seeing what Hank had called the motherland. We enjoyed every inch and minute of our trip together, and we learned much as a family. We were only sorry we couldn't afford to do this when Hank was still alive and able to travel. We missed him every time we entered a new country, remembering how he had enjoyed just entering a new state in the United States.

Henry and I were moved to find that the U.S. ambassador to Togo remembered us both from sermons he had heard us preach in Rankin Chapel at Howard University. He even recalled the topics of our sermons and things we had said.

We were amazed at how easily our children fitted in, showing no signs of culture shock. They always wore their African clothing and showed deep appreciation for African customs. Not unlike their parents, our kids were fascinated by the extended-family character of African society. It served to confirm them in their own custom of calling their parents' dearest friends "Aunt" and "Uncle." From time to time, "Aunt" Lillian and the girls would display their purchases on our hotel beds and model some of their African attire. We were the only audience for our own shows, but it was great fun.

The premier fitter inner was Ken, who made friends and moved about in African circles as if he had lived there all his life. An hour after we registered in the hotel at Monrovia, he was entertaining guests in his room. At Abijan, we had to check out of our hotel room eight hours before flight time. This meant sitting in the lobby half the day with our luggage. Henry happened to strike up a conversation with the concierge, who wanted to know our names. When we said Mitchell, his face lighted up. "Meechell? Do you know Ken Meechell?"

"Of course," Henry said. "He's our son."

"Oh, please don't sit out here all this time," he said, as if he feared he had insulted his friend Ken's parents. "Do let me give you a place to rest in." With that he loaded up all our luggage and ushered us to a nearby room. There was no charge, of course, and he graciously declined our offer of a tip.

H In addition to missing Hank, the other person we greatly missed was my mom, the one who made me so interested in Africa in the first place. I had wished so much to take her there, but when she was physically still strong, we couldn't afford it. By the time I could afford it, she had gone on to her reward. She died suddenly in January of 1973, nine months after Hank. She slept away after working on the phone until after midnight, helping to make arrangements for an even more elderly friend. She herself was almost seventy-nine.

E Mom had been a wonderful mother-in-law. The bond between her and Henry was very strong, but she had never failed to delight in the constant togetherness that Henry and I enjoyed. She was known to remark with pleasure about our spending almost all our time together, without the tensions that arise in marriages in need of breathing space. Her keen observation of us also picked up the interesting fact that, even though we were both preachers, we never competed with each other. Henry got more joy from my triumphs than from his own. And I was so closely identified with him that I enjoyed his successes much more than mine. Both of us were less comfortable when receiving compliments for ourselves.

H When Ella was away for a speaking engagement, I would ask her to phone me a report on how she got along or how the audience responded. Or I'd just call her on my own. I couldn't wait until she got home. When she went to speak at a women's conference in Switzerland, we had a set time to meet by phone and hear her report. Most of the time she would have to tell me to quit bringing up new topics and prolonging the call. I called it filibustering, but the point was simply that I liked to hear her voice. When I was away and she was at home, the situation was little different, except that my voice is not nearly so pleasant.

Without premeditation, our togetherness is taken to what might seem ludicrous extremes, like when we drive together to the post office late at night with urgent mail. It's not for security, especially if

I'm the one with the mail; it's just that we get a great deal of joy out of just riding down the road together. Either one of us will get up and dress just to ride those twenty-five miles to the all-night post office. We even kiss sometimes at stoplights.

There were a few ragged edges to our togetherness. One of them will keep our tale from looking too pretty: the closest thing Henry and I ever had to a quarrel. It was after we both had gotten our doctorates, and we had moved into an apartment near the campus in Claremont, nearly forty miles away from the Center. We had a no-toll phone line to keep in touch with our students in Los Angeles. I formed the habit of sharing Henry's calls, without the caller knowing. It saved a lot of time, and in our happiness at working together, it seemed to help to have me in on everything. As I was eavesdropping on a call one day, Henry signaled me to hang up, and I did. When he had finished, he issued a sharp and unprecedented edict: "Except when I am talking with the kids or students, you are never again to listen in on my phone calls unless I ask you to."

I thought I heard anger in his voice, and I associated it with the fact that he was talking with a rather attractive female friend of ours. Our habit of sharing *everything* seemed suddenly and instantaneously scuttled, in order to protect a privacy neither of us ever sought before. I was annoyed, overwhelmed by an old fear—that I wasn't the "chosen one" after all. I had never before felt that way once we were married.

Rather than put up an argument, I crept out of the apartment in tears. I drove around the block and then hid across the street in the car. When Henry realized I was gone, he called around and hunted for me frantically. Eventually he stumbled upon me, sitting in the car, reading.

"What on earth are you doing parked here and just sitting?" He demanded.

I had actually been watching his movements through the kitchen window, wondering how long it would take him to find out I was missing. "You don't have to worry about me," I told him. "If you don't want me around, there are plenty of places I can go to get out of your hair. All you have to do is tell me."

He was aghast. "You've got to be kidding! You better not even think about leaving me, and you better know there's nobody I'd dream of leaving you for. Whatever this is that has got into your head, I think we need to go upstairs and talk it out."

I went back in the apartment and finally coughed it up. "You should have heard yourself. You sounded so angry at me—more angry than I remember ever hearing you talk to me. I decided it must be over when you raised your voice like that. I was too wounded and too proud to want to stay around."

Henry looked hurt. "I know I raise my voice a lot, but not at you. And I can't believe I raised it *that* much." He took my hand in his. "In any case, please know it's not over. It's not ever going to be over until one of us is gone on to our heavenly home. And please, please forgive my tone of voice. The last thing I want to do is hurt you. I think I've had thirty-some years to prove that."

I was melted already. "You know very well I'm more than happy to forgive you. I promise, I won't overreact again. But you must know that sometimes couples do break up after even more years than that. I did have some reason to be afraid. Oh, yes, and for the future, please, let's reach some understanding about the telephone. I realize that what I was doing was messy at best, especially when it wasn't a student."

We hugged and kissed for a while, and he did something I had never seen him do, except out of bereavement. He actually shed some tears. Those tears meant more to me than the speeches, and I haven't listened in on a phone call uninvited since that traumatic afternoon.

H After that our partnership seemed richer than ever, and our responsibilities spread. Ella retired from the Claremont public schools after seven years as kindergarten teacher, but she continued teaching at the Center. She then became minister of church education at the large Second Baptist Church in Los Angeles, where the nationally known Thomas Kilgore was pastor.

I took on a three-quarter-time professorship in Religion and Pan-African Studies at California State University, Northridge, in addition to teaching and directing at the Center. I drove a hundred-mile round trip from Claremont to Northridge, four days a week. On Friday evenings and Saturdays, I was up to my ears in the Center. I was beginning to think I was very healthy when once again I almost passed out, this time in front of a class at Northridge, March 30, 1982. Cardiograms revealed nothing.

Just before my appointment at Northridge, I started a long and complicated process that would allow me to practice as a therapist with a young and brilliant medical hypno-therapist, Nicholas Cooper-Lewter. His father was the identical twin of Andy C. Lewter, the man who gave Hank the watch. One day when we happened to be discussing the mystery of my illness, Nick asked quite abruptly, "When did you say Hank died? I mean, what was the exact date?" When I told him, he burst out, "That's it! That's it! Anniversary syndrome!" It's common for folks to have a recurrence of deep grief on the anniversary of the death of a loved one. We had seen it annually with Ella. Every year on the anniversary of Hank's death, Ella would either play the audiotape of the funeral or order flowers to be placed on his crypt. I hadn't thought I reacted the same way, but Nick told me otherwise. My fainting was a delayed and accumulated ten-year response to Hank's death.

Nicholas Cooper-Lewter, later to be Ph.D., had good grounds for this diagnosis, and I felt myself opening up to it the minute he began to lay it out for me. He had me record dreams, which he later analyzed and interpreted. In one of them, I had walked up to Hank's coffin and said, "Get out. I'm getting in." Nick's analysis was that I had suffered all these ten years' worth of ingeniously masked, massive depression over Hank's death. The dream revealed that whenever I was losing breath and passing out, I was trying at deepest levels to die in Hank's place. Hank had never been placed in a coffin, but my creative subconscious had put him there anyway. I needed to give Hank up, leave my wilderness, and return to health and life.

Nick and Ella did all they could to help me heal. They thought I could work through my repressed grief in a second funeral service. Such services have often been known to help. The simple realization that my heart trouble had been "broken heart" trouble meant I needed little more. It was as if I had learned the name of the demon who possessed me and so could cast him out. I felt better amazingly soon. I could bring my feelings to the surface and express them in healthy ways. I could be like Ella, letting it out whenever it came up. Now when I hear great choral music and associate it with Hank, I enjoy the music and the tears as well. I cry to my heart's content

E We don't always cry over Hank, we just make no attempt to hide it when we do. Whether we are in the pulpit or driving in the car, wherever, we just let it out and keep going. We enjoy his memory and even have fun recalling some of his antics, especially as a boy.

About this time, California State University at Northridge offered Henry a post as distinguished professor in Pan-African Studies for the next year. He was about to sign on, because Spelman College in Atlanta had withdrawn a tentative offer to me for the deanship of Sisters Chapel, for budgetary reasons. Spelman's president Donald Stewart had said Reaganomics was to blame, and certainly a recession raged that year. Henry had always said that our "last" professional move should be for *my* career, but once again we had only his options before us. Mine had closed. I was very disappointed, but what could I do? I was just glad Henry had prospects of adequate employment where we could be together.

That Mother's Day Sunday, Henry came to Second Baptist in Los Angeles to pick me up for the drive back to Claremont. The preacher that day had been David T. Shannon, president of Virginia Union University in Richmond. The minute he saw Henry he burst out, "Henry Mitchell! Just the man I need to see!"

Six weeks later we moved to Richmond, where Henry was to serve as interim dean of the School of Theology. He had been diagnosed and healed just in time to take on what, three weeks after his arrival, would become his full appointment to be dean. In short order, I was appointed Director of Continuing Education and Associate Professor of Christian Education at the same school. Our offices were side by side, and once again we were together for a good purpose. We thoroughly enjoyed our "professional association."

H Ella should have added that she worked supposedly half time, while replacing a full-time person who didn't include graduate classes in her program load. It wasn't that her new boss (me) tried to exploit her. It was more like she herself had volunteered to double the original job description, carrying it out with joy and great ease.

During our ten-year period in Claremont, Ella and I had become, as it were, sponsors of each other. As a public school teacher, she was earning our only predictable income, the part with which we paid the regular bills. I expressed my gratitude for her new role in a letter a few days just before Christmas in 1974. When she finished her kindergarten class and went to the parking lot, there on her steering wheel was an epistle from Henry Mitchell.

Darling Ella,

As you know, the ceaselessly answer-seeking psyche of your husband tends to look analytically at even the greatest joys. No matter how glad he is, he always wants to know why.

One of the greatest joys of my existence these past few weeks has been the astounding productivity of my quiet, calm, and seemingly casual wife. When I manage on occasion to be equally effective, if I ever do, I seem consistently to make a great scene of it. Yet here you are, with a neck in pain, blazing away on three or four fronts with an apparent ease unparalleled in our blessed thirty years together.

May I hazard three guesses as to how and why you have so dramatically achieved top potential without even being aware of it?

1. You are at work in the school in a satisfying and creative setting, where you can use your best skills and be recognized for it. You are completely at home and at ease in your work. It's your thing. Because you enjoy it you produce far beyond your own awareness of it.

2. For the first time in our lives together you are clearly not the protected female, with a heroic husband whose job is to shield you from all the hazards of existence in and out of the home. You have made no speeches, but in the broadest sense of the word, and the best, you feel responsible for me as much as I have ever felt responsible for you. I suspect that few women ever feel that way, and that this protected status tends to whittle away their personhood. I don't intend to give up the so-called gallantry of opening doors for you, etc., but at a deeper and more substantive level we are genuinely opening doors for each other.

3. We have always been a very busy couple, and we are no

less busy and involved now, but we have been led, perhaps providentially, to an unpremeditated but much more disciplined approach to spiritual and physical togetherness. The richness of it flows both ways, to and from our work. And it affects us both.

I just hope this whole business keeps going, this joyous Christmas and always.

Yo, Henry

At first glance, I couldn't imagine what Henry was up to, putting a note on my steering wheel. I slid into the seat, read it and reread it, and wept for joy. It wasn't just a love letter. It was a message that an unspeakably liberating force was at work in my life. We had entered a wilderness together and, with God's help, made it fertile. Now we could travel to new promised lands.

CHAPTER 17

Together as Deans: Fruitful "Retirement"

H *(Henry)* Just when we were assuming that we had entered the home stretch of our lives professionally, we found ourselves launching two, maybe three or four, whole new careers. I turned sixty-three in 1982, shortly after we arrived in Richmond, and Ella turned sixty-five. A term as interim dean appeared tailor-made to top off what would then be my total of forty years out of seminary. After that I would slow down and retire. The call to move from interim to the full deanship at Virginia Union was a surprise, especially coming so soon after we arrived. And the course of events ever since suggests that a "retirement" will not even be a word in our vocabulary.

Nearly ten years earlier, in 1973, in a restaurant in Los Angeles, I was discussing my career desires with two good friends, the Rev. Drs. Manuel L. Scott and M. C. Williams. At that point, I was assumed to be sick with heart trouble but expected I would be well soon, and I told my colleagues I wanted to be called to serve as pastor of a vitally active congregation. "I don't care how many books I write or lectures I deliver at great institutions," I said. "In my bones I am a pastor and preacher. The other stuff is just the dressing. You guys may honor me as a scholar, and I am grateful, but you know very well you would never trade your churches for a professorship."

Scott's response still haunts me. "You are quite right; we wouldn't trade," he told me. "But that's not because what we have is better or worse. It's a matter of vocation—what God calls you to do. With your gifts you ought to be dean of the School of Theology at Virginia Union. I know you think you've had your fill of administration, but you have never been administrator for a Black seminary and a student body of Black preachers." What he said turned out to be true. As was the case for Ella, this job called on every talent I ever had and fulfilled it.

E (Ella) I did my "deaning" at the Sisters Chapel of Spelman College in Atlanta, several years after we went to Virginia Union. In the meantime, the move to Richmond was for me far more than a change of location. In Los Angeles, I was a part-time minister of church education at Second Baptist Church and teacher of a college-level course at the Ecumenical Center for Black Church Studies. (This promising weekend program offered accredited college degrees in religion, to practicing pastors over age thirty-five.)

In Richmond, I was suddenly upgraded to administrator and teacher in a full-fledged program in a seminary, a graduate professional school. My new title at first overwhelmed me: Director of Continuing Education and Associate Professor of Christian Education. Now that Henry was no longer an invalid, I was also moved out of my role as incognito wife-nurse. It was a radically different workload and world into which I was ushered with little or no warning. Yet I can't honestly say that I was overworked or felt put upon. My assignment was a challenge, and Henry and I were together.

In order not to disturb my Social Security benefits, I held my salary to less than half time, but I didn't restrict my actual time on the job. My office was next to Henry's, and we usually went and came together, a distance of nearly two miles between our house on the college campus and our temporary offices and classrooms at the Presbyterian School of Christian Education. We shared the administrative assistance of Mrs. Ella Grimes, who was the registrar, and Mrs. Frances Turner, then the administrative assistant. We were in close quarters, but we soon became a happy family.

H There were times, of course, when our responsibilities sent us on separate ways, and we then used both of the cars we brought from California, with the help of Betty and Aidsand Wright-Riggins, my first successor at the Ecumenical Center. (He is now the executive director of the American Baptist Board of National Ministries.) Years before that, Ace had asked me wistfully, "Do you think I'll ever get to travel like you and Dr. Thomas Kilgore?" I had forgotten it, but he recalls that I said, "Ace, your gifts will make room for you."

So much of what we were able to do went far beyond our aspirations. The seminary's certificate program for laity, which Ella directed, expanded greatly. The degree section of her continuing ed responsibilities, called the Non-Traditional Hours program (NTH), expanded even more. Ella and I rearranged the class schedule so that a student could take three years of intensive weekend classes and complete all requirements for the degree of Master of Divinity in three calendar years. The appeal to second-career students increased immensely.

In our second year there, the total enrollment for all degree students grew from 96 to 144. NTH students came from hundreds of miles away, in time for the three-hour classes on Friday evenings. Most of them stayed over for the Saturday classes, some of which were scheduled until midafternoon. These nontraditional students did work that was superior in many cases, and they seemed more grateful than the other students for an opportunity to gain fully accredited preparation for service to God.

For almost all the NTH students, seminary was a second career. For the most part, the regular resident faculty taught the courses, and these already professional students (lawyers, college administrators, public school officials, undertakers, teachers, military officers, and so on) were both motivated and gifted.

Imagine a lawyer apologizing abjectly for being late to Friday evening class. He had only driven three hundred miles, from near the West Virginia border, and run into a new drift of snow. That man has moved now from representing the United Mine Workers to sitting as a judge; in another town, he serves as pastor of a church on weekends. For African-American undertakers, Saturday is the busiest day, but one NTH student left his funerary practice and came all the way from Harrisburg, Pennsylvania, to attend class on Fridays and Saturdays. A health science professor at Norfolk State University was already serving a church, even as he pursued his religious studies. The valedictorian of the entire seminary class of 1986 was a sister on the staff of the State Department of Education, who had already earned a doctorate.

Henry and I both found it challenging to foster their development and satisfying to watch it happen. I felt so fulfilled. At chapel I was playing the organ, which for me has always been a great means of self-expression. I was also mothering a brood of students, as well as advising and teaching them. The roles did not seem to clash. And to work alongside Henry meant once again that both our personal lives and our vocation were infused with intimacy.

On the way to chapel one day, I was stopped by a first-year male student in the weekday program. He seemed quite awkward and embarrassed, but he finally succeeded in getting out what was on his mind. "Dr. Ella, I need a hug. I'm at loose ends and upset, and I just need a hug."

He couldn't have asked a more willing mother figure. I gladly replied, "Sure, you may have a hug today, and tomorrow, and any other day you need it." The relief he seemed to receive was amazing. All these years since, whenever I see him, we always hug, even now that he is happily married and pastor of a large church. Candid encounters like this were fairly frequent and very fulfilling to me. When I define my roles, I may be only secondarily a scholar and administrator and primarily a mother.

Precisely because of its function as an extended family, I believe that the African-American church has been able to contribute much to the survival and wholeness of Black people. Training at seminary has to encourage the spiritual and emotional formation that prepares people to serve in this healing and helping model of the extended "family of God." Our concept of the church as family no doubt came from our African-based culture, but that makes it no less profoundly Christian and no less supportive of persons under oppression. I reveled in our campus community's character as a continuation of our African heritage.

However, my life was not restricted to the campus. Apart from seminary duties I served as co-chair of an all–North American Baptist Prayer Conference, held in Columbus, Ohio, the summer of 1984. It was the first time I had ever heard of all stripes and races of Baptists doing anything together. But it really cut into Henry's and my togetherness. In 1981, we had traveled throughout China, with special interest in the recent lowering of restrictions on the nation's churches, with the result that there wasn't even standing room in the sanctuaries. Henry was booked to make the same sort of trip in 1984 in the Soviet Union. But the Russian trip was set for the same time as the prayer conference and I couldn't get away. My only consolation, besides a great conference, is the fact that we have been to Russia together twice since then. Our first of many fiftieth wedding anniversary dinners in 1994 was celebrated with our tour group in St. Petersburg.

With my travel, my prayer conferences, and my varied work at

STVU, I finally began to see myself as something of a scholar. Now, also, I was being invited to do academic lectures at various seminaries. The first one, of course, was the most memorable. Dr. Robert M. Franklin, then of the Colgate Rochester Divinity School faculty, invited me to do the 1984 Mordecai Johnson Lectures there. As I discussed history in the hands of God as opposed to Orwell's 1984 horrific predictions, I had to keep pinching myself to be sure I wasn't dreaming, and I had to act cool, as if I had been doing this sort of thing for years. At Duke Divinity School, I did a lecture on the occasion of Martin Luther King's assassination that was received with a standing ovation. The lecture was later published as "The Middle-Class Captivity of African-American Churches" in *The Other Side* (vol. 26, no.4 [July–August 1990]), and in it I discussed the tendency of established Black churches to identify with their upward-bound membership, failing, in the process, to keep their commitment to the masses.

H Although our stay at Virginia Union was relatively short, I deeply believe that we were supposed to be there providing a kind of climactic expression for all the gifts God ever gave both of us, although when I first heard of such a placement, I opposed it.

An interesting example of this expression of talents came when the Brown and Williamson tobacco company moved its offices out of Richmond, leaving behind a fine, empty, modern office building, only one short block across the track from the main VUU campus. Since no other business wanted to move their offices to the 'hood, the building didn't sell, and Brown and Williamson finally gave up and donated it to the university. They in turn assigned the whole second floor to the School of Theology, and we were able to move from the quarters that the Presbyterian School of Christian Education had so generously provided.

This old tobacco building had a wonderful set of offices, but the

Together for Good

huge rooms at each end had to be redesigned and altered. That's where I came in. I renovated the old accountant pool into a chapel that seated 156. With my own hands I removed the dozens of wires protruding from the floor and helped build the platform I designed for the worship center. The other end of the second floor became our largest classroom, plus another office. Through it all the dean was a happy designer, carpenter, and electrician. Until the day I left, as I passed by my handiwork, I felt good and rejoiced.

Ella and I, busy as we were, both published books during our busy four years at STVU. Ella's first volume of *Those Preachin' Women* (1985), a landmark collection of sermons by Black women preachers that she edited, is still high on Judson Press's sales reports. My *Soul Theology,* coauthored with Nicholas Cooper-Lewter, was published by Harper & Row in 1986 and then at Abingdon. If I had had my druthers and been serving in a church, as I'd earlier thought I wanted to do, neither book might ever have gone to press.

I loved teaching classes in preaching and in American church history. Students often affirmed the opinion of my old friend Manuel Scott; they accused me of preaching better when I was teaching than when I was in a pulpit. The fact is, I never learned to lecture with pomp and dignity and restraint. I went so far as to "preach" my lessons in English grammar and composition, but I like to think the "sermons" were effective.

My most memorable class came when my history students were researching Baptist church history. One day one of our 10 percent of White students stood to report to us, with great joy and a bit of mischief. He knew he had a prize finding to report that would be the envy of every other student. "My time assignment includes the 1770s and 1780s among Baptists of the South," he said. "Their two major factions were the Regular Baptists and the Separate Baptists. All White, the Separate Baptists were more extreme in their expressions, as had be-

242

come common after the First Great Awakening. These Separates were vigorous in planting many new churches, and their preaching was passionate, noted for what historians called a 'holy whine.'"

At that point the class exploded in shouts and excited conversation. "Holy whine" is another name for intonation or "whooping" among Whites. We hadn't known that early Whites did this. It was now obvious that Blacks had heard this White intonation and thought, "With our African tools of linguistic intonation, we can do that, and better." In other words, the White "whoop" legitimated, for Christian purposes, the intonation they had brought with them to America. I was ecstatic myself, since I hadn't made the connection between African lingual intonation and the Black preacher's whoop. Finds like this are delightful to hear when you are standing in front of a classroom, help like this triggers impressive scholarship.

We had many fine faculty people who, like me, stood in front of those classrooms listening to fine students. Many of these teachers, including Ella and me, had previously taught in predominantly White seminaries: John Kinney at Chicago Theological Seminary, Samuel Roberts at Union Theological Seminary, and Boykin Sanders at Andover Newton. They were at the School of Theology of Virginia Union out of commitment, surely not for the salary. These and most of the rest of the resident faculty served churches as pastors, and their pastoral spirits augmented their academic excellence. Faculty meetings, which I had once dreaded, were a pleasure at STVU.

I also enjoyed the role of itinerant dean, preaching in large and small churches, in the cities or in the open country. It was most pleasing to hear the comment so often repeated, "I never heard a dean preach with that much fire!" It was even more pleasing when these churches sent their sons and daughters to STVU to train for ministry, or when they sent offerings for the school's support.

Since I was also the de facto dean of students, I did a lot of counseling, and I relished clearing up confusion and lifting burdens. The only trouble was that so often the students' problems were financial, and Ella and I both felt bad as they left empty-handed. At times we almost seemed to be paying for the privilege of working there: The school's greatest weakness was the lack of scholarship and student aid funds, and Ella and I ended up using our own money to help out some students in dire need.

One Sunday I preached in Ohio. When the young pastor introduced me, he told the congregation at length how he wouldn't have a pulpit if it hadn't been for Dean Mitchell. I was all ears, since I didn't recall anything of that importance. "They wouldn't let me register for my last semester at STVU," he told the church members. "My bill was too high. I couldn't cover it before the registration deadline, and my student loan was just plain late in coming. At that point I went to see the dean. I was almost crying. When I finished talking, he pulled out his checkbook and wrote the school a check for twenty-five hundred dollars! I couldn't believe my eyes! I rushed over to the finance office and paid my money, and I'm here today." I was stunned. I finally figured out how I forgot spending that $2,500. I had postdated the check, to be cashed if the student's loan didn't arrive. It was a good check, but it was never necessary for the school to cash it. I wish we could say the same about most of the checks we wrote, but we can't. We don't regret it, however. Expressions of gratitude abound these days as we travel across the country.

Included in our aid to students was the fact that we almost always had a student or two living in our home on the main campus. A place to stay took the place of the cash scholarship we couldn't offer.

It wasn't always even a kind of scholarship we provided. Floyd Parker, an NTH weekend student from Norfolk, didn't need money. He had a well-established moving van business. His wife, Bertha, was enrolled in the lay-level weekend "Evans-Smith" certificate program. The seminary had provided separate overnight accommodations for females and males, but not for couples. So we invited them to our four-bedroom place on the campus for the first weekend. It worked so well we gave them keys, and they stayed on weekends for the entire three years. They brought their own linens, and even food, at times. They were never any trouble, and they became virtual relatives, whom we have kept in touch with and cherished through the years. When we are in the Norfolk area, we dare not stay anywhere but in their home. A major measure of our relationship can be seen in the fact that the Reverend Floyd Parker flew in an airplane for the first time in his life, just to provide one of the prayers in our fiftieth wedding anniversary ceremony, held at Wild Dunes near Charleston, South Carolina.

H We continue to have an extended family with many STVU grads. We stick together and help each other in cities of the East and Midwest, as well as the South. Alumni help each other in placement, especially with new grads. During a trip overseas I was asked by a graduate of another seminary to help him in moving to another situation. "You Virginia Union guys have a network," he said, "and I need some help. This church I'm in is as cold as a deep freeze, and they don't intend to change."

"That's the culture of the region where they are," I tried to explain to him. " Don't criticize the people's culture."

But that didn't suffice. "I know you could help me," he insisted. "Don't hold it against me because I didn't go to Virginia Union. Remember that woman who told Jesus that even the dogs get the crumbs?"

My answer may have sounded hard, but I didn't know what else to say. "I'll do what I can, but you know we have to help our own first," I told him. "If we have any crumbs left, we'll try to remember you."

I still feel a part of that STVU extended family, after more than a dozen years away. And I heartily agree with Ella: Seminaries ought to prepare us for fulfilling leadership in the caring support network which is the very family of God, the church. A pastor is not a cold, distant professional but first and foremost a spiritual parent figure.

This warmth carried over into our chapel services in a new way, especially after we moved into our own space in the new building Henry renovated. We had heard rumors that STVU chapel, as we led it, was more free and spontaneous than in earlier years. We had to try to free up worship without moving it to the other extreme, because we recognized how the seminary needed to model a relevant yet warmly exciting spiritual worship pattern. On the other hand, our increases in enrollment brought in many more from the opposite direction, whom we had to help adjust to worship that was more focused and ordered. One of these students challenged me for not playing the same song repeatedly—on and on, when the "spirit was high." "Dr. Ella, I love you, but I have to tell you, you quenched the spirit," he said. "We wanted to keep on singing, and you and Dr. Henry made us stop."

I wasn't accustomed to such challenges, but I found an answer. "I love you too, but I have to remind you of what Saint Paul called doing things 'decently and in order.' You want to get carried away with your songs and wreck the class schedule, while you repeat the same three words. You can't really say the Holy Spirit meant for us to sing more of those three words and study less of the New Testament or Christian Ethics, can you?"

"I think the answer to that might be yes at times," he responded. "The Spirit is more important than the letter. And we students need to feel free and full of the Spirit sometimes."

The student had a point. "I need the same thing," I agreed. "But emotion without some biblical substance is just an empty wagon, which is the kind that makes the most noise. It's just as bad as a wagon that is so full it can't move. We need feeling, and religion without it is cold and dead. But we can't have feeling just for feeling's sake. Feeling must help us know God and the will of God, and then heal and empower us to do it."

H A few encounters we had were less critical of us than they were unnerving and scary. Ella had one male student who disrespected her terribly in class, refusing even to take off his hat when she asked him to do so. He also talked in the back row as if she were not saying anything worth hearing. He stopped only after Ella threatened to discontinue the class session, and he was rebuked by his peers. He was too accustomed to being the star of the show. He had a very high intelligence and great musical talent, but it would be fifteen years before this attention addict got around to writing to apologize for his misbehavior.

However, I had a confrontation that was much worse. This student was also very intelligent, but he had a bipolar personality disorder, what we used to call manic depression. He apparently waxed too self-confident and stopped taking his medicine. One morning he invaded a women's dorm on the lower campus and engaged in wild, irrational behavior. He narrowly escaped the campus police, who then called me to warn me of his probable return to the seminary. I found this young man—let's call him Bill—playing the piano in the reception room of the refectory which we shared with the two Presbyterian schools in our consortium of seminaries.

I suggested, as calmly as I could, "Bill, I'd like for you to come over to my office. We need to talk right away."

"I'll come when I get ready. I'm doing something else right now," Bill told me, still intent on his piano. I knew nothing of his illness at this point. I pressed on, remembering my call from the police. "Bill, I insist that you come right now. It's very important."

When he refused all the more vehemently, I put on the pressure. "Bill, it is absolutely imperative that you come with me right now. If you refuse, I'll have to expel you on the spot."

With that, he bounded up from the piano and ran through the dining hall screaming profanely. I had no alternative but to call the police, as well as to take some nitroglycerine for my heart. Before the police could arrive, a group of fellow students sought to save Bill by spiriting him off-campus. Enough money was raised to put him on a plane bound for home. The kind-hearted gesture backfired, however, when Bill went berserk on the plane. When the plane landed, he was finally taken into custody by the police in a city where he had no support system.

None of the persons involved in this incident has ever offered any apologies, which left me a little bewildered, but it was an isolated incident at a place where the feeling of family usually prevailed. Our students challenged us, just as we challenged them. Some of our richest experiences would come as the outside world challenged all of us—as it did in the "Plunge" Ella and I led in Philadelphia in 1984.

Urban Term was a requirement for first-year students. It lasted throughout January, but the part most students remembered best was the Plunge. This event was designed to give seminarians a sensitivity to the needs of people living on the streets of the cities they visited. Each student was allowed cash for only one meal and sent out unshaven, uncombed, ragged, and without identification, to guarantee that they would be considered homeless for the forty-eight hours they roamed the streets. They had to sleep wherever they could. They were rousted from hospital waiting rooms, bus stations, and all-night restaurants.

I was so worried about my students that I alerted my nephew, Benes Lawrence, of the Philadelphia Police Department, that our students would be taking to the streets. He, in turn, set some neighborhood boundaries beyond which our distinguished ragamuffins would have no protection. This was very important, since otherwise the female students were likely to be picked up as prostitutes and their male protectors as pimps.

I myself received a reprimand from this same nephew/officer. Before the Plunge began, we had a briefing session at the Episcopal Church of the Advocate in North Philadelphia, which incidentally was famous as the church where the first women were ordained as priests, in defiance of church canons. (The rector and presenter of the ordinands was Henry's schoolmate and my distant cousin, Father Paul Washington.) As we left the church, I called Officer Lawrence to clear a detail with him. He happened to ask me, "Where are you calling from?" I told this good Episcopal layman where, and he exploded. "Get away from there as quick as you can! That's the worst neighborhood I know, and it's outside your strict boundary! I can't promise anything, if that's where you're going to hang out." During our first Plunge, my sympathies really went out to the two women in the class, especially when eleven inches of snow fell that first night. The men tried to shield them, but without identification their greatest problem was the risk of arrest. It was a great relief when everybody reported back two cold days later, with no casualties.

Whenever the university's board has been tempted to outlaw the Plunge, however, the students have risen up en masse and insisted that the requirement remain. Class after class, they declare this to be the most meaningful experience of the whole three years.

H Just hours before our students went on the street in Philly, we all attended the swearing-in of Robert N. C. Nix Jr. as the first Black to serve as chief justice of the Pennsylvania Supreme Court. Our ragged crew stood out harshly in the posh auditorium of the Academy of Music, among an elite crowd. All of the students received stares that said, What on earth are you doing here? One student, Herman Kemp, was asked by a dowager, "Have I seen you here before?" To which he replied, "No, madam, and you'll never see me here again." His prophecy was doubly certain, for he was both a Black and a Californian.

From that afternoon, I best remember the brief but powerful final address of the inauguration ceremony, which was delivered by a Black pastor and lawyer, Edward K. Nichols, who happened to be my classmate at college and had obtained our tickets for the occasion. His unforgettable words, which made the front page of the *New York Times,* were taken from Psalm 118, verse 23: "This is the Lord's doing, and it is marvelous in our eyes." People were moved to tears as he placed the entire administration of justice in theological context and all progress in race relations as part of the divine hand in history. Yet he did it without offending any religious group or exceeding any boundary set for public or civic occasions. It would be hard to find a better example for our students; it was relevance and excellence in ministry personified.

Two years later, when I left Virginia Union for Spelman College, I agreed with the students that the Plunge was the peak experience of my time at the seminary. But what I valued most was the overall atmosphere at STVU, especially for women. The Baptist General Convention of Virginia had gone on record as supporting the ordination and recognition of women in ministry, and their executive secretary, Dr. Cessar Scott, and their officers were diligent about implementing the Convention's stand. As a result, Virginia is far and away the most hospitable place I have ever seen for Black Baptist women preachers. It was with mixed emotions that I left to become dean of the chapel at

Spelman College, which meant enduring the stone-age treatment accorded women by the Black Baptists of Georgia.

Tempering Georgia's antiquated treatment of females for me, of course, was the fact that Muriel and Liz lived in Atlanta, along with our grandchildren. Muriel worked in city government, and Liz was doing occasional contracts as a legally certified interpreter of French, along with full-time motherhood. A little later, she would travel the world, interpreting for former U.N. ambassador and Atlanta mayor Andrew Young, as they worked to win the votes of the African and other Third World countries that would bring the 1996 Olympics to Atlanta. Ken, meanwhile, was settled in Tallahassee, father of three daughters and working as a subcontractor in the communications industry.

Spelman was different from what I had known before, because it was entirely Black and female. Founded by American Baptists after the Civil War and endowed by John D. Rockefeller, it now has a huge new building, the gift of the Bill Cosby family. Cosby made it famous as the school where the television show *A Different World* was filmed.

Four years after I'd been originally recruited, Spelman President Donald Stewart tracked me down by phone and invited me to come to Spelman. Dr. Norman Rates, the college minister, was going on sabbatical. Henry and I were on our way to Kansas City to teach in the summer program at Central Baptist Seminary. We agreed that I would come back to Atlanta the next weekend for the opening convocation. I would be on a year-to-year contract at Spelman, but it was understood that I was not expected to leave when Rates returned to duty. I would now be spiritual mother or grandmother to seventeen hundred women, while living in the heart of the campus. My meals would be provided in the dining hall. Henry would be welcome to share these perks whenever he could visit. He had a year of teaching under contract in Virginia. My expense account would allow us to meet twice a month, one place or the other, if we so wished. And of course we ached to be together. All this was possible because, again, I kept my salary within Social Security bounds. I wasn't quite seventy yet.

I was in heaven with that many young women to mother. We soon took to one another, and I spent office hours, as well as evenings at home, listening to their trials and tribulations and counseling them about everything from boy troubles to academic worries and misunderstandings with parents, with an abortion and a bereavement or two thrown in for added drama. The presence of an older woman helped them to open up, and I deeply valued the warm relationships I developed.

Sunday chapel attendance at first was very low, with fewer than fifty students bothering to come. Some went to churches out in town, of course, but the total percentage of students who attended worship of any kind was still low. In order to increase interest and attendance, I visited a dorm each week and encouraged the residents to come. That dorm would serve as something like hosts for a particular Sunday, supplying worship leaders and ushers. The school's talented and faithful organist, Dr. Joyce F. Johnson, was always there, and so were some members of the Spelman Glee Club. On Communion Sunday and special occasions, the whole glee club sang in chapel.

A small staff of volunteer and work-study students also helped out. Katherine Stanley played the chimes calling the campus to worship, and Ida Abbington coordinated resources. Twin sisters, Adrianne and Karen Purnell, volunteered to prepare and serve communion each first Sunday, just as their deacon father did back in Los Angeles. The ushers' attendance count began to climb, with normal attendance nearing a hundred, and peaks as high as four hundred. The numbers heavily increased on other occasions, such as Parents' Weekend and Martin Luther King's Birthday, when members of the King family (who were Spelman alums) were the speakers. A Clark College student, our nephew Goro Mitchell from East Palo Alto, California, videotaped the services.

Included in the attendance were many students from Morehouse, the highly rated men's college across the street from Spelman, which boasts such graduates as Martin Luther King Jr. and historian Lerone Bennett. The men were permitted to cross-register in some of Spelman's classes, and the women were allowed to cross-register at Morehouse. There were free times in the hall of the student union when it looked like Spelman was a men's school, so many men were in evidence (or on the hunt). I wasn't sure whether they came to hear the service or just to sit with that special girl. But when there was a group of men from the "House" sitting together, I felt they had in fact come to worship.

The most memorable Sunday of all was Palm Sunday, 1988, when a segment of the Cosby show was filmed in Sisters Chapel. The show's story line featured the "Hillman College" convocation announcing a new female president. Bill Cosby "presided." Filming of eighteen minutes of videotape took almost that many hours, and the twelve hundred people who crowded the chapel as extras were fed two meals. The finally released tape showed my full face several times, and friends from all over the country called to make sure that the woman on their television screens was indeed Ella P. When I asked Cosby for a few of the plants on the set, he gave all the ferns and palms and flowers to the school. When I thanked him the next day, he said, "Ask, and it shall be given" (Luke 11:9) and laughed. I left him working in my office, which he was using as his headquarters during the taping of the show.

Strange as it may seem, underneath this peaceful facade there was a war going on. Our chapel attendance was reduced in part by the fact the many students went to chapel at neighboring Clark and Morris Brown colleges, both liberal arts schools like Spelman. The music and worship in these two schools were warmer and more like what students were accustomed to at home. Our chapel music was arbitrarily chosen by Dr. Roland Allison, who headed Spelman's music department. He refused to allow the glee club he directed to depart from the standard repertoire—Euro-American classics and spirituals—to sing gospel music.

Once again I was faced with a culture clash. At Virginia Union the old guard resented spontaneous audible response and preaching they considered too fiery, but music was not an issue. Here at Spelman, the traditionalists were committed to a repertoire that excluded a popular twentieth-century Black art form. At neither school did veteran faculty members seem aware that faith, hope, and love all *require* an element of emotion that reinforces their substance. Without profound emotion, all of them are dead.

I tried to negotiate with Dr. Allison. Once I told him I was preparing a sermon on "The Stumbling Enemy," a text from Psalm 27:2, and wanted the glee club to sing that great gospel version of "The Lord Is My Light, Whom Shall I Fear?" Dr. Allison, some years my junior, retorted, "Young lady, you know we don't sing those kinds of songs."

"But this is as much an anthem as it is a gospel, and it fits the sermon perfectly," I said.

"Well, it's not in our repertoire, and I don't know it," Dr. Allison snapped.

"Would you please ask the members of the glee club if any of them know it?"

He and I often ate lunch together, and a day later he arrived at our table to announce, "Would you believe they *all* knew that gospel song? But I will not direct it. I will have one of my young ladies do the directing of that number for the service."

Their rendition was magnificent, even though there was no sheet music available, and it flowed with the sermon beautifully. I suspect

Dr. Allison himself was moved by this powerful combination of the Word in sermon and song.

At the end of the year, the issue of what was appropriate church music explained why I would not be retained as dean of the chapel. The prevailing policy was so committed to "proper" middle-class Euro-American culture that my four or five departures from the norm sealed my doom. The choirs I had invited to Spelman, as well as my own requests of selections, were considered countercultural at this great Black institution of higher learning. It didn't seem to matter that chapel attendance had greatly increased during the year.

To my lasting joy, my students supported me; they even talked of a strike or other demonstration to protest my leaving. I strongly opposed that, but I cherish the fact that they dedicated the next yearbook to me. The theme phrase for the entire book was taken from my baccalaureate sermon during the 1987 commencement festivities, "To Whom Much Is Given" (Luke 12:48).

H This mild account of a bloody maneuver omits the fact that Ella's heart was broken. She had never enjoyed any position so much as this professional priesting and mothering of so many young women. My reaction was not quite so gentle. The minute Ella received that fateful letter warning her that her services would not be continued, I began seeking to guarantee that she would be promoted instead of demoted. About that same time, I was being asked to return to active duty by teaching homiletics at the Interdenominational Theological Center, situated in the same Atlanta University complex as Spelman. ITC is the largest African-American seminary in the world, with six constituent denominational schools sharing one faculty.

Now officially "retired," I had been reluctant at first to take on such structured responsibility, but it occurred to me that the job would be far easier if the two of us did it together. Ella and I agreed to teach two courses a semester on condition that we work together as a team. We would accept only one salary and it would go to her, since I had not yet reached age seventy. Later we discovered that the blessing was doubled, since she had not previously built up her Social Security account. This gave her the quarters she needed for full standing. I had succeeded in my quest: Ella was promoted from undergraduate chaplain at Spelman to Visiting Professor of Homiletics at an accredited graduate professional school of religion. When a little door closed, God opened a bigger one.

Out of this maneuver came a phase of our togetherness we had never dreamed we could reach. The more we team-taught, the more fun it came to be. The more we pooled our gifts, the easier the task before us. Ella was the specialist on matters biblical and handled a majority of the paperwork. I did the lectures on the theory of homiletics, using a textbook I happened to be writing at the time. Our first classes were given bound and photocopied manuscripts of *Celebration and Experience in Preaching,* which would be released by Abingdon Press in 1990.

During the 97–98 winter session at Pittsburgh Theological Seminary, we were made more aware than ever of our team teaching and preaching habits: "We have never had any lectures like this, where one starts the sentence and the other finishes it," said one of our students jovially. We realized that when one of us slowed down or briefly faltered, the other would always know what came next and quickly supply the phrase or idea. We were not offended, of course, but we were made somewhat self-conscious. It still happens, but we try not to complete each other's sentences quite so often.

We have team-taught continuously for more than ten years. When there was a three-semester break in our work at ITC, we continued our teaching at places such as the D.Min. program at United Theological Seminary in Dayton, two summer sessions at the College of Preachers at the Washington Cathedral of the Episcopal Church in Washington, D.C., a two-week session in the D.Min. program at San Francisco Theological Seminary (Presbyterian) at San Anselmo, and a week at Cliff College (Methodist) near Sheffield, England.

In 1996, we went to Russia to teach two weeks of undergraduate homiletics at Moscow Theological Seminary, where we labored through an interpreter. It sounds romantic, but it was the toughest job of teaching we have ever had. The interpreter did not know as much English as some of the students, and we were never sure we were getting through. Our rather good rapport with students was suddenly and utterly destroyed by the simplest final exam we ever wrote. They were asked to identify the metaphor in Hebrews 12, about the "cloud of witnesses" as we run the Christian race. Strict Russian Baptist tradition holds even track and field competition to be sinful. When the dean and the president first sided with the students' failure to see the metaphor, we threw in the towel. They changed when I referred them to the original Greek verb: running, not walking. Ella and I gave everybody a well-deserved P for passing and fled back to our home in the States.

E Preaching-teaching has lead to surprisingly increased growth. Sometimes our students seem not to know just how good they have turned out to be. At the Interdenominational Theology Center, Marvin Crawford, M.D., a member of the faculty at Morehouse Medical School, was possessed of a natural, seemingly effortless ability to recount biblical stories. He reminded us of a country preacher, one who was also a fine scholar. Bernice Norman, a computer engineer, seemed to have no idea how powerfully she had employed the principles we had taught. Everybody else in the class could see her superior gifts, but she didn't.

Another one of our students, Kevin Smalls, pastor of a United

Methodist parish in Hogansville, west of Atlanta, preached his sermon in class, rather than present us with a tape he'd delivered in his parish. He started off very casually, as if he hardly knew how to report an amazing phenomenon he had witnessed. He described the impressive countenance of the leader, whose name he didn't know at first. "I saw maybe a dozen guys helping him," he told us. Little by little Kevin drew the whole class into the scene, and when he was finished, we all felt we had almost literally witnessed Jesus' feeding of the five thousand. We were deeply moved. It was clear we had taught him well, but it was even clearer that he had *learned* especially well, and that God was using him in an awesome way to make the Word come alive.

We had another standout, this time in our D.Min. class at United Theological Seminary in Dayton. Richard Wills, then pastor of the Dexter King Memorial Baptist Church in Montgomery, had been too busy to finish the sermon we'd assigned. Henry and I kept postponing his time to preach until all fourteen other members of the class had already completed their work. Henry then asked him, "Haven't you done anything at all to prepare for this final sermon?"

Richard replied humbly, "Oh, yes, sir, I've done most of it. I just haven't had time to put on the finishing touches and print it."

"What's to stop you from preaching from the notes on your laptop?" Henry asked him.

Richard, never one to be disrespectful, answered, "I'll give it a try, sir." With that he placed his laptop on the stand and, with a prayer, proceeded to preach a sermon that flawlessly evidenced the vividness, flow, and charismatic power we sought to instill in all our students.

As we watch the progress of our preachers, we realize we have learned a lot as teachers and grown more aware of how we can still progress. Our deep convictions about the providence of God apply to our teaching also. Some students have learned beyond all we could ask or imagine. Of course, they might have learned so well in spite of their teachers. This much is certain: Although we have tried hard, to God goes all the glory. Like the art of preaching, the art of teaching preaching is truly successful only if blessed by the Spirit.

CHAPTER 18

Flowing Together:
Reflections on Oneness and Trust

H *(Henry)* Strange as it might seem, our present years of supposedly advanced age are in many ways our best years of all. We work fewer hours and take longer naps but accomplish much more in less time and with less effort. Maybe age helps us understand better how to do things and how to accept less strain. We definitely take time to savor each and every day of these bonus years beyond the biblical quota of three score and ten. Call it praising God or simply telling each other how much we enjoy this or that or each other. Joy can't be joy until it is given expression.

E *(Ella)* Our sunset years do include some shadows. I guess much of our joy is just there within us, independent of what is happening on the outside. For instance, I don't recall any panic or tears at the Georgia Baptist Medical Center on July 1, 1991, when Liz and I watched on the monitor as Dr. Calvin McLarin examined Henry's heart. His second largest cardiac artery was 100 percent blocked. Two days later, Liz and I were holding hands in silence again, almost mesmerized, as we saw a balloon inflate to open up the artery. We shed no tears, and neither did Henry, who was watching the procedure on the same screen as Dr. McLarin. In fact, Henry says he almost wanted to shout for joy as he painlessly witnessed the skills of the doctor. He saw the procedure as lengthening out "the brittle threads" of his life. That was truly cause for celebration, even though he was lying on a cold steel table.

In fact, Henry had been quite calm, if not almost lackadaisical, about his heart condition from his first suspicion that something was not right. He was doing his usual vigorous half mile of swimming on June 21 when he noted he had less energy than usual. He went upstairs from the pool to the highly respected Georgia Baptist Rehab Clinic for a checkup. When he had no pain from the stress tests, they told him to stop swimming until they could do some more tests a week later. He never needed the nitroglycerine they gave him, and he worked as hard as ever. He and our two nephews put a floor in the attic over the garage of our new house. Then Henry collected the stuff we had stored in various homes and carried the boxes up the ladder! Imagine the surprise of us all when, on the third test, Dr. McLarin said calmly, "Reverend, you've had a major heart attack. When did you have it?" Henry had no reply. They finally decided it had occurred when he got that gentle warning in the pool, ten days earlier.

When a second angioplasty was required a year later, in July of 1992, we had pretty much the same reaction. The blockage was almost as complete, but it was as easily removed, and the report on Henry's heart has been good ever since. With no heart damage and no pain, Henry has acted almost as if the two heart attacks never happened. His refusal to worry and his inner calm reinforce the trust in all of us.

H My reaction to a diagonosis of cancer was not quite so calm. After daily doses of aspirin had caused some gastric disorders, my gastroenterologist, Dr. Edward Layne, did a lot of tests, ordered removal of my gallbladder, and told me I should see a urologist. When I asked him, "What has a urologist got to do with this?" he confessed that he had thrown in a prostate specific antigen (PSA) test for good measure, and it was high. I ended up having a radical prostatectomy, by my urologist, Dr. Robert Bennett. This operation seemed successful, but a year later my PSA started rising again. When the oncologist ordered thirty-five radiation treatments, my calm began to deteriorate. It might have been much worse if Ella had not insisted on driving me the fifteen miles each way to the cancer clinic. That way I was able to stave off most of those awful feelings that arose each time I heard the radiation zap. Added to the eerie feeling on the radiation machine was the fact that I had been reading about millionaire movie personalities dying of prostate cancer, despite all their wealth and expensive health care. These people were Whites, and here I was a Black, the ethnic group known to have a much higher risk of the disease. Furthermore, my dad and my two brothers had had cancer of the urinary tract. There was good reason to be afraid.

I had to be realistic, I thought, so I started planning my funeral just in case. I wanted to talk it over with my pastor, Reverend Cameron Alexander, but by the time our schedules matched, the treatments seemed to be working and the specter of my funeral had receded. As far as Pastor Alexander was concerned, my worries and plans were completely unnecessary. "Henry, you're liable to be here when all of us are gone," he told me. That was more than four years ago, and my trust has held up better ever since. I'm a calmer believer now.

However, that doesn't mean I couldn't get run over by a truck or have a fatal heart attack. I simply refuse to live under a cloud. I think I really should keep my last will and testament in order and make plans for that funeral. But those are just routine and practical proce-dures, not the products of doom and depression. Faith in the provi-dence of God creates quality of life, not necessarily length of life. A working faith in God's gracious care surely means that while you live, however long, you live abundantly.

E My own trials in more recent years have been chronic but mundane: arthritic deterioration, pinched nerves, and excruciating pain in some of my joints that have left me nearly an invalid. I was resigned to live with my aches and canes and wheelchairs until Henry convinced me to see Dr. Don Morris, his orthopedic surgeon. He made it clear I needed a new knee, and I needed to get it last week—even if it meant missing the commencement for the eight women I had mentored at United Theological Seminary in Dayton who were receiving their D.Min. degrees. I'm not sure the class ever understood my absence from their graduation, since my regrets and graduation gifts of Kente cloth stoles were somehow lost in transit.

I was active sooner than I had anticipated, and blessed to have come out of that with only two limits: I can't kneel to pray, and I'm strictly ordered not to walk in airports. I wish all the other aches could be cured that easily.

When you have endured pain so long, you do whatever you can to survive. You take antiirritants, but there is a limit to their effectiveness. You pray for relief, but God does not grant the prayer, so far as you can see. Finally you realize that this kind of pain requires a different kind of faith from what is required by the prospect of death. God's final no to the prayer for life comes when you are gone. For us the living, pain is a continuing reality, and we have to trust God and maintain morale anyhow. I've learned to focus my mind on the blessings I have and the work I need to do. That raises my threshold of the consciousness of pain, and I "rejoice alway," as Paul advised (Philippians 4:4). Well, almost always. Sometimes I do cry a little, but I've never cried long enough to lose my trust in God's providence.

On December 16, 1996, as I made a left turn by the ITC, I was hit by a speeding car. Our supposedly indestructible Volvo was totaled, yet I came away with only some bruises and a partially paralyzed diaphragm. We since have learned to survive with a single car, which brings us even more together and interdependent. In the light of things like this, I have to declare that the best attitude in the midst of troubles is "holy curiosity," a tendency to wonder just what manner of blessing God's providence will squeeze out of *this*. But note that it is curiosity, not distrust.

We have gone deeper and deeper into faith and trust as the years have passed. This growth didn't just happen. Since the children's departure from the nest in the early seventies, we have had more freedom from interruption. We have been very disciplined about praying together before we engage in anything else, even before watching the news or checking the ball scores. In more recent years, we have added serious devotional materials, which one of us reads aloud, in a scratchy morning voice. Then we chat in reaction, after which each of us prays, ladies first. We always begin by praising God and counting our blessings of the previous day. Then we seek specific guidance for the day before us. We try to be very disciplined about interceding for our family and for others and then close, again in praise and thanksgiving.

In recent years we have been exposed to an interesting and enriching series of writings about third- and fourth-century "desert fathers and mothers," on such topics as prayer and love and work. Liz came across them in her studies with Dr. Roberta Bondi, at Emory University's Candler School of Theology in Atlanta. She gave us copies, as she does with many others. In the process she has spontaneously become for us a kind of spiritual adviser. This adds immeasurably to the variety and enrichment of our devotional life.

It would be unwise to offer here a list of what we think of as the results of our praying. God gets the glory, and we dare not claim publicly that any good thing happened to somebody else because we prayed for them. We only know that we have the privilege of privately believing our entreaties to the Lord make a difference, and we deeply believe in prayer. We try to follow biblically based habits of talking with God, and we know that Jesus taught us to ask for what we need.

One of our most memorable prayer projects lasted for months, as we pled daily with God on behalf of a student we knew. She was being mercilessly and arbitrarily abused by academic structures and authority and had been denied graduation. As happens too often, there was seemingly no higher appeal or redress available from anywhere in her school. Her career appointment was at stake, and yet the powers that be seemed unable to care. The only apparent direct result of our praying was the emotional support that came from our friend's knowledge that we were so constantly engaged in prayer on her behalf.

With this worry hanging over her head for a whole semester, it was a miracle that she could concentrate on her studies at all. Then suddenly, at the midnight hour so to speak, she received a call. The legal and moral injustice of the treatment given her had been detected, and she was certified to graduate. We are still celebrating. And when we plead with God for seemingly hopeless weeks or months or years, our faith is strengthened by the memory of this sudden and completely unexpected answer.

In both the pleading phase and the celebration phase of our prayer project, Henry and I enjoyed a kind of comradery in prayer, which was a blessing in itself.

H When friends come to visit, Ella will often steer conversation to the Cosby show episode in which she can be seen several times on the screen. "Did you happen to see the segment when they announced the new president of Hillman?" she asks. If the answer is no, Ella will follow up with, "Would you like to see it? It takes only a few minutes." With that she quickly inserts the videotape and shows the places where she is most interested because she is given greatest exposure.

Just as Ella rewinds to the moments that please her, again and again, so in our devotional life we rerun the blessings, primarily, in gratitude to God. Our thanks to God amounts to repeatable awareness of blessings, with the advantage of repeatable joy, requiring only the time required to praise God.

We happily share together another repeatable devotional activity: religious music. Our taste spreads all the way from our late son Hank's love for Beethoven's Ninth Symphony (part of which was sung at his funeral), through spirituals and hymns, to such beautiful recent gospel songs as "Order My Steps in Your Word." Ella and I used to love to sing together, especially as we drove on trips. We don't do many duets now, since my baritone has just about lost all its upper range. Bass and soprano make a poor duet. But we do dearly love choir singing.

We have lived our lives in choirs: from Durham, to Ella's choir in Berkeley, to the Christmas choirs at First Baptist Church in Oakland, to holiday choirs in Fresno and Santa Monica, to year-round singing with the Charles Walker Chorale at Rochester. Hank and Liz joined us in this group, and we sang in a concert in Carnegie Hall in New York City, less than three months before Hank passed. In Los Angeles we sang with the fine choir at Second Baptist Church and with a community chorus that performed a gospel music concert accompanied by the L.A. Philharmonic under the baton of Zubin Mehta.

I used to sing to myself aloud a lot, but not any more. I have finally figured out that my audible praise died after Hank died. But my joy is not all gone. I still sing hymns in my head all day long, without being quite happy or energetic enough to burst out singing aloud. Meanwhile, Ella sings often, and my heart is warmed as I know that she must be happy to sound like that. Her sister Lurline had a theory that sounds accurate to me: "When people sing while they work, listen, 'cause mean people don't know no songs."

One of our ambitions as a family was to have four-part harmony at the dinner table, singing grace instead of saying it. When Hank sang bass, I would shift to tenor. It sounded wonderful, but it lasted only briefly. First they went off to college as soon as they could really hold a part, and then Hank passed. However, I do plan to sing with him again in heaven.

Our most memorable singing experience may well have been a spontaneous grouping in the High Sierras. We Mitchells arranged with my college classmate, Roy Nichols (later a United Methodist bishop), and his family of three children, including Dr. Ruth Nichols's mother, Mrs. Richardson, to camp at the same time in Tuolumne Meadows in Yosemite. The Mitchell party was joined by the four children and a niece of Drs. Jesse Jai and Pearl McNeil, who were vacationing off the coast. One evening, we walked over to the Nicholses' campsite and had a joint campfire sing. There were a dozen youth among our seventeen voices, and most of them sang parts just like the adults. It sounded very good.

At the next campsite over, there were thirty White American Baptist youth from southern California. They loved our singing, and behold, their youth minister had studied under Ella in the seminary at Berkeley. They asked if we would sing the next evening, and if they could join us. We happily agreed, and they gathered with the Nicholses and us at the Mitchell campsite. We had fifty voices! We sang our way through fun songs, hymns, and spirituals, and finally ended with Handel's Hallelujah Chorus. The parts were sung flawlessly, with no sheet music and no light save the stars. The harmony flooded the thin air for what seemed like miles. A huge crowd gathered, and our choir itself increased in the dark to maybe a hundred voices. I had to stop singing bass for a bit, while I wept for joy.

The next morning a woman appeared on the path above our campsite and asked, "Is this where the singing was last night?" When I assured her that it was, she wept. "That was the most beautiful thing I ever heard in my life. Heaven must be like that."

E Our life together has been enriched by music over almost all the world. Before we ever thought of marriage we went to performances in New York. We have heard the music of Mozart in his original salon in Salzburg, Austria, following in Hank's tracks over there. We have heard liturgical choirs in London's Westminster Abbey and Rome's St. Peter's Basilica. The many huge choirs and orchestras of the Youida Church in Seoul, South Korea, have astounded us. We have rejoiced as we listened to the rich bass of the Russian church choirs, and we have ecstatically joined the amazing harmony of whole congregations in West and South Africa. We look for the spiritual joy of music wherever we go, whenever we can.

H Whether or not we sing along, we feel joyously together riding in the car and listening to great music. We must have played Bach's Toccato and Fugue on CD a thousand times. We have dearly loved the music of great pipe organs ever since we were exposed to it at Union Seminary, with organists like Clarence Dickinson, Hugh Porter, and T. Tertius Noble. Music like this is not ordinarily associated with romance, but I listened while driving for thousands of miles, holding the steering wheel with my left hand and holding Ella's hand with my right. I didn't dare look deep into her eyes the way I wanted to; I still had to steer the car at sixty-five miles an hour. But the very air in our car was charged.

Both music and travel give us great feelings of togetherness, even if at times travel is stressful. Shifting scenes and cultures, and the haps and mishaps of public planes, trains, and accommodations often rub people raw. It takes a very flexible and adaptable person to remain unwaveringly pleasant while wandering far and wide. Ella is that person. I hate to leave home without my traveling buddy.

Ella was transported as we walked where Jesus walked in the Holy Land. As I almost always do, I caught her spirit. Our hands squeezed together on the Via Dolorosa, on the way to the place of the Cruci-fixion. There was no music this time, but the location and all we had been taught about it flooded us with a prayerful awareness of the Presence. Travel like this is blessing beyond description.

If our abundant travels suggest that we have wealth, let me clarify. Almost every trip we have taken overseas in the past ten years has been on bonus tickets from our frequent flyer miles. Many trips before that, to West Africa, Zaire, and Kenya, were professionally sponsored. We bought bargain tickets to Australia, but our trips to Japan, Korea, England, South Africa, Alaska, and Bermuda, and our teaching tour of duty in Moscow, were all flown business class at no cost to us. We don't earn great honoraria, but we do accumulate bonus miles from our many flights. We also get points for credit card purchases, even at the grocery. Ella is the family travel agent, and she really knows how to sit on the phone for hours and massage the system, so we can ride where and when needed, often first class!

E We have lived all these years very frugally. In 1997, my dream of celebrating my eightieth birthday in South Africa was realized, busi-ness class, with frequent flyer bonuses. We spent two nights in the Umtata home of Gastor Sharpley, who lived with us in Atlanta while on a government service internship. A marvelous ten days in Johannesburg were spent in the palatial home of Bishop C. G. Henning, our old friend and colleague (board chair) from our Ecumenical Center days in Los Angeles. Our extended family covers the planet, and we try to visit as often as we can.

On occasion, we still wear garments we bought at rummage sales unashamed. We have cut each other's hair for years. Henry resists all my efforts to send him to a professional barber, and I seem to have be-come an even better stylist since my hands were disabled by carpal tunnel syndrome. Henry also cut our grandsons' hair until recently.

There was a time when he even rebored and rebuilt his own car motor, and I teamed up with him to lay tile and hang Sheetrock when we built our own home in Berkeley, California. Even at that time, however, we were systematically giving to the Lord's work more than a tithe, and we have enjoyed giving "off the top" together all these years. This could never have happened if either of us had had any reservations about our level of stewardship.

We had a test of our unity in this matter back about 1947. Henry had asked his mentor, Dr. Hubbard, for an offering from his congregation to help complete a building for a young church in the San Joaquin Valley. Dr. Hubbard willingly scheduled Henry to preach and receive an offering. When Henry asked that the appeal be made for the church, Dr. Hubbard declined. "Henry, those people know *you*. They don't know that church. When you receive the money, it's yours. You do with it what you wish." Henry still asked that his check be written to the church, but the treasurer declined, based on the wording of the appeal. He asked me, "Sister Mitchell, don't your children need shoes? Wouldn't you have a lot of good uses for seventy-five dollars [a lot of money then]? You're not going to let him give that money to that church, are you?" With that he cashed the check and handed the money to me.

I hate to seem ungrateful, but I knew Henry had asked God for that money for a specific purpose, and he wanted to put it where he promised God he'd put it, so I handed him the money. "I do appreciate your concern, and I thank you so much," I told the treasurer. "You asked the people for our sakes, but Henry asked God for the sake of that country church. I believe we would be more blessed if we did what we promised to do." When Henry heard my unqualified support, the gratitude on his face was worth more than $75.

Being so much of one mind and wired together is a great joy, but it poses for us some interesting problems in these later years. For instance, we find it hard to discard clothing. We always want to find a *couple* who can both wear suits from one of our many matching outfits. We know we should give away anything we haven't worn in a year, but it's hard. Our early conditioning from the Great Depression and the first half of our marriage makes us want to give to students or some other couple that we know, rather than to an agency. But we can't find couples who match our sizes. The result is closets jammed full of matched clothing we never wear. The same could be said of our overloaded bookshelves.

H Today, our general lifestyle is more stoic than frugal. We seriously follow the diets prescribed for us, avoiding cholesterol, red meat, and fried food. We use no salt, except when we cook for company. We exercise regularly, three times per week, when we are at home in Atlanta; that means water aerobics for Ella and a half-mile swim for me. We take a nap almost every day, and then we get up and go back to work. Our joy in being together is greatly enhanced by being in something like vigorous health.

The day will come when we will have to slow down considerably. But when I see a ninety-year-old woman working out in the pool twice as long as we do, I take hope. When we have to, we'll enjoy the rocking chair together, as much as we have enjoyed the swimming pool.

I don't dread that day. I saw Ella's parents do the rocking chair with grace and great joy. They died at ninety-four and ninety, after sixty-four years of marriage. In their later years, a brief period of which was spent in Santa Monica, they stayed in the same room in the rest home and then in the same bed at our house. We saw them sit for hours holding hands, and during their devotions they sang together. They continued this comradery when they returned to South Carolina to live with Ella's sister Jess and her husband, Fred. It lasted until Papa passed in 1968. Later, when Jess's health began to fail, Mama had to be placed in a Presbyterian rest home, which was near Ella's sister Ermine, in Walterboro, South Carolina. Mama passed away on Papa's birthday, February 22, 1976.

E We have some other resources for staying "young" besides exercises and diets. They are called grandchildren, and they live almost across the street. Liz's sons, Art and Mitch, are teenagers and will go away to school fairly soon, but for the moment we thoroughly enjoy them, whether I am serving as their taxi driver or feeding them, or Henry is working with one of them in the toolshop, or they join us in the swimming pool. We love just to talk with them and watch their minds grow. And they seem to enjoy us too. Art's seventeenth birthday dinner had teen peers and grandparents in equal parts of four, at his request.

Our three granddaughters, Ken and Carla's girls—Danielle, sixteen, Kim, fourteen, and Marri, twelve—live in Tallahassee, and we invited them to spend two weeks of their vacation with us. They are almost unbelievably cooperative and well-behaved. They can't stop thanking you for whatever you do for them, so you can imagine their response when we flew them to New York City to visit Aunt Muriel. It was their first plane ride. We wish they lived closer, to help in keeping us young.

Our first grandchild, Muriel's daughter Stephanie Mitchell-Smith, graduated from the U.S. Naval Academy at Annapolis in 1995 and is now at sea on the USS *Enterprise,* as a lieutenant senior grade in the Naval Supply Corps. She, too, finished growing up nearby, down the street here in Atlanta. Earlier on, some of Henry's and my richest times together were spent riding up the California coast, with visiting Stephanie, age six or seven, poking her head between us from the back seat. She has gone forth in the world, but she still calls us by the names she first gave us, which the others use also: Nana and Papou. She too is good medicine for old folks and often uses our house for a home port.

Times of intimacy with grandparents are a matchless ingredient in the raising of any child. We wanted to move east from California to be near our grandchildren, and we have remained in Atlanta for that purpose more than any other single reason. We're happy we did.

H Ella is the quintessential mother and grandmother, as I often remind her. On the phone and in person, she happily spends quality time with them almost every day, local or long distance. She often invites me to join. "Papou, pick up the phone, line two." But as much as I dearly love the brood, I don't seem to linger with them like she does. My workdays seem to be too crowded with writing, both books and presentations, and also with Ella's typing. But I do love the rascals dearly, and I'm determined to have more time as soon as this very book is completed.

Whether playing with our grandchildren or preaching from a pulpit, Ella and I are as different as day and night in personality, but our values and principles are identical. Her voice is sweet; mine is rough. She is very careful how she says things; I tend to feel that the truth is the best help you can give a student or anybody else. She is warmly relaxed and permissive with people and with herself. I tend to be precise and exact, and to follow rules and schedules. I will help a person to the hilt, in an effort to help him or her meet standards or make a grade, but I refuse to alter the rules out of false compassion.

Ella's personality leaves room for creative ideas to flow in ways that sharply contrast with my own creativity. She has the patience to follow details and do meticulous research in ways that would tax my patience to the limit. As a writing team, we function amazingly well because our gifts are so complementary.

Many couples in the same profession end up competing with each other. Their divorce rate is high for this reason. Ella and I, however, have a strange habit of identifying with each other's victories more than we enjoy our own. I often find myself impatiently waiting to hear how Ella did in a speaking engagement or sermon. Sometimes I ask her to call and report as soon as possible, even though she may be coming home that same evening or the next morning. She does the same for me.

Our empathetic responses are not something we planned, or some discipline we employ to keep the peace. We just woke up one morning and realized that this was how we identified together. For me, it is at least part of a small deficit in self-esteem that makes me a bit uncomfortable when I am given high praise. I'm more comfortable when it's showered on Ella.

People who hear us both preach can't resist the temptation to try to set us into a contest about who is the better preacher. This is especially true when we speak at the same church on the same day. One Sunday when we lived in Richmond, a recent summa cum laude graduate of the School of Theology invited us both to speak for Family Day at the church where she served, in Dinwiddie County, below Petersburg. Ella spoke at 11 A.M., and I was to speak in the afternoon. At eleven I preached at a church in Richmond. Then I drove to Dinwiddie, assuming I would have time to eat before the afternoon service. I arrived a shade after 2 P.M. and strolled toward the social hall, only to find that the afternoon service was already in progress. I pulled myself together as quickly as I could and soon found myself preaching.

When the service was over, a tall, straight octogenarian approached me and shook my hand. "Reverend," he said, "when your wife spoke here this morning, I just had to tell her, 'Madam, you are a great preacher.' She thanked me modestly, and then said, 'But wait till you hear my husband. He can *really* preach.'"

There was a long pause. It was obvious he was having a hard time saying what was on his mind. I waited patiently, wondering why Ella had happened to make that comment. As far as I knew, she had never said it before and hasn't said it since. Finally the good deacon gave up and just blurted out his opinion. "You may be louder'n her, but you sure ain't no better."

I thanked the brother warmly. It was a great remark, and I have used it dozens of times to place audiences at ease. They need to know I am extremely proud of the preacher's daughter I met in New York City those many, many years ago.

E Just as we found it wise to begin teaching together in 1988, we were moved to team-preach. Our first invitation came from the Duke University Chapel in 1991. Henry had written a sermon published in *Pulpit Digest* (1989), which consisted of a visionary dialogue between King David and himself in heaven. I took Henry's part, and he played King David. The huge, packed audience was rapt. We decided we should try it again sometime. The next invitation came in 1994, from the Riverside Church in New York City. The pastor, Dr. James A. Forbes, a doctoral grad in the King Fellows program we directed, asked us to do a dialogue sermon. This time we wrote one for the purpose; I was the woman at the well in Samaria, while Henry spoke the part of Jesus. The format began to attract attention, and we have had several invitations a year ever since.

In October 1996, we did a dialogue sermon for Seniors Day at Saint Philip's Episcopal Church in Brooklyn. Pastor Pruitt, whom we had taught at the College of Preachers, Washington Cathedral, thought we were old enough to suit his purpose. "Christian Maturity" offered hope for abundant living for the elderly. We were very surprised at the response: these high-church Anglo-Catholics stood and cheered when we finished. We knew then what sermon to use when we were invited to preach a dialogue on TV, for the Chicago Sunday Evening Club's

Thirty Good Minutes. It aired there on December 7, 1997, and two days later on the Odessey Network, an ecumenical national cable outlet.

H Our latest common joys have come from writing together. There is an awesome arithmetic at work, giving two individuals a total sum of much more than two. In symbolic numbers it amounts to something like "1 + 1 = 5." Our synergy spurs surprising creativity. Not only do we come up with the same idea at the same time, we seem to get gems from heaven far better when sitting at our adjacent posts than when we are working alone. "Where two or three are gathered together in my name" (Matthew 18:20), our Lord joins the group and, of course, enriches the two or three minds immeasurably.

This joint effort produces virtual miracles even in our drudge work. I once received a set of galley proofs for one of my books. I had a week to return them, and Ella was in San Francisco, preaching the ordination sermon for Martha Simmons, our former student and recent co-author. I do truly hate to read proof, and besides that I'm slow. Since I would be doing it by myself, I foresaw a dull time-consuming task, and I worried I'd miss the deadline. I shared my pain with Ella by transcontinental phone early Sunday morning, and started the job that Sunday night.

About six the next morning I was awakened by somebody fiddling with the front door lock. I leaped to my feet and looked for something to defend myself with, only to behold Ella. She had skipped the reception after her evening sermon and dashed to catch the red-eye special back to Atlanta. After flying all night, she was more prepared to proofread than I was. She got me to working, and we were finished by late afternoon the next day. Not only that, we had far greater confidence in the quality of our work than would have been the case with either of us alone. Still more importantly, it was fun: We sat side by side and clowned around as eagle-eye Ella caught my mistakes.

There is a pattern here we have only recently become aware of. We tend to rush almost instinctively to supply each other with the support the other one needs. It isn't something we plan, not the result of a covenant we consciously entered into. We just do it. When I raced to the car wreck Ella had, I don't recall any concern whatever about the car that was totaled. When she tried to express concern about it, I was almost impatient. This sort of thing has to be a gift from God. I'm not naturally that unselfish.

E And neither am I. What we have tried to share in these pages we can hardly offer as a model for others, if by model you mean "how-to." So much of what has blessed us has not been the direct result of our wisdom or effort, but of God's. If our story motivates and inspires the reader, it may well be in spite of our limitations in wisdom and spirit. Perhaps this witness of praise and thanks can be in itself a kind of catalyst for us *all* to realize anew that we are joined to God and to each other—together.